Keeping the Peace in the Village

STUDIES IN GERMAN HISTORY

Keeping the Peace in the Village

Conflict and Peacemaking in Germany, 1650–1750

MARC R. FORSTER

OXFORD
UNIVERSITY PRESS

Great Clarendon Street, Oxford, OX2 6DP,
United Kingdom

Oxford University Press is a department of the University of Oxford.
It furthers the University's objective of excellence in research, scholarship,
and education by publishing worldwide. Oxford is a registered trade mark of
Oxford University Press in the UK and in certain other countries

Published in the United States of America by Oxford University Press
198 Madison Avenue, New York, NY 10016, United States of America

British Library Cataloguing in Publication Data
Data available

Library of Congress Control Number: 2023943249

ISBN 978–0–19–889847–4

DOI: 10.1093/oso/9780198898474.001.0001

Printed and bound by
CPI Group (UK) Ltd, Croydon, CR0 4YY

For Sara, Max, and Zinnia, Jenny and Josh

Contents

Acknowledgements

This book has been more than a decade in the making, and in that time I have accrued many debts. The staffs of the *Generallandesarchiv* in Karlsruhe and the *Hauptstaatsarchiv* in Stuttgart have always been helpful and professional. Special thanks go to Wolfgang Zimmermann, the *Abteilungsleiter* of the *Generallandesarchiv*, for his advice and friendship over the last twenty years. Peter Wallace read the whole manuscript, and his thoughtful suggestions have made it a better book. The anonymous readers for Oxford University Press gave the manuscript a careful and thorough reading. Other colleagues have given advice and suggestions over the years, especially Kay Edwards, Joel Harrington, Bridget Heal, David Luebke, Susan Karant-Nunn, Mary Lindeman, and Laura Smoller.

At Connecticut College, the Henry B. Plant Endowed Chair has funded many research trips to the archives in Germany and to conferences to present ongoing research. The interlibrary loan office has found obscure books and articles efficiently and professionally. Many colleagues have been friends and supporters throughout my thirty-three years at the College. I want to especially thank the administrative assistants in the History Department, Nancy Lewandowski, Ellen Mahoney, and Rosa Woodhams. Thank you to my faculty colleagues, especially Geoffrey Atherton, Roger Brooks, Leo Garafalo, Luis Gonzalez, Anthony Graesch, Karolin Machtans, Frederick Paxton, Donald Peppard, Catherine McNicol Stock, Lisa Wilson, Marc Zimmer, and the late Dirk Held.

My students have been at the heart of my professional life for decades, in office hours, discussions of senior theses, and in evening French Revolution seminars. My greatest inspiration has been the students in Posse 13 from Chicago, Cam, Emiliano, Fernando, Gosia, Ian, Jangael, Kelley, Maricela, Miguel, and Pluto. I have learned more from them than I could ever have taught them.

My aunt and uncle, Gisela and Horst Cyriax, have kept my German in top form and, even more importantly, have always been my homebase in Germany.

My parents were a part of this book from the beginning, as inspirations, editors, and interlocutors. My father, Robert Forster, died before the book was finished, but our many discussions of history have left their mark all over my work. My mother, Elborg Forster, read and edited every word of the manuscript as I wrote it during the Covid lockdown of 2020–1. The book is clearer and less jargony because of her excellent stylistic advice. It was also finished more promptly because of her ability to motivate her son.

Tina has lived with this project, and all my other scholarly projects, from the beginning. After more than forty years together, she knows more about German peasants than she would ever admit publicly.

This book is dedicated to the young people in my life, our daughters and their husbands, Sara and Max, Jenny and Josh, and our new granddaughter, Zinnia. The world is in excellent hands.

Glossary of German Words

Amman: *Amtmann* in the local dialect

Ammänin: wife of the Amman

Amtmann: village headman or mayor, plural *Amtmänner*

Amtshaus: administrative building

Amtsknecht: court servant

Bannwart: boundary guard

Bauern: propertied farmer

Beklagte: defendant in a court case

Bescheid: decision in a court case

Biedermann: an honest man

Bodensee: Lake Constance

Bueb: boy

Canzlei: chancellery, office

Dieb: thief

Dorfgericht: village court

Fastnacht: Carnival

Frevelgericht: local or village court

Friedbott: call for peace

Frondienst: corvée, unpaid labor service. Sometimes just *Fron*

frühzeitiger Beischlaf, zu früher Beischlaf: sleeping together too soon, pre-marital intimacy

Gelage: ritual drinking

Gemeinde: commune, plural *Gemeinden*

gemeine Sage: common knowledge

Gerede: common talk

Gericht: court

Gerichtsamman: same as *Amman*

Geschrei: widely and loudly spread rumor

Geschwätz: gossip. Often *Weibergeschwätz*: women's gossip

Gulden: gold coin. Standard denomination of currency

hausen: domestic economy

Hausfrieden: protected space of a private house

Hausvater: house father, patriarch, plural *Hausväter*

herausfordern: to call someone outside

Herrschaft: lordship

Hexe: witch

Hexenmeister: master of witches, a male witch

Hochgericht: upper court, here referring to the highest court in a territory

Hochstift: ecclesiastical territory

Hofmeister: an administrative official at a monastery, a kind of chief operating officer

Hur: whore

Jäger: local official, supervisor of hunting and forests

Junker: nobleman

Ketzer: heretic

Kirchweih: parish festival

Kirmesse: parish festival

Kläger: complainant in a court case

Leibeigenschaft: serfdom

Mädle, Mädlein: girl, maid

Mass: liquid measure

Maultaschen: slap

Niedergerichte: lower court

Oberamtmann: district official, plural *Oberamtmänner*

Oberamt or Oberamtsgericht: district court, the primary court of the lordships of Mainau, Rot, and Salem

Oberamtsprotokolle: minutes of the district court

Obervogt: district official

Obrigkeit: the secular authority, plural *Obrigkeiten*

Öffentlichkeit: public sphere

Pfleger: financial officials

Practikant: lawyer in training

Pranger: stocks

Protokolle: minutes or protocols

Rathaus: town hall

Rossbueb: horse herder

Sage: common knowledge

salva venia, salva honore: “begging your leave”

Schelm: scoundrel, rogue

Söldner: small farmer, sometimes a cottager

Stube: (main) room

Torwart: gatekeeper

Unparteiischer: mediator

Vergleich: settlement, plural *Vergleiche*

Verhörprotokolle: minutes or protocols of a (court) hearing

Vizekanzler: Vice chancellor, an important secular official

Wallfahrt: local pilgrimage procession

Wirt: innkeeper, tavernkeeper, publican, female: Wirtin, plural: *Wirte*

Wirtshaus: tavern, inn

Introduction

The Thirty Years' War in Historical Memory

Settled societies place great value on peace and order, probably never more so than in the aftermath of great wars and the social dislocation, disease, and destruction that accompanied them. Germany experienced two of these terrible wars in the twentieth century, and those experiences have dominated the memory of war for Germans and all Europeans ever since. But before the cataclysms of 1914–45, it was the Thirty Years' War that symbolized the trauma and destruction of war for central Europeans. Perhaps, as historians have come to argue, it was (only) "a myth of all destructive fury" that gripped both the popular classes and the cultural elite, yet that myth was powerful.[1]

And yet, even if the myth exaggerated the destruction, the long war deeply scarred central Europeans of all social classes. Lives, property, and wealth were destroyed on an unprecedented scale. The demographic impact of the war was devastating, with a loss of 20% of the population across the Holy Roman Empire. Southwest Germany probably suffered worse, since reliable sources estimate that in Württemberg the population declined by 57% between 1634 and 1652. The population of Bavaria, which like Württemberg bordered the region studied here, lost 30% to 50% of its people.[2] The psychological impact of the war was arguably even more long-lasting. Survivors rebuilt their villages and towns, cleared abandoned fields and returned to their workshops, and life gradually returned to normal. But people did not forget the war—indeed its destructiveness, cruelty, and barbarism became (and remain) the stuff of legend.

The stories, myths, and memories of the Thirty Years' War became deeply embedded in German culture. Jacob Christoffel von Grimmelshausen's 1668 picaresque novel *Simplicius Simplicissimus* probably did more than any other text in creating a particular kind of memory, a story of uncontrolled and never-ending violence.[3] Grimmelshausen's depictions of rape and pillage by ferocious mercenaries were highlighted by his famous passage about the "Swedish Drink." "They

[1] Hans Medick and Benjamin Marschke, eds. *Experiencing the Thirty Years' War. A Brief History with Documents* (Boston and New York, 2013), pp. 95–109; Geoff Mortimer, *Eyewitness Accounts of the Thirty Years' War* (Houndmills, 2002), esp. ch. 14.

[2] Peter Wilson, *The Thirty Years' War. Europe's Tragedy* (Cambridge, MA, 2009), pp. 786–9.

[3] Hans Jakob Christoph von Grimmelshausen, *Der abenteuerliche Simplicissimus Teutsch*. Available at: https://www.gutenberg.org/ebooks/55171.

Keeping the Peace in the Village: Conflict and Peacemaking in Germany, 1650–1750. Marc R. Forster, Oxford University Press. © Marc R. Forster 2024. DOI: 10.1093/oso/9780198898474.003.0001

laid the bound servant on the ground, stuck a wooden wedge into his mouth, and poured into his belly a bucket full of foul manure water, which they called a Swedish Drink." This torture, used to force peasants to reveal the location of hidden treasure or food supplies, along with the very real experience of rape, and the many (unsubstantiated) stories of cannibalism, created a memory of a society reduced to barbarism.[4]

Memories of the war continued in popular culture into the twentieth century. Especially in Alsace and in southern Germany, parents disciplined disobedient children by telling them that "the Swede will come for you" unless they behaved properly. Paul Nagler from Sindelfingen remembered from his childhood growing up in the *Ostalb* (the eastern Swabian Alb region) the verbal threats of the adults if he had misbehaved. First, they would call on the "bad wolf," and then if that did not work, they spoke of the Sechta Bear, named after the local stream. Nagler reports, "when none of that helped, then they said 'the Swede is coming.' And for that threat the children had great respect (*einen Heidensrespekt*)."[5]

Bertolt Brecht's *Mother Courage and Her Children* brought together the popular memories of the war and the cultural tropes that grew out of the reading of Grimmelshausen.[6] Written right after the German invasion of Poland in 1939, *Mother Courage* was first performed in 1941 in Zürich and filmed in Germany in 1959/1960. Brecht called up the deep memory of the Thirty Years' War to produce a modern anti-war play. The war was the ideal setting for Brecht's "epic theater," a didactic and overtly political work, in which Brecht could emphasize that wars were not natural disasters, but instead caused by humans and exacerbated by people trying to profit from them.

Peace, Order, and Conflict

The memory of the war was especially powerful in the century after 1648, first in living memory and continuing after the last survivors of the war had died off. The memories and the lessons people drew from them had consequences for diplomatic relations, confessional tensions, military organization, and state formation.[7]

[4] The Nazis also drew on these images to frighten people about what would happen if/when the Russians invaded. Grimmelshausen and others often referred to rampaging mercenaries as "Croats" or "Swedes," people from the "less civilized" margins of Europe, a cultural trope the Nazis exploited as well.

[5] Arnold Rieger, "Der Schwede kommt! Der Schwede als Kinderschreck," *Stuttgarter Nachrichten*, October 8, 2009. Available at: https://www.stuttgarter-nachrichten.de/inhalt.der-schwede-kommt-der-schwede-als-kinderschreck.d1dee74c-458e-49bb-9851-a6888577429b.html

[6] Bertold Brecht, *Mutter Courage und ihre Kinder. Eine Chronik aus dem Dreißigjährigen Krieg* (Frankfurt am Main, 2018) and many other places.

[7] Pierre Nora, *Realms of Memory: Rethinking the French* Past, 3 vols. (New York, 1996). Original: *Les lieux de memoire*, 1984–1992; Neil MacGregor, *Germany: Memories of a Nation* (London, 2014); Andy Wood, *The Memory of the People. Custom and Popular Senses of the Past in Early Modern England* (Cambridge, 2013).

The common folk, especially the rural people who are the subject of this study, urgently sought peace, order, and stability after the war ended. A close look at the administration of life in the villages reveals the ways in which this emphasis on peace played out in daily life. The large numbers of court protocols that have survived from the period after 1650 show people negotiating settlements to disputes and increasingly using the judicial system to resolve conflicts. Furthermore, in this process they shaped the courts to their needs. By using these institutions intensively, people participated in bringing peace and also in legitimizing the states that provided the courts, staffed them, and enforced their decisions. These developments can be seen in even the smallest of the many territories that dotted the German landscape.

This study examines the population's response to the war and to the development of the state. For the common folk were at once promoters of peace, order, and stability, subjects of increasing state authority, and participants in the "rise of the state." As Peter Wilson emphasizes, the fact that "social and political structures were intertwined" means that the political story of Germany in the wake of the Thirty Years' War is also a story of how people lived together in local communities.[8] Furthermore, as historians have come to understand, any story of the development of state institutions must be examined in light of its reception at the local level.[9]

A widespread desire for peace and order, expressed frequently in depositions before local courts and in the decrees of local and regional governments, clashed constantly with the reality of frequent conflict at the local level and in private life. Violent interactions were common, particularly tavern brawls and street fights, but also domestic disputes, sexual assaults, and home invasions. Even more frequent were verbal conflicts, slanderous words about other people's honor, and crude statements about a neighbor's virtue or behavior, often expressed as attacks on someone's honesty or their sexual behavior. This tension between the desire for peace and the reality of conflict was a defining characteristic of village life, and is a focus of this study.

Yet despite the high level of conflict, in the century after 1650 a system of conflict resolution developed that allowed rural society to achieve a measure of stability. This "system" was really a set of practices that incorporated formal elements, such as legal proceedings, within a wider set of informal mechanisms of dispute resolution. A key practice was the search for a settlement, a *Vergleich*, that could

[8] Peter Wilson, *Heart of Europe. A History of the Holy Roman Empire* (Cambridge MA, 2016), p. 637.

[9] See especially: Jürgen Schlumbohm, "Gesetze, die nicht durchgesetzt werden: ein Strukturmerkmal des frühneuzeitlichen Staates?" *Geschichte und Gesellschaft* 23 (1997): 647–63; André Holenstein, Daniel Schläppi, and Wim Blockmans, eds. *Empowering Interactions. Political Cultures and the Emergence of the State in Europe, 1300–1900* (Abingdon, 2009); Ronald G. Asch and Dagmar Friest, eds. *Staatsbildung als Kultureller Prozess: Strukturwandel und Legitimation von Herrschaft in der Fruhen Neuzeit* (Köln, 2005); Michaela Hohkamp, *Herrschaft in der Herrschaft. Die vorderösterreichische Obervogtei Triberg von 1737 bis 1780* (Göttingen, 1998).

satisfy all parties. These settlements were informally negotiated and then sometimes brought to a local or district court to be recorded. People, usually but not always men, brought legal actions to enforce such agreements or started proceedings to force a settlement. The system of conflict resolution thus contributed to a juridification of society, but only partially and incompletely.

There is significant evidence that people used the local and district courts more intensively as time went on. This is a trend found throughout the Holy Roman Empire, as well as in England, Italy, Sweden, and elsewhere.[10] However, it is important that historians examine this development in the context of actual social practice. In Southwest Germany, a more frequent use of courts does not necessarily indicate the imposition of state authority on local society. Instead, it reflects the ways in which local people used, even exploited, these institutions for their own purposes. Of course, it often happened that the aims of the state and those of influential members of society overlapped, so that the activity of some state institutions appeared to be less of an intrusion and more of a government service people appreciated.

Importantly, it was not exclusively powerful men—big farmers or master artisans—who appealed to the courts. Women, farm laborers, apprentices and journeymen, even servants, brought cases, especially for slander, but also in attempts to enforce work agreements and punish abusive employers. Not surprisingly, they were often disappointed in these legal actions, but not always. State authorities almost always considered some groups, youths in particular, as suspicious and in need of disciplining, whether by courts or local officials. But many people from most elements in rural society could see the benefits of using institutions like local and regional courts. They might also appeal to local officials or even directly to their prince.[11]

Agents of Conflict Resolution: The Authorities

In the century after 1650, the small states of Southwest Germany participated in the Europe-wide effort to strengthen and deepen the rulers' ability to project

[10] England: Tim Stretton, "Written Obligations, Litigation and Neighbourliness" in Steven Hindle et al., eds. *Remaking English Society, Social Relations, and Social Change in Early Modern England* (Cambridge, 2013), pp. 180–210; Bernard Capp, "Life, Love, and Litigation: Sileby in the 1630s" *Past and Present* 182 (2004): 55–83. France: Jeremy Haghoe, *Enlightened Feudalism. Seigneurial Justice and Village Society in Eighteenth Century Northern Burgundy* (Rochester, 2008). Italy: Caroline Castiglione, *Patrons and Adversaries. Nobles and Villagers in Italian Politics, 1640–1760* (Oxford, 2005); Carlo Ginzburg, *The Cheese and the Worms. The Cosmos of a Sixteenth Century Miller* (Baltimore, 1980). Germany: Gerd Schwerhoff, *Historische Kriminalitätsforschung* (Frankfurt, 2011) with bibliography. Sweden: Jan Sundin, "Cooperation, Conflict Solution, and Social Control. Civil and Ecclesiastical Justice in Preindustrial Sweden" *Historical Social Research* 37 (1986): 50–86.

[11] David Martin Luebke, *His Majesty's Rebels. Communities, Factions, and Rural Revolt in the Black Forest, 1725–1745* (Ithaca, 1997).

power into the villages they governed. The four lordships that are the focus of this study, the Commandery of the Teutonic Knights at Mainau, the Premonstratensian Abbey of Rot an der Rot, the Cistercian Abbey of Salem, and the Prince-Bishopric of Constance, were independent of all authorities except the Emperor. The first three of these entities governed fairly compact territories. Their rulers' authority within these territories was not absolute, however, since in some places other princes held some elements of legal jurisdiction. The Bishops of Constance's ecclesiastical court, for instance, held power over various kinds of legal cases, such as disputes over marriage promises. Furthermore, in some places neighboring princes held higher jurisdiction, that is, the right to try cases of murder and rape.

The small states were lightly governed. Their central administrations were small. The prince-abbots and the commanders were often personally engaged in day-to-day governing, assisted by monastic officials and a few lay administrators. The most important of these, from the perspective of local people, were the *Oberamtmänner*, the chief district officials. In these small territories there was only one of these, and he usually served as the judge of the District Court as well. Directly below the *Oberamtmann* were the *Amtmänner*, known as the *Amman* in the local language. There was one *Amman* in each village, usually a prominent man from the community, often a big farmer who controlled lots of land, but also sometimes a master artisan, a miller, or an innkeeper.

The citizens of each village elected a communal council (the *Gemeinde*), which met regularly to regulate village affairs. Some councils also functioned as a village court or elected a subset of its members to preside over that court, such as the *Frevelgericht* at Wollmatingen. While in theory the legal system was hierarchical, with village courts subordinate to district courts, in practice the system was less structured. Few villages retained village courts in the late seventeenth century, or at least their records have not survived. At the same time, district courts here were not far away, and were accessible to the population, so that they could function as local courts in many ways.[12] The local nature of government in these small states can be seen in other ways. One aspect was that the Abbots of Rot and Salem were regularly present at court sessions and sometimes attended personally to issues coming out of the villages. These men were usually of peasant background themselves, which at the very least meant they understood the concerns, motivations, and emotions of their subjects.

The court records that underpin this study show that governance operated close to the ground. Court meetings, even though they were held in the abbeys or

[12] The court system was more structured and hierarchical in some larger territories, such as in Württemberg. See David Warren Sabean, *Power in the Blood. Popular Culture and Village Discourse in Early Modern Germany* (Cambridge, 1984). Legal structures in *Vorderösterreich* district of Triberg were similar to these territories. Hohkamp, *Herrschaft in der Herrschaft*.

at the Teutonic Knights' stronghold at Mainau, were face-to-face proceedings. Particularly after 1700 there are indications that lawyers were sometimes present, but in most cases rural people testified, argued, and were sentenced in person. Relations with the local representative of the state, the *Amman*, were even more personal, since he lived in the community and interacted with his neighbors on a daily basis.

Interactions between local people and their rulers increased in quantity and intensity after 1650. People used the district courts to record agreements and settlements, including property transactions, marriage contracts, and inheritances, in part because these courts were now keeping better written records. They took disputes over these issues there when less formal resolutions failed, or in an effort to force a settlement. The authorities also increasingly attempted to discipline local life, whether it was to enforce rules about sexual behavior, to suppress popular appeals to the supernatural, or to insist on obedience to the established rulers. What did not happen in these places, however, was the establishment of a more distant, rules-oriented, and structured system of government. Perhaps by the early eighteenth century the university-educated district officials, even in provincial backwaters like Mainau, Rot, and Salem, dreamed of a professionalized, rational administration. However, just like the people they governed, in practice these men remained knee-deep in the pragmatic, complex, and idiosyncratic world of local village life.[13]

The Needs and Purposes of the Population

A top-down kind of social discipline had very little impact here, and any real state-building managed by state officials was limited as well. Nevertheless, there was a change in the way the institutions of governance were used and (most likely) viewed by the population at large. In the aftermath of the Thirty Years' War, the heightened desire for peace and order increased the awareness of the constant conflict that afflicted communities and made the need for conflict resolution more apparent to people. The tools for finding settlements, such as informal negotiations, the use of mediators, and the appeal to judicial instances were

[13] On more intensive interactions, see Rudolf Schlögl, "Kommunikation und Vergesellschaftung under Anwesenden: Formen der Sozialen und ihre Transformation in der Frühen Neuzeit" *Geschichte und Gesellschaft* 34 (2008): 155–224; Rudolf Schlögl, *Anwesende und Abwesende. Grundriss für eine Gesellschaftsgeschichte der Frühen Neuzeit* (Konstanz, 2014); Hohkamp, *Herrschaft in der Herrschaft.* On flexible and pragmatic courts, see Govind Sreenivasan, "Prosecuting Injuries in Early Modern Germany (ca. 1550-1650)" *Central European History* 47 (2014): 544–84 and Patrick Oelze, *Recht haben und Recht behalten. Konflikte um die Gerichtsbarkeit in Schwäbisch Hall und seiner Umgebung (15.–18 Jahrhundert)* (Konstanz, 2011), esp. pp. 15–25.

all engaged more intensely. Furthermore, people certainly used courts in cases where their interests and those of the authorities coincided or overlapped, for example in the disciplining of unruly youths, but they also brought cases about issues of little interest to state officials.

Consider the issue of honor disputes. Local people wanted courts to help resolve such conflicts, many of which may have struck judges and district officials as petty and unimportant. On the other hand, these men were part of this world themselves, and they surely knew the central place of honor in the life of rural communities. As a result, they did their best to get to the bottom of such conflicts, which was not an easy matter. Probably many honor disputes were resolved informally, but people seemed to have needed courts to adjudicate the more thorny and persistent conflicts. And the courts did so, always demanding the parties reconcile and make peace at the end of such cases.

Other kinds of conflicts came to the courts, most of them at the initiative of local people. Conflicts over border markers, the use of pastures, and other aspects of agricultural life were important for village communities, which sometimes took them to court. Local political conflicts, usually between the village council and the *Amman*, also needed adjudication. Disputes over inheritances were common, as were difficulties over the sale of land and livestock. Villagers came to the courts because they needed them for their purposes, which were primarily to keep or restore peace and order in the areas of life that mattered to them.

Even when issues of public order came to the courts, such as tavern brawls and street fights, often caused by a man calling another out of his house (or the tavern) to fight, it was usually villagers themselves who reported the cases and demanded punishments. The evidence certainly indicates that conflicts were often bloody and dangerous in these villages, but that did not mean that people accepted or approved of the violence. In this area, as in many others, most people's interest in promoting peace and order coincided with the desires and policies of the authorities.

State Formation from Below

The story presented here begins with the end of the long and destructive war. As in many places after a time of social trauma, people placed great value on peace as they worked to rebuild their communities. Of course, peace and order were timeless, elusive, and probably impossible goals, even if they were highly valued. After the long war, people reconstituted traditional forms of conflict resolution and sought respected members of the community and parish priests to help settle disputes. But they also increasingly used the courts provided by the small states that ruled them.

The authorities were surely aware, as they had been for centuries, that the ability to effectively dispense justice brought prestige to the state they served. The local and district courts studied here were effective, providing rapid, inexpensive, and reliable decisions. Furthermore, these courts did not compete with traditional aspects of conflict resolution, but rather complemented them. As this system matured in the decades after 1700, it provided a basis for a kind of state formation, where state institutions functioned with the broad support of the population.

This story, then, is one of growing appreciation for the public services provided by these small states. This did not mean, of course, that Southwest Germany became a happy, well-governed world. There were always conflicts between the authorities and the population over taxes and the burdens of serfdom, especially transport services required by the monasteries. Tensions between the big farmers and the poorer villagers also increased after 1700. And daily life probably did not become less violent, as evidenced by the continuing reports of brawls and fights, insults and slander. Nevertheless, the intervention and activity of local courts in that daily life increased, as part of a broader intensification of state-society interactions. In the eighteenth century, the village was more deeply governed than it had been in the previous century, the result not so much of the efforts of rulers, but rather of the desires of the population.

The idea of state formation (or state-building) from below has gained currency among historians in recent years, although it remains a controversial idea. A 2005 conference in Ancona, which led to the 2009 volume *Empowering Interactions*, brought together a large number of scholars to discuss this idea. It is perhaps not surprising that Swiss historians were pioneers of the idea that state structures responded to and served the needs of the wider population, and not just the elite, since that is how the Swiss like to understand the development of their state. What is clear from *Empowering Interactions* is that research since the 1990s by historians of Italy, France, Germany, and England has deployed this perspective to force historians to think differently about the "rise of the state."

André Holenstein's introduction to *Empowering Interactions* emphasizes the process of state formation from below.

> Such processes occurred because specific state instances reacted to complex social problems, because they answered to the demands and claims of various groups and members of the society, because they rendered services to these groups and helped bring about what these groups expected from a higher political power—for instance the settling of disputes and the solution of conflicts, support for carrying through specific interests, or the implementation of specific concepts of public and social order.[14]

[14] Holenstein et al., eds. *Empowering Interactions*, p. 5.

This perspective is supported by the role the peasants who are the focus of this study took in their own governance. Other studies from both Germany and across Europe also show the "common folk" participating in the development of governmental structures. Holenstein himself, in his studies of local government in Margraviate of Baden in the eighteenth century, shows how people increasingly used local courts, the *Frevelgerichte*, to solve disputes and bring order to local communities. In Baden, he argues, the state developed in a dialectical process that incorporated the claims and demands of the population.[15] In another study of a smaller polity in southern Germany, Michaela Hohkamp's detailed book on the Further Austrian district of Triberg shows the leading local official, the *Obervogt*, balancing pressures from higher authorities in far-away Vienna, the demands of local elites, and the needs of local society.[16] These are just some examples of a wealth of local and regional studies that posit a strong role for local people in the development of the state.

The formation of states from below was not just a characteristic of the small territories of southern and western Germany, or of the cantons of Switzerland, or provinces of the northern Netherlands. Historians of England have always posited that the English state had local or "country" roots. Even studies of France, traditionally the classic example of a centralizing modern state, have shown the weaknesses of royal power and ways in which the central government had to cooperate with the nobility and other local elites to govern. These new ways of talking about the state and governance and its relationship with local society all result from examining the process of political development at the local level, a perspective central to this study as well.

Wolfgang Reinhard, an influential German historian of state development in Europe, criticizes this new perspective in *Empowering Interactions*. While agreeing that "localized micro-perspective is more than essential for the study of early modern politics and political systema," he also insists that "by definition state-building is a top-down process, because it originates from and is based upon the interests of the people at the center."[17] More convincingly, I think, he criticizes state-building from below for its failure to transcend the obsession with the rise of the modern world that has long dominated the political history of early

[15] André Holenstein, "Klagen, anzeigen und supplizieren. Kommunikative Praktiken und Konfliktlösungsverfahren in der Markgrafschaft Baden im 18. Jahrhunderts" in Magnus Eriksson and Barbara Krug-Richter, eds. *Streitkulturen. Gewalt, Konflikt und Kommunikation in der ländlichen Gesellschaft (16.–19. Jh.)* (Köln, 2003), p. 339. See also: André Holenstein, "Ordnung und Unordnung im Dorf. Ordnungsdiskurse, Ordnungspraktiken und Konfliktregelungen vor dem badischen Frevelgerichten des 18 Jahrhunderts" in Mark Häberlein, ed. *Devianz, Widerstand und Herrschaftspraxis in der Vormoderne. Studien zu Konflikten im südwestdeutschen Raum (15.–18. Jahrhundert)* (Konstanz, 1999); André Holenstein, *"Gute Policey" und lokale Gesellschaft im Staat des Ancien Régime. Das Fallbeispiel der Markgrafschaft Baden(-Durlach)* (Epfendorf/Neckar, 2003).

[16] Hohkamp, *Herrschaft in der Herrschaft*.

[17] Wolfgang Reinhard, "No State Building from Below! A Critical Commentary" in Holenstein et al., eds. *Empowering Interactions*, pp. 299, 302.

modern Europe.[18] This study, and others from across Europe, seek to mitigate these concerns in several ways. First, discussions of the development of state structures have to take both a bottom-up and a top-down perspective. No one denies the efforts of state-building from rulers and their officials.[19] Secondly, a good "localized micro-perspective" (in Reinhard's somewhat condescending language) has to examine state development in relation to and in the context of the ways local societies functioned in a daily basis. Finally, by conceptualizing the development of the state as "state formation," as I do here, scholars have turned their focus away from the plans and programs of theoreticians and government officials to emphasize instead a dynamic and organic process that involved all of society.

In order to examine how local societies interacted with the state, one must engage with ***the history of crime and of the justice system***, a perspective required by the source base for this study, local court records. Steve Hindle's analysis of English political culture emphasizes the "widespread participation in the process of governance" and the "ubiquity of the forms and rhetoric of law."[20] Hindle also asserts that "the desire for order and peace did not merely 'trickle down,' but actually 'welled up' within society itself."[21] Central to this process, he argues, was the fact that the legal system was widely accessible in England and was used by people to solve conflicts.

Michael Breen finds similarities to Hindle's England in early modern France.[22] Surveying revisionist studies of the French legal system, Breen concludes that "the administration of justice as depicted in these studies, especially at the intermediate and local levels, bore little resemblance to the horror stories with which modern scholars have been familiar. On the contrary, it was quick, inexpensive, and satisfactory."[23] In his discussion of local courts, Breen points to a number of studies that show that "local justice was surprisingly flexible and well adapted to local needs and concerns." One study shows that for the courts "repressing deviant behavior and imposing social discipline took a marked back seat to restoring and maintaining social harmony."[24] Since local courts in Southwest Germany, both those studied here and those studied by Holenstein, operated in a similar

[18] Reinhard, "No State Building from Below!," p. 302.

[19] Jon Mathieu, "Statebuilding from Below—Towards a Balanced View" in Holenstein et al., eds. *Empowering Interactions*, esp. p. 309.

[20] Steve Hindle, "Law, Law Enforcement and State Formation in Early Modern England" in Ronald G. Asch and Dagmar Friest, eds. *Staatsbildung als kultureller Prozess* (Köln, 2005), pp. 211–12; Steve Hindle, *The State and Social Change in Early Modern England, c. 1550–1640* (New York, 2000).

[21] Hindle, "Law, Law Enforcement and State Formation in Early Modern England," pp. 220–8.

[22] Michael Breen, "Law, Society, and the State in Early Modern France" *The Journal of Modern History* 83 (2011): 346–86.

[23] Breen, "Law, Society, and the State in Early Modern France," p. 360.

[24] Breen, "Law, Society, and the State in Early Modern France," pp. 377–8.

fashion, this study reinforces the revisionist view of early modern legal history outlined by Breen.

A related area of fertile research in the history of early modern European rural society has been in ***the history of conflict and violence***. These studies have moved beyond a (usually tentative) calculation of the levels of crime, or the ways that institutions of justice functioned. Instead, they increasingly look at the meaning of conflict and violence—and I would add peacemaking—in order to develop a deeper understanding of how communities operated on a day-to-day basis. An excellent example of this new kind of history of violence is Malcolm Greenshields' study of the Haute Auvergne.[25] He shows that "much can be learned about societies, behaviors, and attitudes, as well as crime and justice, from a careful scrutiny of justice records." Furthermore, "violence informed and expressed the vitality of society and culture...."[26]

Karl Härter's *Policey und Strafjustiz in Kurmainz* (2005) is an example of the many studies of legal history in the German historical tradition, with its focus on institutional developments.[27] Like Reinhard, Härter is skeptical about the participation of the population in the development of the state. Yet he also argues that the regulatory and legal policies of the Electors of Mainz were characterized by "ambivalence, flexibility, and leeway in making decisions (*Entscheidungsspielraum*)." His conclusion, which fits well with the situation in Southwest Germany as well, is that the legal system in the Mainz Electorate did not operate to discipline society from above, but rather created "possibilities for communication and interaction with many social groups and subjects in society and even gave them limited influence and participation, which also meant integration and acceptance."[28] Thus even scholars in an older tradition of legal history have accepted that legal developments in the early modern period always involved a process that included the wider population.

This study also makes a contribution to our understanding of ***the role of honor*** in early modern societies, a subset of the studies of social conflict. Despite important studies by scholars like Martin Dinges on the working people of Paris, or Laura Gowing about women in London, scholarship on the role of honor tends to focus on either the nobility or on Mediterranean societies.[29] German peasants, like the working people of London and Paris and the peasants of the Haute Auvergne, were deeply concerned with defending their honor.[30] This study reveals

[25] Malcolm Greenshields, *An Economy of Violence in Early Modern France: Crime and Justice in the Haute Auvergne, 1587–1664* (University Park PA, 1994).

[26] Greenshields, *An Economy of Violence in Early Modern France*, p. 18.

[27] Karl Härter, *Policey und Strafjustiz in Kurmainz.*

[28] Härter, *Policey und Strafjustiz in Kurmainz*, esp. 1124–58, quotes pp. 1129, 1158.

[29] Martin Dinges, " 'Weiblichkeit' im 'Männlichkeitsritualen.' Zu weiblichen Taktiken in Ehrenhandel in Paris in 18. Jahrhundert" *Francia* 18/2 (1991): 71–98; Laura Gowing, *Domestic Dangers. Women, Words, and Sex in Early Modern London* (Oxford, 1998).

[30] Greenshields, *An Economy of Violence in Early Modern France.*

a widespread German or northern European culture of honor characterized by a deep concern by men for their standing as an "honest man," and women's defense of their sexual reputation. Furthermore, women always defended themselves against accusations of being a witch, and they did so themselves, including bringing slander suits in court, rather than depending on male relatives to do so.

The court records that underpin this study provide a new ***understanding of the ways rural society functioned.*** The role of violence, the importance of honor, the methods of adjudicating disputes, the place of rumor, interactions between people and their rulers, are all part of understanding the development of state and society in the century after 1650. When one examines state formation at the local level, there is little doubt that local people were agents as well as subjects in this process. Furthermore, how local society and governing structures interacted in daily life at the level of the village did much to determine the nature of the state. The nature of conflict, violence, and peacemaking, and the instrumentalization of courts, was common across Europe. At the same time, different political and institutional contexts mattered for longer-term state development and for the relationship between state and society. An appreciation of and support for effective state institutions, so much a part of the political culture of Germany since the eighteenth century, had roots in the developments discussed here.

To argue that the state developed, in important ways, "from below" does not discount the efforts of rulers and state officials to penetrate local society more effectively and consistently. One must also problematize the idea that Germans were, by nature or because of their historical experience, "obedient subjects," a point made decades ago by Peter Blickle in *Deutsche Untertanen: Ein Widerspruch.*[31] The subjects of this study, the peasants, artisans, farmworkers, and servants who populated the villages of Southwest Germany, may have used local courts and (mostly) respected their decisions. But they also protested taxes and fees, ignored unwelcome regulations of their social life, and organized local life with limited interference from the "state," such as it was. Their descendants in the nineteenth and twentieth centuries were not always obedient either, as studies of socialism and the labor movement, or of opposition to the *Kulturkampf*, have shown.[32]

Although this is in one sense a local study, based on the sources from a number of small Southwest German territories, it is my contention that the developments traced here are representative of developments across (at least) western and southern Germany. Comparable studies have been published over the last twenty years, many of which have inspired and informed this research. If each place and time has its own particular character, common patterns can be found,

[31] Peter Blickle, *Deutsche Untertanen. Ein Wiederspruch* (Munich, 1981); *German Subjects. A Dissent.*
[32] See Stefan Berger, *Inventing the Nation: Germany* (Oxford, 2004), esp. ch. 3.

particularly in the agency of the common folk in creating the political structures that governed their lives. Beyond its contribution to an understanding of German developments, I hope this study also tells us about the way rural communities functioned in the past, not only in Germany, but across western Europe.

The Structure of the Book

This book begins with an overview of the local and district law courts whose records underpin this study (Chapter 1). The courts handled a wide range of cases involving everyday life at the village level, most often in response to complaints brought by local people. Interpersonal conflicts dominated court dockets, but people also brought cases that emerged from agricultural life, from boundary disputes to illegal taking of wood, to disputes over the grazing of animals. These courts remained places of face-to-face interaction throughout this period, with testimony occurring in person. The punishments assessed were traditional, involving fines and shaming, and the courts almost always issued decisions that appealed explicitly to a desire for peace and order.

The next pair of chapters deal with the issue of honor, which was almost always present in conflicts. Chapter 2 focuses on male honor and the range of issues that led to slander cases being brought to court. The courts were embedded in this world of personal honor, and the judges and juries accepted and understood the stakes involved. Honor disputes could and did lead easily to fisticuffs or worse, and there is no doubt that interpersonal violence, physical and verbal, was common. People also saw value in going to court to resolve disputes or force an apology for an insult, since the courts were public spaces where resolution or reconciliation could be made to stick.

Women were very much a part of this discourse on honor (Chapter 3). Insulted as whores and witches, women defended their honor in a variety of settings. The ubiquitous witch insult lost some of its danger by about 1700, but it continued to be used to label some women as dangerous outsiders whose behavior and speech threatened others. The whore insult was even more common and had the effect of making all assaults on women's honor primarily attacks on their sexual behavior. Women were active participants in this world of insult and slander and resorted to the same practices, including filing lawsuits, that men used to defend themselves. In honor cases, the courts and the people were almost always in agreement on the importance of honor and how it needed to be defended.

Chapters 4 and 5 turn to the places and spaces where conflict occurred in these communities. The central importance of publicity is a key theme here. Not surprisingly, a dispute carried out in public had a wider significance and a greater chance of devolving into a long-standing feud than a dispute that was less widely known. Taverns were one of the most public of spaces, as well as places where (mostly) men paraded their status before others. Furthermore, taverns were ritualized spaces, where long-standing traditions governed the purchasing and sharing of drinks. Drinking added to the volatility of tavern sociability, and the presence of "outsiders" made them communications nodes as well. As a result, many local disputes originated in words or blows exchanged in taverns or other drinking locales.

People came into conflict in other public places, in front of the church, in the village streets, even on roads between villages. Chapter 5 highlights the complexity and variety of conflicts that ended in court cases. One obsession of the authorities, as well as the population, was with the role of gossip and rumor in spreading stories. Local officials, even state officials all the way up to the prince-abbots of the monasteries, wanted to prevent the spread of slanderous stories. They invested time and resources investigating the channels that led gossip to spread as rumor and eventually become widespread enough to be called "common knowledge." Here again we see the significance of publicity, of the circulation of stories from village to village, and the development of what Beat Kümin has called a "peasant public sphere."[33]

The ubiquity and drama of interpersonal conflict can obscure the widespread desire for peace and order. This desire was reflected in the variety of methods people used to resolve conflicts (Chapter 6). Disputes could be resolved informally, through mediation, or in court. Deeply embedded in the culture was an appreciation of the settlement, a *Vergleich*, which would bring people together, reconcile enemies, and solve difficult disputes. Not all conflicts were settled of course, nor was there enduring peace and quiet in the villages. But the persistent effort to achieve peace was part of life in the village, as was the reality of constant conflict.

The focus of this study is on social practice and on the agency of the common people in both initiating and resolving conflict. However, the rulers and officials of the small territories of Southwest Germany were also active, attempting to discipline the population and bring people's behavior into line with the proscriptions of the Catholic Church and the ruling elite (Chapter 7). This disciplinary program was quite limited, however, focusing on disciplining sexual behavior, suppressing public disorder created by young people, and enforcing obedience to state authorities. These projects had some success, primarily because they were supported by powerful elements within village communities such as wealthy farmers, master artisans, millers, and innkeepers. Where Church or state regulations clashed with the needs of the local population, as they did for example around the issue of

[33] Beat Kümin, *Drinking Matters. Public Houses and Social Exchange in Early Modern Central Europe* (Houndmills, 2007), ch. 6.

pre-marital sexual activity between courting couples, a compromise was reached. An extensive campaign of disciplining the population did not occur, but state structures like the local and district courts became more important. It is in the interplay of these institutions and their officials with social practice at the local level and the needs and desires of rural people that one can see state formation from below.

1

Lower Courts and Conflicts in the Village

In the century after 1650, lower courts operated in various forms across the Holy Roman Empire. There were village courts where peasant judges and juries adjudicated cases, noble courts presided over by *Junkers* and their officials, and city courts run by city councils. Lordships of all kinds, from large territorial states such as Bavaria to independent monasteries, ran court systems and presided over lower courts. This study is based on research in the court records of several smaller, primarily rural, Catholic ecclesiastical territories in Southwest Germany. Comparison with other case studies indicates that the function of these courts was not peculiar to these polities or this region.

Lower courts functioned at the intersection of several kinds of tension in the rural society of the post Thirty Years' War period. The first of these was the constant tension between the reality of social conflict and the broad desire for peace and order. Conflicts of all kinds were common in villages, but also, as André Holenstein argues, "there was a great social demand for the arbitration of disputes and the resolution of conflicts."[1] Studies of rural communities, particularly of those regions where courts were local and easily accessible, all describe a situation where people sought to resolve disputes in a variety of ways, using forms of non-judicial conflict resolution as well as going to court, sometimes interchangeably and often simultaneously.[2] Martin Dinges goes a step further and argues that rural folk went to court primarily to pressure the other party, with the goal of reaching an informal agreement rather than a formal judgment from the court.[3]

Peace and order were important values for villagers, as they were for their *Obrigkeiten*, state officials and local lords. Whether we refer to efforts to keep communal peace as "self-regulation," or as "the maintenance of social order," villagers drew on traditions of self-government to participate actively in keeping communal peace.[4] All recent studies show that neither informal conflict resolution

[1] Holenstein, "Klagen, anzeigen und supplizieren." Julia Haack emphasizes conflict, but also points to the desire for peace and order: Julia Haack, *Der vergällte Alltag: zur Streitkultur im 18. Jahrhunderts* (Köln, 2008).

[2] Barbara Krug-Richter, "Konfliktregulierung zwischen dörflicher Sozialkontrolle und patrimonialer Gerichtsbarkeit. Das Rügegericht in der Westfalischen Gerichtsherrschaft Cannstein, 1718/19" *Historische Anthropologie* 5 (1997): 227–8.

[3] Martin Dinges, "Justiznutzungen als soziale Kontrolle in der Frühen Neuzeit" in Andreas Blauert and Gerd Schwerhoff, eds. *Kriminalitätsgeschichte. Beiträge zur Sozial- und Kulturgeschichte der Vormoderne* (Konstanz 2000), pp. 503–44, esp. pp. 540–4.

[4] Krug-Richter, "Konfliktregulierung," emphasizes "conflict resolution." Dinges, "Justiznutzungen als soziale Kontrolle," emphasizes the goal of social control.

Keeping the Peace in the Village: Conflict and Peacemaking in Germany, 1650–1750. Marc R. Forster, Oxford University Press. © Marc R. Forster 2024. DOI: 10.1093/oso/9780198898474.003.0002

nor courts functioned primarily as instruments of social discipline from above and that they were not effective tools of state-building.[5] Conflict and conflict resolution were, above all, local matters within the village community.

In the century after 1650, villagers and local officials together found a balanced solution to the tension between conflict and the ideal of communal peace, developing a flexible and evolving mix of tools for resolving conflicts. To understand how this system worked we need to look at the rituals and practices of conflicts and their resolution. It is also important to examine the spaces where these conflicts took place and where they were resolved. Spaces were important above all because of their *Öffentlichkeit*, or public nature, which was a key element in determining the impact of disputes and hence was essential in resolving conflicts. How taverns and inns, marketplaces, the local church, and the administrative building (the *Amtshaus*), as well as the streets and houses of a village, functioned as spaces of conflict and resolution is a major aspect of this study.[6]

The second tension around the role of courts was between their regulatory role and their importance for settling disputes in rural communities. Lower courts regulated rural life, enforcing the rules that allowed the village economy, society, and political system to function. Some of this regulation took the form of social discipline, as when courts punished adulterers and fornicators, or couples who became pregnant before marrying. Lower courts also fined people, mostly the young, for a variety of "victimless crimes," such as dancing on Sundays or public drunkenness. More often, regulation meant punishing people for violating the local rules that governed agricultural practices, such as the use of pastures, hayfields, and woods, or the setting of boundaries and the placement of paths and fences.[7]

This regulatory role could clash with the role courts played in the resolution of conflict. Courts were part of an interlocking set of practices that prevented (or tried to prevent) interpersonal conflicts and violence from destroying the community. Personal insults and interpersonal violence were a significant element in the social practice of these small communities, among women as well as men.[8] Honor conflicts were common and public and often led to physical violence. A mix of informal resolution by family members and local people and "going to court" provided mechanisms to end such conflicts, restore honor, and prevent further escalation. Courts performed this function mostly at the behest of the villagers and in cooperation with them, which is another indication of the

[5] Schwerhoff, *Historische Kriminalitätsforschung*, esp. pp. 105–12.

[6] There were no courthouses as such in German villages, but more *Amtshäuser* were being built in the eighteenth century. Courts also met in taverns since they were the only large public buildings, other than the church. Kümin, *Drinking Matters*, pp. 126–30.

[7] Blickle, *Deutsche Untertanen*.

[8] Schlögl, "Kommunikation und Vergesellschaftung under Anwesenden"; Schlögl, *Anwesende und Abwesende*; Rainer Walz, "Agonale Kommunikation im Dorf der Frühen Neuzeit" *Westfälische Forschung* 42 (1992): 215–51.

role of the common folk in the formation of the state. An examination of the actual work of lower courts further elucidates these tensions.

Salem, January 1700

In January 1700, the Salem *Gericht*, or lower court, met on Saturdays, on the 9th, 16th, and 23rd.[9] The court convened in the *Hochgericht*, a building situated at the gate of the monastery complex at Salem, or Salmansweiler as it was known in the early modern period. The second ranking secular official of Salem, the *Vizekanzler* Dr. Reuthershauser, presided, assisted by the secretary and a "*Practikant*," a lawyer in training. The court protocols (or minutes) were recorded by the *Gerichtsschreiber*, Johann Franz Felbinger, in a neat, clear hand.[10]

The Salem *Gericht* was one of two legal venues local people from the monastery's territory could use during this period. Local artisans and farmers also brought complaints to the *Oberamt*, a kind of administrative court presided over by the *Oberamtmann*, the chief district official.[11] The *Oberamt* was not really a court, but rather an administrative body that (among other activities) heard and adjudicated disputes. People brought similar cases to the *Oberamt* as they did to the *Gericht*, and its protocols read like court protocols, referring to complainants (*Kläger*) and defendants (*Beklagte*). Its cases ended with a decision (*Bescheid*), just as the *Gericht*'s cases did.

In January 1700 these two instances heard twenty cases, fourteen in the *Gericht* and six at the *Oberamt*. All were from the local area, either from the community at the monastery or from villages under the monastery's legal jurisdiction. All were the kind of cases that lower courts throughout Germany dealt with, involving local and family disputes, questions of slander and honor, and property conflicts of various kinds. A brief survey of the court cases adjudicated at Salem over one month gives a sense of the role of these courts in daily life.

[9] On Salem: Katherine Brun, *The Abbot and his Peasants. Territorial Formation in Salem from the late Middle Ages to the Thirty Years' War* (Stuttgart, 2013); Erika Dillman und Hans-Jürgen Schulz, *Salem. Geschichte und Gegenwart* (Salem, 1989); Erika Dillman, *Stephan I. Fundamente des Barock. Salem an der Wende zum 18. Jahrhundert* (Tettnang, 1988); Erika Dillman, *Anselm II. Glanz und Ende eine Epoche. Eine Studie über den letzten großen Abt der Reichsabtei Salem* (Salem, 1987); Hermann Baier, "Die Stellung der Abtei Salem in Staat und Kirche" *Freiburger Diöcesan Archiv* 35 (1934): 131–54.

[10] Abbreviations for archives: GLAK = Generallandesarchiv Karlsruhe; HStAS = Hauptstaatsarchiv Stuttgart. GLAK 61/13342, pp. 1–26. These *Protokolle* are clearly clean copies of the notes Felbinger must have taken during the court sessions. David Warren Sabean, "Peasant Voices and Bureaucratic Texts" in Peter Becker and William Clark, eds. *Little Tools of Knowledge: Historical Essays on Academic and Bureaucratic Practices* (Ann Arbor, 2001), pp. 67–94; David Warren Sabean, "Village Court Protocols and Memory" in Andreas Würgler et al., eds. *Gemeinde, Reformation und Widerstand. Festschrift für Peter Blickle zum 60. Geburtstag* (Tübingen, 1998); Francisca Loetz, *A New Approach to the History of Violence. "Sexual Assault" and "Sexual Abuse" in Europe, 1500–1850* (Leiden and Boston, 2015), pp. 21–4.

[11] GLAK 61/13341, pp. 1–8.

Table 1.1 Cases Heard at Salem, Gericht, and Oberamt[12]

	Jan. 1681	Jan. 1696	Jan. 1700	Jan. 1710	Jan. 1720
Slander/Honor	4	4	4	2	3
Agricultural issues (Wood, haying, residence)	0	2	7	1	1
Property issues					
Sales	2	1	0	0	1
Debt	1	2	3	3	0
Inheritance	0	1	2	0	0
Family disputes			2	0	0
Sexual crimes/pregnancy	0	1	1	1	1
Political conflicts (Disobedience, taxes, *Gemeinde*)	2	2	1	0	0
Total:	9	13	20	7	6

The *Gericht* regularly dealt with disputes among the artisans working at the monastery. A large fire had destroyed many of the Cistercian monastery's buildings in March 1697, so by 1700 the complex was a busy construction site, as the abbots invested in extensive new Baroque and Rococo buildings. Artisans were notoriously touchy about their honor, because any stain—a moral failing, sexual misdeed, or legal difficulty—could ruin their ability to work in their craft, since it made them ineligible for membership in a guild. It was in the context of a monastic complex teeming with young artisans and their families that a number of disputes erupted.

On January 9, Hans Georg Grotz, a journeyman locksmith, along with some companions, brought a complaint against the journeymen carpenters, citing in particular Joseph Hueber and Ulrich Vogler.[13] The dispute among the journeymen was about a New Year's Eve tradition at the monastery. On this evening, monastery officials gave money to young men who went around the complex "singing in the New Year." The locksmiths and weavers had led the singing, at least according to Grotz's testimony, while other journeymen had avoided participating but wanted a share of the money collected just the same. After hearing the initial complaint, the court ordered all involved parties to return the following week to testify.

On January 16, more witnesses were heard. It became clear that the carpenters had not appreciated that the locksmiths and weavers had been unwilling to share the proceeds from the singing. According to the weavers, the carpenter Hueber

[12] 1681: GLAK 61/13335, pp. 5v–9r; 1696: GLAK 61/13337, pp. 137–60, GLAK 61/13338, pp. 67–77; 1700: GLAK 61/13341, pp. 1–8; 1710: GLAK 61/13345, pp. 450–4, GLAK 61/13346, pp. 431–3; 1720: GLAK 61/13350, pp. 459–72.

[13] GLAK 61/13342, pp. 7–10.

had said "if the master weaver keeps the money from the singing, what does he do with bigger things?" This amounted to an accusation of corruption. The master weaver demanded that his honor be restored after this insult. Hueber denied the charge, stating that he and his companions had not insulted anyone, although the weavers had slandered them. They had only said that they should get the money they deserved. The court was clearly confused by what had happened and, in an exasperated tone, handed down an indecisive decision. "...A punishment will lead to further conflict and hate, so the insulting words are cancelled (*aufgehebt*) by the lordship."

Honor disputes of this kind were the regular business of all lower courts. On January 23 the *Gericht* handled a straightforward case.[14] Melchior Löhlin from the village of Mimmenhausen brought a complaint for slander against Sebastian Bürenbaum from Weildorf. Witnesses had heard Bürenbaum call Löhlin a *Schelm* (scoundrel) in front of others at the gates of the town of Meersburg. Bürenbaum denied the insult, saying that he considered Löhlin an honorable and honest man ("*ein ehrlicher Bidermann*"), adding that "if he had said such a thing while drunk, he is very sorry." The court brought the case to a close by stating "we will let this issue end with this statement [from Bürenbaum], and therefore Löhlin has nothing more to complain about, and furthermore many people, before the court and elsewhere, have defended him as an honorable man." In these honor cases the Salem court emphasized its role in publicly setting aside or solving disputes, rather than punishing slanders or criminals.

The *Oberamt* used rather more heavy-handed methods in a case brought before it on January 11. Hans Georg Baumann, a journeyman carpenter, brought a complaint against Hans Georg Keüsch, who "called him a s.v. dog's...and as a result the other artisans no longer want to eat with him."[15] The accused admitted the insult and the *Oberamt* fined him 30 *Kreuzer* and ordered the insult canceled. The quick decision and fine may reflect the more administrative character of proceedings before the *Oberamt*.

These courts considered it appropriate to interfere directly in family disputes, here again looking for solutions as well as punishments. Thus, the *Oberamt* engaged directly in a long-running feud between Elizabeth Schneiderin and her son-in-law, Joseph Knörlin.[16] The two could not get along, even though the protocol records Elizabeth giving Knörlin 100 *Gulden* and also paying off a fine he owed. The court then stated, "because these people live in permanent conflict, the lordship hands down the following order for the prevention of further misery, that Knörlin must find another residence and should move out of the little house

[14] GLAK 61/13342, pp. 25–6.

[15] GLAK 61/13341, pp. 3–4. The actual insult was "dog's cunt," usually elided for propriety's sake in the court minutes. s.v. means *salve venia*, "begging your leave." See below, Chapter 2.

[16] GLAK 61/13341, pp. 7–8.

within two weeks." Not only did the *Oberamt* actively seek to regulate domestic conditions, it was also clearly cognizant of this family's interactions and even the size of the house.

To get another sense of how these courts worked, let us examine "a day in the life" of the court.[17] In winter the court probably did not begin hearing cases until 8 a.m.[18] On January 16 the court began its work by hearing witnesses in the dispute among artisans about the gratuities for singing on New Year's Day. This was a continuation of the case, which was originally brought to the court the week before, and it brought quite a few men, parties to the dispute and witnesses, into the court. The court next dealt with a dispute over a small debt of 2 *Gulden*, followed by an issue with a disputed inheritance, where the court ordered that a proper inventory of the inheritance be made. Then the court took up a dispute from the village of Oberuhldingen about how the money needed to pay off a communal debt should be raised, a dispute that set the big-landed farmers (the *Bauern*) against the small farmers (*Söldner*). Finally, the court ended its day's work by fining a man for illegally housing a "foreign" weaver, that is, someone from another lordship.

The workings of the Salem courts described here are quite typical of lower courts found in the smaller territories of Southwest Germany. They handled a mix of low-level cases, involving slander, property disputes, and other interpersonal conflicts.[19] The Salem courts worked fast, for example dealing on January 9 and 16 with a dispute that took place on January 1. Other cases also often came before the court within days of the incident that initiated them. The courts were sensitive to and knowledgeable about local conditions in the villages and often sought resolutions that would prevent further disputes. Particularly in cases involving debts, the courts sought to arbitrate instead of handing down hard and fast decisions. Villagers who brought cases to these courts could expect a resolution, but did not have to fear that a punishment was the only possible outcome.[20]

When the courts did make decisions, they never referred to legal principles and only rarely to statutes or ordinances—these were common law courts.[21] Local knowledge, rumors, and hearsay were considered, but were also checked by testimony from the parties and by witnesses. While local notables, such as wealthy farmers or *Amtmänner* (often the same people) surely were given special

[17] GLAK 61/13341, pp. 7–17.

[18] Brun, *The Abbot and his Peasants*, p. 259.

[19] Compare other studies: Barbara Krug-Richter, "Von Rügebrauch zur Konfliktkultur. Rechtsethnologische Perspektive in der Europäische Ethnologie" *Jahrbuch für Volkskunde* N. F. 28 (2005): 27–40; Michael Frank, *Dörfliche Gesellschaft und Kriminalität: das Fallbeispiel Lippe 1650–1800* (Paderborn, 1995); Holenstein, *"Gute Policey" und lokale Gesellschaft*.

[20] Martin Dinges highlights how and why people used courts, see "Justiznutzungen als soziale Kontrolle," pp. 503–44.

[21] John Jordan, "Rethinking Disputes and Settlements: How Historians can use Legal Anthropology" in Stephen Cummin and Laura Kounine, eds. *Cultures of Conflict Resolution in Early Modern Europe* (Farnham, 2016), pp. 32–3.

consideration, poorer and less powerful men and women also had their day in court. If local people preferred courts with local perspectives, and that operated rapidly, cheaply, and fairly, the Salem courts fit the bill.[22]

Niedergerichte—Lower Courts

The lower courts of Southwest Germany all shared these basic characteristics of being local, meeting frequently, and adjudicating and mediating personal disputes, property conflicts, and community tensions. At the same time, in accord with the political particularism of the Holy Roman Empire, each court had its particular mix of jurisdictions and functions. As we have seen, the Salem court operated parallel to and probably in cooperation with the *Oberamt*. The *Oberamt* of the Premonstratensian monastery at Rot an der Rot operated in a similar fashion as the *Oberamt* at Salem, but there is no evidence of another court at Rot. The *Verhörprotokolle* (minutes of the hearings) from Rot include not only decisions made in disputes brought before the *Oberamt*, but also recordings of various official acts, such as marriage contracts, inheritances, retirement agreements (*Leibgedinge*), payments required of serfs (death payments, fees for manumission from serfdom, etc.), and tenancy agreements. They thus frequently functioned as an administrative or even notarial body.[23]

The *Oberamt* of the Commandery of the Teutonic Knights at Mainau also maintained a court, and the protocols of this institution have survived from the 1660s on.[24] These protocols, unlike those from Rot, usually do not record marriage contracts, inheritance arrangements, and the like because Mainau kept a second series called *Contractsprotokolle*.[25] This division reflects a greater administrative sophistication and division of labor at Mainau, which was embedded in the larger organization of the Teutonic Knights. Like other lower courts, the Mainau court dealt with disputes from a group of villages under Mainau's jurisdiction and, just as at Salem, the court met weekly to hear cases mostly brought by villagers and village *Amtmänner*.

The courts in these ecclesiastical territories had small staffs. We have seen that at Salem in 1700 the vice chancellor presided over the court, assisted by a secretary, a *Praktikant*, and the scribe. The *Praktikant* was an addition to the personnel, since in 1698 Dr. Ruetershauser, at that time just *Oberamtmann*, had only two

[22] Dinges, "Justiznutzungen als soziale Kontrolle," pp. 515–20. Anthony Crubaugh, *Balancing the Scales of Justice: Local Courts and Rural Society in Southwest France, 1750–1800* (University Park, 2002).

[23] HStAS B486, Bd 13–15, 18.

[24] GLAK 61/7599–61/7606.

[25] These kinds of contracts are sometimes found in the *Verhörprotokolle*, mostly in cases where disputes about them were brought there for adjudication or mediation.

assistants.[26] The court at Rot was similar, although in the seventeenth century the abbot himself at least sometimes presided. So, in 1684 the abbot, the cellarer, and the *Oberamtmann* were the judges, probably assisted by a scribe.[27] In the 1670s, the Commander of the Mainau House of the Teutonic Order presided over the court there as well, along with the chancellor.[28] The Abbot of Salem also occasionally presided over the court there. The direct participation of these imperial princes in their courts shows how small these territories were; it also shows that the abbots and commanders considered their courts important.

The *Gericht und Frevel Protokolle* from the village of Wollmatingen are rather different.[29] This was a true village court, which met yearly in the fall, usually in early November, but sometimes as early as September. Wollmatingen was under the jurisdiction of the Bishops of Constance, whose *Hochstift* was small, geographically fragmented, and lightly governed. Cases at Wollmatingen were adjudicated by the village *Gericht*, a group of men chosen by the villagers from among the citizens of the village. In the 1690s, nine men were listed as *Richter* (judges), and most of them were also members of the village council (*Rat*).[30] The annual *Frevelgericht* seems to have usually been overseen by an official from Constance who traveled once a year to Wollmatingen, which is a one-hour walk north of the city.[31]

The *Frevelgericht* handled minor crimes and violations of the village agricultural rules. At the court session on December 1, 1700, for example, one person was fined for fighting, a widow was fined for holding a dance party, three couples received hefty fines for getting pregnant before their weddings (*zu früher Beischlaf*, pre-marital intimacy), two slander cases were adjudicated, and five people were fined for the violation of agricultural rules, such as illegal grazing or improper taking of wood.[32] In 1701, agricultural issues predominated even more, with eight fines for illegal taking of wood and three fines for drying flax inside houses (a fire danger) being imposed, and several disputes over paths through fields being resolved.[33] The village court also handled disputes and punishments between meetings of the annual court, often less routine cases that required testimony of witnesses and thus could not be held over until the end of the year.

The court of the Amt Rotteln, another district of the *Hochstift* Konstanz, also functioned as a kind of village court. The protocols from 1659 call it "the village court held at Thengen." Listed are the seven *Urteilsprecher* ("judgment speakers") and the *Index* or secretary of the court, all local men.[34] This court pronounced

[26] GLAK 61/13340, pp. 191, 196. The *Praktikant* was presumably a lawyer in training.
[27] HstAS B486/Bd 15, pp. 141r, 142r, 152r, 165v. [28] GLAK 61/7600.
[29] GLAK 61/13268. [30] GLAK 61/13268, pp. 35–7, 39–40, 47–8.
[31] Johann Baptist von Kolb, *Historisch-statistisch-topographisches Lexicon von dem Großherzogthum Baden*. Band 3. p. 398.
[32] GLAK 61/13268, pp. 64–8. [33] GLAK 61/13268, pp. 68–71.
[34] GLAK 61/6958. No pagination.

Table 1.2 Wollmatingen Frevelgericht 1669–1727: Overview of its Work[35]

975+ total "entries."
Public order
Insults, swearing: 98 Fights and violence: 87 Drunk and disorderly: 60 Taverns: 17 A small number of cases of disobedience to authorities Note: there are some blasphemy cases mixed into the insults category.
Moral issues Pregnancy before marriage, sexual crimes: 37
Regulating agriculture Illegal grazing: 229+ Illegal taking of wood: 88 Illegal haying: 38 Stealing fruit, acorns, grapes: 34 Boundaries and right of way: 16
Economic issues Collecting debts: 13 A few inheritance disputes

judgments and assessed fines in cases of illegal grazing and other agricultural violations, as well as insults and slander, and also debts. In addition, it recorded sales of property, particularly livestock, for which there was a lively market in this area. The court also published ordinances and regulations, sometimes coming from Constance and at other times from communal authorities.[36]

These courts shared a number of characteristics. They all adjudicated cases of lower justice, that is, crimes that were neither capital offenses, nor, since these were Catholic territories, offenses reserved for the Church courts, such as broken marriage promises. They all dealt as well with civil cases, particularly slander, but also economic issues like the payment of debts and disputes over the buying and selling of property. Most of them were administrative bodies as well, issuing ordinances and decrees, recording the appointment of local officials, including midwives, and registering marriage contracts and wills.

Moving from the daily and weekly work of the lower courts to the annual docket of one of these courts, the Mainau *Oberamt* in 1710, we get a further sense of their work.

[35] GLAK 61/13268. "Entries" seems a better category than "cases," since not all of the issues dealt with at the *Frevelgericht* were actual legal cases.

[36] The *Gerichtsprotokolle* from the Amt Bohlingen (another Constance district) are similar. I have only sampled them. GLAK 61/5174.

Table 1.3 Cases Before the Lower Court of Commandery of Mainau of the Teutonic Knights, 1710[37]

Property issues	
Property transactions	28
Marriages	14
Pregnancy	2
Inheritance	14
Debts	41
Wage disputes	4
Apprenticeships	2
Interpersonal conflicts	
Insults and honor	14
Conflicts with neighbors	1
Conflicts with outsiders	5
Agricultural conflicts	
Wood	7
Haying	1
Grazing	1
Paths and fences	3
Communal issues	
Appointments	3
Conflicts in commune	4
Miscellaneous	7
Total	161

The court at Mainau dealt with a large number of property cases. One cluster of these involved disputes over the sale of property, both land and livestock. In these cases, the standard dispute involved a problem with payment, since most of these transactions were made on the basis of promises of future payment. Purchasers sometimes could not or would not pay, and the seller brought the case to court, often in order to arrange a payment schedule. The largest number of cases involved debts, mostly cases of creditors seeking payment. Many debt payments were apparently in arrears in 1710, when this region was suffering from poor harvests exacerbated by the quartering of troops during the War of the Spanish Succession. Creditors sent representatives to Mainau in an attempt to get their debts paid. So, for example, a baker from Constance came to Mainau on August 23 as the wine harvest was being collected and sought payment on five different loans in Mainau villages. He seems to have sought the payment of considerable overdue interest, but the court only ordered debtors to pay small amounts of wine, the best that was possible in what the court called "bad times."[38] The Mainau court frequently dealt with these kinds of debt claims, and it often protected local

[37] GLAK 7696, pp. 1r–68v. *Verhörprotokolle*, "hearing protocols."
[38] GLAK 7696, pp. 49v–50v.

Table 1.4 Lower Court Cases, Overview of Selected Sources

Court records	# of cases	Insults, violence	Taverns
Deutschordenskommende Mainau Verhörprotokolle, GLAK 61/7599 May 1661–April 1663	63	18	5
Deutschordenskommende Mainau Verhörprotokolle, GLAK 61/7602 Jan 1685–Jan 1687	168	63	12
Hochstift Konstanz Amt Rotteln, GLAK 61/7958 1659–63	81	13	2
Hochstift Konstanz Wollmatingen, GLAK 61/13268 Sept. 1669–Dec. 1695	218	63	??
Kloster Salem Gerichtsprotokolle, GLAK 61/13334 1669–72	124	84	24

villagers from creditors, citing poor harvests and pointing out that it was impossible for many to pay even the interest on loans.

Other property conflicts in 1710 involved inheritances and marriage agreements. The cases recorded in the protocols in Mainau sometimes involved adjudicating disputes, while at other times the parties to an agreement brought it to Mainau to have it recorded. It appears that in 1710 the separate protocol of contracts and marriages was either not kept or only sporadically so. This means that important documents were recorded in the court protocols, as happened in other lordships as well.

Personal conflicts were also adjudicated at Mainau, particularly from the surrounding villages of Allmannsdorf, Dettingen, Dingelsdorf, Litzelstetten, and Staad. The court was close enough to be fairly easily reached on foot, and men and women brought charges of slander and insults to their honor there. As we shall see, most interpersonal conflicts had an honor component, and the Mainau court, like all lower courts, played an important role in adjudicating and resolving these disputes.

This basic survey of a selection of lower court records from small Catholic territories in Southwest Germany shows that about a third of all cases these courts handled involved not just conflict—after all, most court cases were about some sort of dispute—but personal conflicts that involved insults, attacks on someone's honor, and physical violence.[39] Some courts, like the village court in Rotteln, adjudicated fewer cases of violence, perhaps because there were other instances that handled such cases. These courts were very busy keeping the peace. Between 1669 and 1672, eighty-four of the 124 cases adjudicated by the court of the Abbey

[39] GLAK 61/7599 (*DO Mainau*) 1661–3, GLAK 61/7602 (*DO Mainau*) 1685–7, GLAK 61/13334 (*Salem GerichtsProt.*) 1669–72, GLAK 61/13268 (*Wollmatingen*) 1669–95, GLAK 61/6958 (*Rotteln*) 1659–63.

of Salem dealt with the more violent disputes. This court closely supervised both the tavern at the abbey and the large population of artisans, servants, and laborers attached to the monastery, a population that seems to have generated many conflicts involving insults and physical violence.

These courts all had the authority to impose and enforce punishments. Punishments ranged quite widely, from admonitions to keep the peace, to reprimands and shaming punishments, to fines, imprisonment, and banishment. These lower courts were limited in the physical punishments they could use, and of course they could not impose the death penalty, as these were penalties reserved for higher courts ("blood courts"). Some of the lower courts did enforce aspects of church discipline, for example punishments for a failure to attend church services, but other cases (particularly disputed marriage promises) were reserved for the ecclesiastical courts.[40]

At the end of the cases, courts admonished people to bury their enmity and, if there was any honor dispute involved, the decision stated that "all insults were removed by the lordship." Sometimes people were let off with a warning, as was Joseph Felder, accused in 1671 of impregnating a maid.[41] Accepting Joseph's somewhat garbled defense that he had slept in the woman's bed, but had not had sex with her, the court let him go with a "strong warning."[42] Two women from Uhldingen were brought in front of the Salem court in 1706 for verbal conflicts that "caused disorder throughout the village."[43] They were told "from here on out to leave each other and other people in peace and quiet" or else face serious punishment. When Jörg Kräss and Christian Knöbelspiess appeared in court after an exchange of insults, they were admonished to make peace, which they did.[44] "They agreed to be friends, confirmed peace with several *Mass* of wine, and swore a pact of peace." Since these courts were heavily involved in negotiating agreements, mediating economic disputes (particularly debt issues) in other aspects of their work, it is not surprising that they could also work to diffuse interpersonal conflicts without using a heavy hand.

Fines were the most common punishments, across all of the courts. These ranged widely, starting with the very small fines of fractions of a *Gulden* assessed by the Wollmatingen Village Court for violations of grazing regulations or for illegally taking wood. All of these courts handed out serious fines for rebellious words, as the Salem court did in 1671.[45] Fines for pre-marital sex were also consistently high, between 7 and 15 *Gulden*, an indication of the authorities' concern for improper sexual behavior. The court at Salem assessed eighty-three fines

[40] See Satu Lidman, *Zum Spektakel und Abscheu. Schand- und Ehrenstrafen als Mittel öffentlicher Disziplinierung in München um 1600* (Bern, 2008).
[41] GLAK 61/13334, pp. 99–100.
[42] This practice was known as "bundling" in England and in colonial New England.
[43] GLAK 61/13346, pp. 21–2.
[44] GLAK 61/13334, p. 108.
[45] GLAK 61/13334, pp. 111–13.

between 1669–72, as compared to twenty-two punishments of other kinds. The other courts operated in a similar fashion.

The second most common form of punishment was imprisonment. The court at Rot an der Rot used imprisonment more than the other courts, perhaps because it was a small lordship, with all its villages clustered around the monastery. Imprisonments at Rot ranged from the eight days served in "the tower" by a repeat offender in 1669 to the six hours served by Peter Guglmayer and Michael Hellmann for a tavern brawl.[46] The court also sometimes gave convicted men a choice between a fine and a prison term. Hans Schödle's son was given the option of spending a day and a night in the tower, or paying a fine of 3 *Gulden*.[47] He chose the fine, probably to avoid the long-term damage to his honor caused by imprisonment.

Men were generally punished with fines or imprisonment. Women often suffered shaming punishments. These included exposing women in the pillory or the stocks (the *Pranger*) or in the *Halsgeige*, a metal collar.[48] In most places these instruments were set up in front of the church on a Sunday. The village court in Wollmatingen used these punishments, but also regularly punished men with the "Spanish Coat," a kind of barrel placed over the guilty party, who was then paraded through the village.[49] This was the favored punishment for men convicted of adultery or pre-marital sex.

A variation on the shaming punishments were the church punishments. In a fairly extreme punishment, Basche Romer and Caspar Georg were sentenced to stand before the parish church in Wollmatingen for a whole day, one in the Spanish Coat and the other in a "Schnabel," a metal beak-shaped mask.[50] This was a punishment for fishing on Corpus Christi Day, rather than attending church and the annual procession. More commonly, men and women were required to donate wax to the parish church as punishment for missing church, or for getting drunk on Sundays or feast days. Several children in Wollmatingen were ordered to publicly pray the Rosary as punishment for stealing twelve beets.[51]

The use of pilgrimages and praying the Rosary points to the survival of penitential elements in the judicial culture of these Catholic territories.[52] Work punishments had this character, as did shaming punishments, since they were framed as a showing of public repentance for moral failings. Monastic lordships like Rot

[46] HstAS B486/Bd 14, pp. 127r, 145r–146r. [47] HstAS B486/Bd 14, p. 99v.

[48] Isabel Hull, *Sexuality, State, and Civil Society in Germany, 1700–1815* (Ithaca, 1991), pp. 77–88.

[49] GLAK 61/13268, pp. 66, 108, 173r–173v, 1717, 2 January. Women punished with the "collar" were also sometimes paraded through the village.

[50] GLAK 61/13268, p. 33.

[51] GLAK 61/13268, p. 169v. See also pp. 23, 165v for other examples of people ordered to pray the Rosary.

[52] Xavier Roussuaux, "Entre accommodement local et contrôle étatique. Pratiques judiciaires et non-judiciaires dans le reglèment des conflits en Europe médiévale et modern" in Benoît Garnot ed. *L'Infrajudiciaire du Moyen Age à l'epoque contemporaine* (Dijon: 1996), p. 98.

and Salem often referred to penance quite directly by sentencing men to imprisonment "on bread and water."

Work punishments were widely used, particularly by Salem and the village court in Wollmatingen in the early eighteenth century. It is possible that these punishments were imposed in cases of men who could not pay the fines. This may have been what happened when Franz Greüz had his fine of 20 *Gulden* "moderated" to six days of work for the lordship.[53] Similarly, Jerg Allmayer, who stole a small amount of wood, was punished with two days of work "in consideration of his poverty and his miserable condition."[54] Furthermore, these punishments fit with the idea of creating a disciplined and productive workforce and were used as an alternative to imprisonment.

The most serious punishments meted out were banishments. In all cases, banishments were given to women who were found guilty of sexual crimes, adultery, and sex outside of marriage. In 1671, Catherina Dürrin, a thirty-year-old servant, admitted to having sex four different times with Jacob Seüter, who was also related to her in the third degree.[55] Both Dürrin and Seüter were banished. Maria Hubennestlerin testified in 1710 that she had been seduced by Hans Jerg Mayer and was banished from the Mainau lordship "as an example."[56] The Wollmatingen court used exile on several occasions, sending women out of the lordship for one year as a punishment for getting pregnant out of wedlock.[57] As noted above, the men in these cases only received shaming punishments.

As with much of the work of the courts, there was a tension in their administration of punishments. The court decisions almost always stressed a desire for peace and reconciliation, expressing the idea that a court decision should put an end to conflicts and disputes. Yet the use of shaming punishments tapped into the deep concern in this society for personal honor and were intentionally dishonoring. It seems unlikely that the people exposed in the stocks, paraded through the village in the "Spanish Coat," or put in prison felt a sense of closure. The fact that people brought up old punishments, including prison time and fines, when they wanted to attack someone's honor, highlights the ongoing stain that punishments left behind.

Conflicts in the Countryside

A broad survey of lower court records makes it clear that German villages were riddled with conflicts, conflicts that often spilled over into verbal and physical violence. There were tensions and conflicts within families, over inheritance,

[53] GLAK 61/13268, p. 157r. [54] GLAK 61/7607, p. 22r.
[55] GLAK 61/13334, p. 55. [56] GLAK 61/7606, pp. 15v–16r.
[57] GLAK 61/13268, pp. 173r–v, 183v, 190v–191r.

sexuality, and power, between neighbors over boundary lines, the husbandry of animals, and the organization of agricultural life, and between villagers over debts, property sales, and control of local institutions. Young people and their parents disputed promises of marriage and came into conflict over unexpected pregnancies. Villagers fought outsiders over a drink with words and fists and opposed distant institutions and their lords who sought to collect dues or taxes. Poor villagers and servants demanded pay from their employers, usually richer farmers in the village, and landed farmers fought with their servants and farm workers over conditions of labor. These conflicts frequently led to verbal insults and quite often to physical violence. As Barbara Krug-Richter states, village "communication structure and culture were strongly characterized by conflict."[58]

Yet it is difficult to say whether German villages in the century after the Thirty Years' War were any more conflict-ridden than they were earlier or later. The fragmentary nature of court records from the period and the overlapping and conflicted jurisdictional setting makes any broad statistical survey almost impossible. Local studies come to a variety of conclusions. In the Austrian District of Triberg, studied by Michaela Hohkamp, the number of conflicts that came to the local court was fairly stable between 1650 and 1750.[59] Eva Lacour's study of the Eifel region in western Germany also shows stable levels of conflict and violence for much of this period.[60] Some scholars see more conflict developing in the later eighteenth century, particularly over issues of property.[61] Historians who focus on social and economic developments rather than the history of crime argue that there was increasing fuel for social conflict in the villages over the course of the eighteenth century. Population growth put pressure on resources where communities practiced partible inheritance, and in regions of impartible inheritance economic differences grew between those peasants with access to land and the growing group of landless peasants, farm laborers, and servants.[62] Whether and to what extent the evolving social and economic situation led to increased conflict in villages is impossible to quantify, and the sources used in this study only give an impressionistic sense of the frequency of conflict in rural society.

Lower courts played an important role in the communal regulation of agricultural life. Courts fined people for the illegal taking of wood and the improper

[58] Krug-Richter, "Konfliktregulierung," p. 220. She is referencing Walz, "Agonale Kommunikation."

[59] Hohkamp, *Herrschaft in der Herrschaft*. Hohkamp identifies a growing number of honor conflicts after 1750. Triberg is in modern Baden-Württemberg, between Freiburg and Karlsruhe.

[60] Eva Lacour, "Faces of Violence Revisited. A Typology of Violence in Early Modern Rural Germany" *Journal of Social History* 34 (2001): 649–67. Eva Lacour, *Schlagereyen und Unglücksfälle: zur historischen Psychologie und Typologie von Gewalt in der frühneuzeitlichen Eifel* (Frankfurt/M., 2000).

[61] Peter Wettmann-Jungblut, "Modern Times, Modern Crimes. Kriminalität und Strafpraxis im badischen Raum 1700–1850" in Rebekka Habermas and Gerd Schwerhoff, eds. *Verbrechen im Blick. Perspektiven der neuzeitlichen Kriminalitätsgeschichte* (Frankfurt, 2009), esp. pp. 154–5.

[62] Govind Sreenivasan, *The Peasants of Ottobeuren. A Rural Society in Early Modern Europe* (Cambridge, 2004); David Warren Sabean, *Property, Production, and Family in Neckarhausen, 1700–1870* (Cambridge, 1990); Frank, *Dörfliche Gesellschaft und Kriminalität.*

grazing of animals. They also investigated and mediated disputes over property boundaries and the use of paths and rights of way, and enforced other rules regulating economic activity. This kind of work was central to the docket of courts based at the village level, like the court at Wollmatingen, but the court at Mainau and the courts at the monasteries also dealt regularly with the regulation of agricultural life.

At the *Frevelgericht* of 1703 at Wollmatingen, the peasant judges fined four people for drying hemp in the oven, a serious fire danger forbidden by local statute.[63] Three women, probably from the poorer families in the village, judging by the small amounts of hay they had stolen, were fined for illegal haying. Fines were handed out in ten cases for illegal grazing of animals or for letting cattle or horses get loose so that they damaged the arable or the vineyards. In this period there appears to have been considerable conflict between the farmers who focused on animal husbandry and those whose income depended primarily on viticulture. This was a fairly common mix of violations of the agricultural regulations faced by this court.

The illegal grazing of livestock was a major issue for the annual court session in Wollmatingen, particularly after 1700. At the annual court in 1717, about 20% of the cases involved illegal grazing of various kinds.[64] Most often, the crime involved horses or cattle being let out to graze in communal pastures that were not open for use. Farmers let horses graze illegally at night, presumably when they were not needed for plowing or hauling. The fines were not large, and one has the impression that wealthier farmers, those who could afford horse teams, considered these fines part of the cost of feeding their animals and they paid them without protest. More serious conflicts between villagers arose when animals got into fields and vineyards and damaged crops.

All lower courts dealt with the regulation of the use of forests. The monasteries and the Teutonic Knights at Mainau understood the forests as important sources of income for the lordships and in many cases for the local communes as well. Local officials reported those who stole wood to the courts, which routinely fined them.[65] The local official called the *Bannwart* (boundary guard) often brought woodcutting cases to the Mainau court. These cases involved men who took larger amounts of wood, a large tree or more, often for the purpose of selling it elsewhere. In 1710, for example, a man in the village of Allmannsdorf was found in possession of five recently cut oak trees. Over the course of two court hearings, it became clear that he had purchased them from a *Bauer*, a big tenant farmer, who had cut them down in order to extend a field.[66] The court issued fines and forbade the farmer to expand his fields.

[63] GLAK 61/13268, pp. 83–6. [64] GLAK 61/13268, pp. 187r–193r.
[65] Some examples: GLAK 61/7600, 1672, 16 January, 1672, 11 June, 1673, 3 May, 1675, 8 June.
[66] GLAK 61/7606, pp. 23r, 23a v, 24r.

At times villagers attempted to justify or explain why they cut down a tree. In January 1684, Jacob Baumbgartner, from Allmannsdorf, said he cut down a cherry tree because it "stood in the middle of the path and hindered the passage and in any case it was small and did not bear fruit. He used the wood in his house."[67] The court did not accept this explanation, perhaps because Baumbgartner had a reputation for being disobedient. "He is earnestly warned that, since he does not pay much attention to either orders or prohibitions (*weder um Gebott noch Verbott vil frage*) and has shown himself to be very disobedient in all things, should he be found out in such things again, he will be banished from the territory."

Lower courts often dealt with the nitty gritty of agricultural life in villages. In 1684 a couple complained that their neighbor had planted eighteen fruit trees in the garden next to their vineyard, damaging their vines, presumably by bringing shade.[68] The defendant claimed that the garden had "orchard rights" and he should be allowed to plant fruit trees there. The court ordered a mediator to be appointed to examine the situation and make a ruling, with the costs of the mediator paid by the loser of the dispute. In 1710, a dispute over a newly built fence, which blocked a pathway to a pasture, required the court to send someone to personally inspect the location in question.[69] When a farmer in Bachen failed to participate in the cleaning of the drainage ditches, complaining that they were too far from his fields, he was cited by communal officials at the court at Rot. The court's judges, the *Oberamtmann* and two monks, the prior and the cellarer, ruled that the farmer had to pay a fee to help clean the ditches, but that they (the ditches) should be adjusted to serve his fields better.[70]

The cases point to several characteristics of these courts. First, they operated very close to daily life, adjudicating the kinds of issues that caused conflict in an agricultural community. Secondly, the judges and jurors understood the implications of a new plantation of fruit trees or the illegal grazing of livestock. These courts were operating from within this rural world, not as outside forces.

Disputes over property and debts did not have to lead to personal conflicts or violence, and they were often settled through arbitrated agreements. In a typical case, the Teutonic Knights' court in Mainau ordered Christian Schulter from Dettingen to pay off his debt of 57fl, 20kr by paying 10fl each fall at the time of the wine harvest.[71] Such agreements were particularly common in the case of widows, who had presumably inherited the debts and had limited means to make payments. In 1663 a widow and her creditors were asked to come to an agreement outside of court.[72] In 1685, Regina Rauchin from Egg owed the Franciscan

[67] GLAK 61/7602, pp. 6v–7r. [68] GLAK 61/7602, pp. 11v–12r.
[69] GLAK 61/7606, p. 36r. See also pp. 38v–39r.
[70] HSTAS B486/Bd 14, p. 121v. 1668. Monks at places like Salem and Rot were often of peasant background, so they would have understood the issues involved in these disputes.
[71] GLAK 61/7602, 1686, 2 March. [72] GLAK 61/7599, pp. 94–7.

convent in Constance 82fl in back rent on a vineyard. "Because the widow does not have this money on hand, nor will she ever have it, the convent should look to find a purchaser for the vineyard." The court stated that the convent had a legal right to this debt, but nevertheless the debt would not be paid. The authorities in Mainau also excused payment of 50fl for the mortgage Mainau held on the same property.[73] In the 1660s, courts usually ordered agreements where debtors had to arrange to pay off the capital, but interest accumulated during the previous decades of war was to be forgiven.[74]

Disputes over debts could, however, cause further conflict, leading to the typical escalation of insults and physical violence. In 1671 a dispute over a debt resulted in a fight when one man hit another over the head with a rake.[75] A tavern dispute over money owed on a bar tab could easily lead to insults and violence. When Hans Dreher insisted that his drinking companion Hans Miller owed 5 *Batzen*, Miller burst out "if he says that he owes him something, then he is not speaking like an honest man (*ein Biedermann)* but rather like a scoundrel (*Schelm*)."[76] In court Miller said he could not deny having said this and that he had been drinking so heavily that he had no memory of the insults.

Conflicts that arose over debts are a subset of conflicts over property more generally. The lively market for both land and livestock in southern Germany meant that country people at all levels of society were involved in property transactions.[77] A person's reputation for personal integrity was essential to their ability to function in this market, for it made everyone sensitive to rumor, public discussion, and intimations of dishonesty. In this context, insults like *Schelm* (scoundrel) and *Dieb* (thief) were not just used generically, for they were often deployed as the opposite of *Biedermann* (honest man).[78] In a dispute over property, calling someone a thief was a pointed insult aimed at one's reliability in a property transaction.

Property disputes could and did lead to interpersonal conflicts, including exchanges of insults and violence. In 1659, Hans Schädler from Kirchdorf (near the Abbey of Rot an der Rot) appeared at five in the morning at the house of Georg Palster in the village of Unteropfingen.[79] The two men were pitted against each other in a property dispute, and Palster asked Schädler if he had any new information about their law case. Schädler said no, he had heard nothing, but went on to say that Palster and Georg Kueff, the *Amman* in Kirchdorf, were "fine scoundrels" (*schöne Schelmen*) and that they were bad mouthing him with the

[73] GLAK 61/7602, 1685, 7 July, pp. 47v–48r. [74] GLAK 61/7599, pp. 29–30, 38, 46–7.

[75] GLAK 61/13334, p. 103. [76] GLAK 61/13334, p. 6.

[77] Sreenivasan, *The Peasants of Ottobeuren*, esp. ch. 6.

[78] Barbara Krug-Richter, "Von nackten Hummeln und Schandpflasten. Formen und Kontexte von Rauf und Ehrenhändeln in der Westfälischen Gerichtsherrschaft Cannstein um 1700" in Eriksson and Krug-Richter, eds. *Streitkulturen*, pp. 290–5. See GLAK 61/6958, 1663, 16 January.

[79] HStAS B486/Bd 13, pp. 223r–224v.

monks at Rot in order to acquire Michael Staigmiller's property.[80] Palster retorted that he was tired of Schädler calling him a scoundrel and a thief all around the region. Witnesses stated that Schädler had spoken to officials at the monastery and that he had brought up the dispute in several different taverns. On meeting Kueff in a tavern, Schädler was heard to say, "he would rather hang from the nearest gallows than allow this to happen to him" (ie. Have the legal decision go against him). Schädler did not recall this confrontation, allowing that all parties had been drinking.

Property disputes like this one (it would appear) involved well-off farmers. The Schädler-Palster dispute must have been widely known, since the men discussed it in several different taverns. Officials at the monastery were drawn into the dispute and had apparently been lobbied by both sides. No physical violence was involved, but Schädler in particular used strong insulting language and implied that his opponents were somehow using unfair influence with higher authorities.

Even more common were day-to-day disputes over the purchasing and selling of land and livestock. The court of the Amt Rotteln dealt with the buying and selling of livestock and property at every meeting, often recording the sales, but sometimes dealing with disputes over sales as well.[81] In 1684 a series of legal cases were adjudicated in Mainau between Jacob Mayer "hebraer von Aulendorf," probably a Jewish livestock dealer, and a number of villagers over the sale of horses and cows and the payment of a number of debts.[82] None of these cases had caused verbal or physical violence, and the court ordered a series of agreements between the parties, lowering some payments, but also enforcing earlier sales agreements.[83]

The herding of livestock provided another frequent source of conflict in villages, particularly when animals broke into fields and damaged crops. Often this problem was the fault of the herders, usually boys. The records of the *Dorfgericht* in Rotteln are full of fines for these minor crimes.[84] These cases could cause confrontations. In Wollmatingen in 1669, the horse herders were blamed for damage done in fields, leading to an exchange of insults between the *Rossbuben* and the farmers.[85] A particularly heated clash occurred between two women in 1686 in the village of Dingelsdorf.[86] Hans Mayer's wife accused Mathes Thumb's wife of allowing her cows to go into the Mayers' garden, damaging some young trees. When told to remove her cows, Thumb's wife (referred to here as the *Thumbin*) called Mayer's wife a witch.[87] The *Thumbin* had said "that no one else but the

[80] Probably a case of acquiring a tenancy that belonged to the Abbey.
[81] GLAK 61/6958. [82] GLAK 61/7599, pp. 12r–14v.
[83] See also GLAK 61/7599, p. 21v. [84] GLAK 61/6958.
[85] GLAK 61/13268, 1669, 10 September. [86] GLAK 61/7602, 1686, 23 February.
[87] Usually women were referred to by their birth names, with the feminine -in added to the name. But in this case the woman was called by her husband's name, in the feminine. Confusing this issue further, sometimes women were referred to by their position, so the *Wirtin*, wife of the innkeeper, or the *Ammänin*, the wife of the *Amman*, the village headman.

plaintiff had bewitched her calves." There was another conflict behind this exchange, over interactions in the marketplace, which the court did not address, instead ordering the *Thumbin* to pay a fine for the insults and apologize to Mayer's wife.

Family Conflicts: Inheritance, Marriage, and Domestic Violence

Conflicts over property could split families, as did conflicts over power within the family. In closely knit villages these disputes could easily end up as subjects of public discussion and sometimes in adjudication before lower courts. It should come as no surprise that family members fought over inheritances. A 1685 case from the village of Allmannsdorf demonstrates how these disputes could escalate. Caspar Renckhen brought a complaint that his brother-in-law, Jerg Hamman, had called him a scoundrel for stealing 10 *Eimer* of wine from the inheritance.[88] Hamman admitted that he had no evidence for this charge and had heard the story from a third party. Renckhen went on to claim that another heir, a young woman, had taken a silver belt that was therefore not properly divided among the heirs. Witnesses were called who testified that Hamman had in fact insulted Renckhen in the tavern in Immenstaad, stating "he wants to make another into a scoundrel, lest he become one and be one."

It seems hard to believe that Hamman's small fine for insulting his brother-in-law was going to end this family dispute. Hamman's final and somewhat enigmatic statement seems to reflect the idea that he did not want to be fooled in the inheritance dispute and that someone was behaving dishonestly, in his opinion Renckhen. Renckhen was also on his guard, worrying about what his relatives were saying in taverns, while also tossing around accusations about smaller items like the belt.

The same Jerg Hamman was present for another family dispute some months later.[89] A longer quote from the court records gives a feel for the event.

> This past Sunday, Jerg Hamman the younger, from Allmannsdorf, held a baptismal meal (*Tauff Suppen*) or meal of peace (*Fraidmahl*) and he had also invited his father, Caspar Hamman to join. Since they were in the best spirits together Jacob Manz joined them too. His wife had cooked all afternoon, but he (Manz) did not want to leave her there, but asked her twice to come home with him, and when she did not agree, Manz hit his wife in the face.

[88] GLAK 61/1685, 20 June, 7 July. pp. 46r–47r. 10 *Eimer* is a fair amount of wine, 1/3 of a *Fuder*, or 500 liters. Brun, *The Abbot and his Peasants*, p. ix.

[89] GLAK 61/7602, 1686, 26 January.

> Caspar Hamman got involved in the dispute, since she (Manz's wife) is his daughter, and during this dispute and tumult Caspar was hit twice in the face by Manz, his son-in-law. He does not know if this was done intentionally or not intentionally.
>
> In response, Jacob Manz, as the defendant, said that he can say in good conscience that he had not meant to hit his father-in-law. It happened in great disorder (*Tumult*), as he had to defend himself against three or four women at the same time...

Manz took his punishment, a fairly modest one, and was ordered to apologize to his father-in-law.

Family gatherings for major events like baptisms, weddings, and funerals were (and are) occasions for both "good spirits" and for family strife. The implication in the court protocols is that it was unusual for the father to come to such occasions and perhaps for Manz as well. Probably Manz had spent enough time with his in-laws and was ready to leave. Does the fact that he was set upon by (presumably) his wife's female relatives (sisters? Mother?) indicate that he already had a reputation for hitting his wife? Or was such behavior unacceptable in any case? What was the role of alcohol in this fight? We will never know for sure. Because the case was brought to court, not by one of the parties but by the *Amman* in Allmannsdorf, it is clear that this family brawl was a public scandal.

Family conflicts frequently erupted in situations where multiple generations of adults lived together in the same house.[90] The transfer of property between generations and the transfer of authority within the household, particularly between mothers and daughters-in-law, was almost always a source of tension.[91] Furthermore, multiple marriages often brought stepchildren into a family, a further potential source of conflict.[92] In 1684 Caspar Renckhen came to blows with his brother-in-law, Joseph Hamman.[93] Renckhen came to the defense of his sister, Hamman's wife, when Hamman hit her. In the confrontation Hamman insulted Renkhen and also hit Renckhen's mother. According to Renckhen, behind the conflict was the fact that Hamman was living in his mother-in-law's house and she wanted him out.

Hamman's perspective was of course different. He stated that Renckhen and Renckhen's sister Salome "have been going around the village calling him a scoundrel, thief, and heretic." Living in his mother-in-law's house was also not easy, for the woman he had married had children by an earlier marriage. "The worst was that his stepchildren don't want to obey him, but instead immediately

[90] Krug-Richter, "Von nackten Hummeln und Schandpflasten," pp. 286–7.
[91] See Sabean, *Property, Production, and Family* and Sreenivasan, *The Peasants of Ottobeuren*.
[92] Compare Lisa Wilson, *The History of Stepfamilies in Early America* (Chapel Hill, 2014).
[93] GLAK 61/7602, 1684, 9 October, pp. 24v–25v.

appeal to their grandmother...." The court sought a compromise, with Hamman moving out, but getting paid appropriately for his share of the house. The court particularly admonished everyone to properly "bring up the children in discipline, fear, and honor." As we saw above, a year later the Renckhen and Hamman family engaged in a dispute over an inheritance.

Women could bring their husbands to court for failing to support the family. This is what happened in 1670 when Anna Drescher filed a complaint against her husband, Johannes Junckere.[94] Anna testified that Johannes "lay around too long in bed, worked little, and what little he earned he drank up." She no longer wanted to live with him. Johannes said that "he had no peace in his house, she fought with him all of the time, and when he appropriately wanted to have a drink with honorable people, she did not let him forget it for days." The court at Salem "spoke to them earnestly, and finally they both agreed to live together in peace." This outcome reflects the general desire of authorities to keep families intact and preserve marriages.[95]

Cases of abuse and violence between husbands and wives are an important subset of family and domestic conflicts.[96] This was a society that firmly believed in the right of husbands to discipline their wives, with blows if necessary. In practice, however, neither wives nor bystanders always accepted the husband's right to hit his wife. Cases found in the court records sometimes reflect efforts to stop husbands from beating their wives.[97]

A tragic story from the Mainau court in 1701 shows that serious abuse of wives by husbands did occur.[98]

> About a half a year ago, Peter Ehrenguet's wife gave birth to a monstrous creature (*Missgeburt*) such that it looked more like an animal that creeps on the earth, but which had no life.
>
> As a result, the midwife Maria Eschenbacherin was sworn in and heard and asked what the nature of the birth was. To this she said she could not say what it looked like, it was an unformed piece of flesh, more like a creeping earth animal (*kriechendten Erdenthier*) than a child. (The midwife) suspects it was a cursed birth since her husband irresponsibly swore and cursed at his wife.

[94] GLAK 61/13334, p. 49.

[95] For a similar case, GLAK 61/7606, 1713, 11 January. Thomas Robisheaux, *Rural Society and the Search for Order in Early Modern Germany* (Cambridge, 1989); Thomas Max Safely, *Let no Man Put Asunder: The Control of Marriage in the German Southwest, 1550–1620* (Kirksville, 1984).

[96] Overview of these issues in Julie Hardwick, "Early Modern Perspectives on the Long History of Domestic Violence: The Case of Seventeenth-Century France" *Journal of Modern History* 78 (2006): 1–35, esp. pp. 1–5.

[97] Compare Elizabeth Foyster, "Male Honour, Social Control and Wife Beating in Late Stuart England" *Transactions of the Royal Historical* Society 6 (1996): 215–24; Dinges, "'Weiblichkeit' im 'Männlichkeitsritualen'"; Holenstein, "Klagen, anzeigen und supplizieren," pp. 352–8. Domestic violence was surely a hidden crime, but perhaps less so than in modern times.

[98] GLAK 61/7604, pp. 84r–84v.

> Peter Ehrenguth's wife said that she brought the pregnancy to full term and it came into the world at the normal time, but it was an unfortunate (*unglükhselig*) birth. She cannot deny that her husband often swears and curses at her, but does not think anyone should be given the blame for this unfortunate birth.

This case and the one that follows show the emotions surrounding procreation, as well as the vulnerability of pregnant women.[99]

People also talked about men who had a reputation for treating their wives badly. In 1707 Joseph Bürling brought a defamation charge against Jacob Morgen, because Morgen "had not only called him a scoundrel, but had also said that he (Bürling) had gotten his wife pregnant six times but every time had beaten her so badly that she had a miscarriage (*dz sie abortieren müessen*)".[100] Morgen denied the charge, but added that he had been told that Bürling had said "when he gets himself a wife, he would step on her so hard that her insides would come out." A witness testified that all Morgen had said was that if this statement were true, then Bürling is certainly a scoundrel. Here again, it is clear that if men violated community standards of behavior, or even language, their reputation became a topic of discussion in public places. Bürling's violent language had clearly shocked Morgen, and perhaps the court too, which ruled Morgen innocent of defamation.

Women who had powerful family members could find protection from a violent or abusive husband. This seems to have been the case in Wolmatingen in 1681, where the court sentenced Thomas Wiser to two days and nights in the tower.[101] He was found guilty of continuous conflict with his wife; he called her a witch, and insulted her whole family, including the *Amman*, calling them scoundrels, thieves, and heretics. After he was sentenced, Wiser promised to improve his behavior, drink less, and stop insulting his in-laws. There is no mention of physical violence in this case, but the violent insults aimed at important local people, some of whom were his wife's kin, were enough to land Wiser in jail.

Despite some interventions on behalf of abused wives, protecting women was not always the priority of the court. The farmer-jurors at Wollmatingen revealed their priorities in an April 1720 case.[102] "Jacob Weber did not hear Mass on the day of the Commune of Wollmatingen's procession, beat his wife, swore, and cursed. He will be publicly displayed and will repent by wearing a placard that says 'thou shalt not blaspheme' for one hour." Blasphemy was the issue, not abuse.

Women who were considered "difficult" were not always treated sympathetically by lower courts, although they were allowed to testify in their own defense. Ursula Bonauerin came into conflict with her brother-in-law Mathias Waldtpardt

[99] On monstrous births: Philip Soergel, *Miracles and the Protestant Imagination: The Evangelical Wonder Book in Reformation Germany* (Oxford, 2012).

[100] GLAK 61/13346, p. 136. It is striking that the complainant was willing to air these rumors in court, indicating that he felt they were already circulating widely.

[101] GLAK 61/13268, 1681, 21 July.

[102] GLAK 61/13268, p. 296v.

because she blamed him for difficulties in her marriage, calling him a "marriage wrecker" (*Ehevertrenner*), and blaming him when her husband hit her because of her "unbearable mouth."[103] Waldtpardt brought a complaint of defamation to the Mainau court, seeking to have the insults removed. Bonauerin claimed that Waldtpardt was partially to blame for the conflict, but failed to prove her case. The court sentenced her to stand in front of the church in the stocks and ordered her to get along better with her husband. The two parties were also told to stay away from each other and no longer to enter the other's house. Ursula Bonauerin was given her day in court and the court made some effort to diffuse the conflict, but she was punished for her insults and was not protected from the blows she received from her husband.

A final area of conflict we might call personal and family related circled around issues of marriage. Courts dealt regularly with cases of young people who became pregnant before marriage. This was a crime, and the guilty parties were fined and often had to do public penance in the form of standing before the church with a lighted candle. These cases rarely led to wider conflicts, however, since pre-marital sex between men and women who were intending to marry was generally tolerated.[104] However, there were exceptions. "Balthasar Weber badly beat his future son-in-law Georg Stadelhoffer, because he met him one morning at 7:30 in the morning standing with his daughter."[105] And, not surprisingly, fathers who found young men in their daughters' beds when there was no promise of marriage were often violent. In August 1669, the innkeeper in Salem physically ejected two young men from his house when he found them in his daughter's room.[106] The young men, both apprentices, were drunk and insolent. One of them stated that he had been invited in by the daughter, and the father later admitted his daughter shared the blame for the incident. Both apprentices denied doing anything "dishonorable" with the daughter, claiming they were just sleeping off the wine. The court sympathized with the father, but still fined him, a fine that was then forgiven by monastery officials.

Conflicts did erupt over promises of marriage. Lower courts did not have ultimate jurisdiction in these cases, since authority to determine the legitimacy of a promise of marriage lay with the ecclesiastical court of the Bishops of Constance. Nevertheless, lower courts in places like Salem and Mainau fined people for sex outside marriage, while also strongly encouraging them to marry. A case heard before the Mainau court in 1685 provides a standard example. Martin Wieler Bentz brought the case against Joseph Baumbgartner.[107] "He (Baumbgartner) got his daughter Catherina pregnant and now does not want to make an honorable

[103] GLAK 61/7602, 1684, 24 April, pp. 15r–v.
[104] See below, Chapter 7, for more on the issues around pre-marital sex.
[105] GLAK 61/13268, 1680, 30 January.
[106] GLAK 61/13334, pp. 4–5.
[107] GLAK 61/7602, 1685, 27 December, pp. 32v–33r.

woman of her, so he humbly asks for the *Obrigkeit's* assistance." Baumbgartner said that he had been willing to marry Catherina, but she left him for other men. He claimed to have even caught her in bed with one of them. Catherina denied this, saying "she would not free him or let Joseph get away." The court fined Baumbgartner for sleeping with Catherina and ordered him to decide if he wanted to marry her or provide the money required by law for the feeding and upbringing of the child. Catherina was sentenced to a Sunday in the stocks as an example to the others.

The goal of these courts, as with other courts that dealt with marriage cases, was usually to get the couple to marry. In 1663 Maria Sulgerin and Johannes Schroff agreed to marry, despite the fact that they had broken off their initial engagement (which they admitted had included sleeping together) and each had subsequently found other lovers.[108] Both families supported the marriage, which may mean the young people were under pressure to marry. Occasionally the outcome was different, as in the case of Joseph Felder, who admitted having sex with the servant girl Maria Bucherin, but denied he had promised to marry her.[109] According to the court, Bucherin was a "wanton person" who had even been involved with a priest, and Felder was let off with a strong warning. Not surprisingly, a woman from an established village family had a good chance of marrying the man who had impregnated her, while the servant girl with a sullied reputation had little chance.[110]

One dispute over a marriage, this time between a father and a young man, opens up many questions:

> Andreas Bonawer from Litzelstetten complains against Martin Bentz from there.[111]
>
> The defendant's daughter got pregnant by a servant and could have had a good marriage, [but] he [Bentz, the father] never wanted to make that possible. After [that] the complainant said that Bentz was at fault that the daughter became a whore, for which Bentz often called him (Bonawer) a (begging your leave) scoundrel. He [Bonawer] wants his honor restored.
>
> The defendant Bentz admits to the complaint, but [says that] Bonawer started the dispute, because he could not stand it that he [Bentz] disciplined his daughter for her mistakes.
>
> Decision:
>
> Since the complainant has no right to interfere in the blows the father gives to his daughter and is the one who started the conflict, he is deservedly fined 1lb.d

[108] GLAK 61/7599, pp. 104–8. [109] GLAK 61/13334, 1671, 20 June, pp. 99–100.
[110] Dinges, "Justiznutzungen als soziale Kontrolle," esp. pp. 523–30.
[111] GLAK 61/7602, 1684, 9 October, pp. 25v–26r.

and since the defendant Bentz was excessive in his way of responding he is fined the same amount and the injuries are removed ex officio [ie. The court officially forgives the insults].

While the entry in the court records does not quite say so explicitly, the implication is that Bonawer wanted to marry the daughter, but Bentz would not allow it. Why was Bonawer unacceptable to Bentz as a son-in-law, even when his daughter was pregnant? Was he not from a proper family or insufficiently propertied? Bonawer's desire to protect the daughter from her father's "discipline" seems to us heart-warming, but was it perhaps a cynical attempt to lure a vulnerable (and perhaps rich) girl into a marriage? We will never know.

It comes as no surprise that family conflicts were common in these communities. What is perhaps more unexpected is that people took at least some of these disputes to court, airing intimate family disputes in a public space. This dynamic reminds us that the boundaries between public and private, between family and community, were unclear in these villages and small towns. And the judges and juries were often part of, or at least very familiar with, local dynamics. We cannot be sure, for example, how much the court in Salem knew about the Renckhen/Hamman family who appeared before the court multiple times in the 1680s, but it would not be surprising if the authorities considered the family a problem. This closeness to local society surely contributed to the pragmatic way the courts operated.

Local Politics

Disputes, even fights, could arise as a result of political and religious discussions in taverns. In 1706 a man named Franz Amele made extremely inflammatory comments in the tavern at Maurach.[112] He asserted that the Apostles were liars, as are the priests in their sermons. Furthermore, he said, the Bavarian Elector had a just cause, a reference to the ongoing War of the Spanish Succession when the Bavarians fought with the French against the Holy Roman Empire. Several men with whom Amele was drinking took offense and demanded he "step outside." Eventually, Amele did end up fighting one of these men on the street. Interestingly, the court ruled that Amele's words had gone too far, but so had the man who attacked him. Amele was sentenced to five hours in prison.

A brawl erupted in 1671 in the tavern in Owingen when Jorg Moser complained about his taxes and said that he did not have to obey the Abbot of Salem, but rather the Lord of Unterbodmann.[113] Jacob Vogler, the miller, "remembering

[112] GLAK 61/13346, 1706, 4 December, pp. 91–3.
[113] GLAK 61/13334, 1671, 19 December, pp. 108–13.

his duty," took offense and attacked Moser. The men wrestled on the floor, with Vogler on top. Witnesses confirmed the disloyal words, and one said that Moser had said similar things on an earlier occasion. The innkeeper had asked Moser if he was just joking, to which Moser responded, "if he were joking about this, then he would get on a horse and ride off to war to fight the Turks." Moser's only defense was that he was drunk and "when he is drunk he is unable to control himself and he was beside himself because of his many debts." The court referred his case directly to the abbot.

Political discussions could cause conflicts, even when they were fairly abstract, as with Amele's theological comments and his discussion of the current war. These conversations could also be more concrete, about local issues, such as taxes and the power of local lords. Conflicts within communities over local political power often developed as criticism of local officials. In the 1650s Martin Langegg, a former *Amman*, took a neighbor, Oswald Wideman, to court because the neighbor had criticized him in a local tavern, implying that Langegg had resigned his position under pressure. Langegg was not able to prove his charge, admitting the story might be "purely women's rumors."[114]

Amtmänner were frequently subject to criticism, which is not surprising given the nature of their position as intermediaries between the lordship and the village community. These men were also familiar with the lower courts and made use of them to defend themselves against criticism. In October 1681, the *Amman* from Haslach cited Hans Schimpfessel's wife at Rot for slander.[115] She had stated publicly that the *Amman* "did not run the commune like an honorable man and that he favored his friends," a charge she could not prove. The court protected the *Amman* and the defendant was punished with the *Geigen*, the stocks.

Communes could use the lower courts as a place to bring complaints against *Amtmänner* as well. In 1681 the *Gemeinde* of Karzdorf brought an extensive complaint to Rot about their Amman, Schwalt Widemann.[116] Among other things, members of the commune charged Widemann with allowing dancing in his house during the parish festival (*Kirchwey*), illegally selling beer and wine, and failing to report a brawl that occurred in his house to the court. He also farmed a field that was not his, burnt charcoal without permission, and took wood he should not have. The *Amman* countered that the leader of the *Gemeinde*, Hans Hörlin, had come to his house and insulted him. The members of the commune all testified individually, and the court ruled that the *Amman* was too selfish and did not deal well with the *Gemeinde*, but that Hörlin had been disrespectful and, especially when drunk, tended to "say more than he can answer for." The ruling included the requirement that the *Amman* and *Gemeinde* come to an agreement on several disputed issues, that Widemann cease to sell wine and beer, should pay

[114] HStAS B486/Bd 13, pp. 122r–122v. *lautter Weibergeschwätz.*
[115] HStAS B486/Bd 15, p. 29v. [116] HStAS B486/Bd 15, p. 33r–v.

for the charcoal burning, and should stop holding dances. Hörlin was fined for his insulting language. The court functioned here as a location for the mediation of a village-level political dispute.

In some cases, these conflicts could get violent. In 1684 Jakob Echten objected to the collection of taxes by the officials of the Abbey of Salem (the *Pfleger*), stating that if they put a tax lien on his wine harvest, he would burn down their houses.[117] The two *Pfleger* took the threat seriously and demanded that he be punished severely, or that they be allowed to resign their posts. Echten spent two days in the tower on bread and water, was required to apologize to the whole village commune, and was threatened with exile if it happened again. Fire was a great danger in these villages of wooden houses and arson a very serious crime.

Conflicts could also erupt within the village communal bodies. The cost of quartering soldiers exploded into a serious dispute in the meeting of the commune of Litzelstetten in 1685.[118] A group of men accused the *Amman* and *Pfleger* of cheating the commune and gaining a profit from the collection of money to feed the soldiers. "If they were not getting a profit together, they would not want to be *Pfleger* so much, they cheat the *Gemeinde* like others do." The "ringleaders" (as the court called them) also threatened one of the *Pfleger* physically. The accused only admitted that they had opposed the additional tax of 5 *Gulden*, but multiple witnesses testified that they had accused the communal officials of cheating the commune. They were fined.

In 1686 an even broader conflict over taxation in Lipperatsreute split the tenant farmers, the *Bauern*, from the *Söldner*, or smallholders.[119] The smallholders, who included the *Amman*, were often artisans who felt they were taxed disproportionately. The *Amman* himself complained about being taxed for both his butcher shop and the tavern he ran and that his cows were taxed alive and then again when they had been slaughtered. It is not clear from the court case how the tenant farmers explained this situation, but the Mainau officials who heard the case argued that something needed to be done about the "inequality of the assessments." This was clearly a dispute over taxes that divided the village along social and economic lines and led to a legal challenge to the local tax structure.

Local political disputes sometimes reached the courts. Here too the courts operated in a pragmatic fashion, sometimes listening to, and even acting on, complaints against *Amtmänner*. More often than not, however, the courts backed up local officials and punished any behavior that smacked of disobedience. The fining of the "ringleaders" in Litzelstetten in 1685 is a classic example of this situation. But even in that case, the authorities did not make a dramatic example of the troublemakers, but rather fined them and moved on.

* * *

[117] GLAK 61/7602, 1684, 9 October, pp. 24r–24v.

[118] GLAK 61/7602, 1685, 31 December.

[119] GLAK 61/7602, 1686, 23 October.

The local courts, as we will see in more detail throughout this study, were imbedded in local society. The officials and jurists who made decisions in Mainau, Salem, and Rot showed considerable flexibility in their decisions and in the kind of punishments they imposed.[120] This style was even more apparent among the peasant-jurors in Wollmatingen and Rotteln. These courts did not primarily function in response to princely edicts or legal principles; instead they operated pragmatically, with the goal of keeping the peace and enforcing obedience to the authorities. In some ways this was a very conservative legal system, aimed at preserving the status quo.

But these courts were also part of a changing world, and they gained a more important role in rural society in the century after the end of the Thirty Years' War, as people sought better ways to maintain or restore peace. The peacekeeping role of courts can be seen most clearly in the many honor disputes that came to their dockets. These cases, however, also highlight the ambiguous way the courts functioned. After all, an honor dispute aired in a court hearing likely made that dispute even more public, and a court decision might not bring the conflict to an end. Yet, this was a society riddled with honor conflicts, and any set of peacekeeping practices had to engage those disputes.

[120] Govind Sreenivasan, "Prosecuting Injuries in Early Modern Germany" *Central European History* 47 (2014).

2
The Honor of Peasants

Almost every dispute involving insulting language and physical violence was construed as an attack on someone's honor.[1] At the same time, such honor conflicts often resulted from a pre-existing conflict or set of issues, a dispute over property or a debt, political divisions in the community, or contested social interactions and sexual relations.[2] While a study of the place of honor can function to deepen our understanding of a number of tensions in rural society, it is also difficult and probably misleading to analyze the concern with honor separately from other conflicts.

The courts in Southwest Germany understood the significance of honor in the daily lives of the population. But the jurors, judges, and local officials also had the difficult job of deciding if an insult delivered over glasses of wine in the local tavern was worthy of a fine or some other punishment, or whether it was the ensuing fight that was the real crime. At other times, the courts found themselves investigating underlying disputes in search of malfeasance somewhere else in the lives of rural folks. In the end, they often administered multiple punishments, for slander, for violence, or for other illegal activity. The interplay of honor disputes with other kinds of conflict creates a tension in any analysis of peace and conflict at the local level that requires careful attention to the context of particular conflicts.[3]

Historians have emphasized that honor as deployed in early modern Europe was a "rhetoric" rather than an inflexible code as it is sometimes presented by anthropologists.[4] All kinds of people chose to use the particular language of honor when they felt it was useful and they certainly emphasized their honor in testimony before courts. In any case, honor was real in the sense that both men and women felt a strong need to defend their reputation and to restore their honor, through self-defense, mediation, or adjudication in court. Emotion,

[1] Karl-Sigismund Kramer, *Grundriß einer rechtlichen Volkskunde* (Göttingen, 1974), pp. 46–60.

[2] See Krug-Richter, "Von nackten Hummeln und Schandpflasten," for a useful discussion of this issue.

[3] Barbara Stollberg-Rillinger, "Rang vor Gericht. Zur Verrechtlichung sozialer Rangkonflikt in der frühen Neuzeit" *Zeitschrift für historische Forschung* 28 (2000): 385–418; Ralf-Peter Fuchs, *Um die Ehre: Westfälische Beleidigungsprozesse vor dem Reichskammergericht, 1525–1805* (Paderborn, 1999).

[4] Scott Taylor, *Honor and Violence in Golden Age Spain* (New Haven, 2008), p. 9; Allyson Creasman, "Fighting Words: Anger, Insult, and 'Self-Help' in Early Modern German Law" *Journal of Social History* 51 (2017): 272–92.

Keeping the Peace in the Village: Conflict and Peacemaking in Germany, 1650–1750. Marc R. Forster, Oxford University Press. © Marc R. Forster 2024. DOI: 10.1093/oso/9780198898474.003.0003

particularly anger, was also part of this rhetoric (or discourse) of honor, and could be used to both explain and excuse behavior.[5]

Recognizing the centrality of honor in rural life, courts explicitly, if usually somewhat formulaically, ordered the restoration of honor and "friendship" at the end of many cases. Sometimes these statements demanded personal action: "The accused should recognize the complainant as an honorable man and shake his hand...."[6] At other times, the reinstatement of honor was more formal and official: "The insults used against each other are removed by the lordship."[7] These judicial interventions reflected the realities of rural life, but here too there was a tension, as the juridification of honor disputes inevitably altered how honor functioned in society.[8] Of course we cannot be sure if the removal of insults by officials was always effective.

The discourse on honor was usually very explicit. People talked about their honor and the honor of others in public, and any questioning of one's honor required a response. Women and men also responded to rumors that were spreading in the village and in the wider region, since reputation was threatened in this way as well. Furthermore, memories were long, and dishonorable moments in the past, perhaps a punishment for stealing or an earlier unresolved attack on a woman's sexual honor, could be revived at any time. Honor and reputation were certainly personal, but they were also attached to a family or kin group, and dishonor could be inherited from generation to generation. This tendency was particularly dangerous for women, since a reputation for witchcraft was certainly passed from mother to daughter.[9]

Insults

July 1671: The wife of Jorg Maister, a shoemaker in Neufrach, came into the house of Nicolaus Hetnig of Autingen looking for Hetnig's wife. She said (or perhaps yelled), "where is that immoral person, that wanton whore (*leichtfertige Hurenhaus*), that servant deserving of the hangman (*henckhermässig gesind*), that barracks whore, [for] she was a barracks whore before her marriage." This virtuoso set of insults prompted a respond from Hetnig, as it had to. "He called her a horse thief, an unrooted person (i.e., a vagabond), her mother stole eggs and then threw them away...."[10]

[5] Creasman, "Fighting Words," Part II.

[6] HStAS B486/Bd 13, p. 83r.

[7] *die gegen einander gebrauchte schmach worth von obrigkeits wegen augehebt.* GLAK 61/13340, 1699, 28 November, p. 396.

[8] Stollberg-Rillinger, "Rang vor Gericht."

[9] See, in particular, Thomas Robisheaux, *The Last Witch of Langenburg. Murder in a German Village* (New York and London, 2009).

[10] GLAK 61/13334, p. 106.

August 1681: Hans Mercken's wife charged the *Wirtin* (innkeeper's wife) in Haslach with slander. "Not only the *Wirtin* herself, but also her children, often insulted the complainant (*Clägerin*), begging your leave, as a debauched beggar whore, and also called her all kinds of other damaging words. The *Wirtin*'s children had recently come to the front of the complainant's house with a flaming torch, threatening to burn down the house. The *Wirtin* most recently yelled at her (*vorgeruft*) that her husband is an orphan maker (*Weisenmacher*), a *Strükl Trager*, a catcher of scoundrels (*Schelmen fanger*)." The *Wirtin*, said Frau Merkhen, had made other threats as well. The *Wirtin* defended herself, saying that Frau Merkhen had publicly accused her of a pre-marital sexual relationship.[11]

July 1705: Men seem to have been somewhat less imaginative with insults. Martin Fux filed a complaint against the *Amman* from Litzelstetten, "that he, during the meeting of the commune called him (Fux) a, s.v. [*salva venia*], scoundrel and a thief and with other insults injured him, which he can prove [by calling as witnesses] other honorable men."[12]

May 1704: "Johannes Rohmer [or Römer] from Überlingen is strongly charged by *Amman* and Mayor of Wollmatingen, [who described] how, yesterday, on the public streets of Wollmatingen, he insulted and affronted the *Amman*, [the authorities], his superiors, and whole commune. [He] also swore and blasphemed. After many earnest warnings he also pulled out a knife as if he were going to stab someone. And what is more, to their great insult, he openly said that the Wollmatinger are all ass lickers."[13]

October 1704: Johann Boll was charged with insulting the *Torwart* (gatekeeper) at the monastery of Salem. "The defendant swore terribly, and used this formulation: thunder and lightning should strike him in the head, and using his finger pointed to where it should hit him. Furthermore, [he said] the *Amman* is a scoundrel."[14]

These examples show the range of insults used in this period. As was the case across Germany, the standard insults used against men were *Schelm* and *Dieb*. *Dieb*, thief, clearly indicated a man's criminal character. *Schelm*, usually translated as rogue or scoundrel, has a more complex meaning. It references a lack of trustworthiness needed to interact socially, economically, and politically in the local community. Karl-S Kramer argues *Schelm* has stronger meanings as well, referencing death and disease, as well as meaning a villain or a traitor.[15] The words scoundrel or rogue do not quite capture those all meanings. By the early eighteenth century, men were also regularly insulted as "not a *Biedermann*," that is, "you are not a respectable man," a new phrase that probably reflected a growing

[11] HStAS B486/Bd 15, pp. 179v–180r. The reference to a *Strükl Trager* is unclear.
[12] GLAK 61/7604, pp. 191r–191v. s.v. = [*salve venia*], meaning "begging your leave." See below.
[13] GLAK 61/13268, p. 87.
[14] GLAK 61/13344, pp. 387–8.
[15] Karl-Sigismund Kramer, "Hohnsprake, Wrakworte, Nachschnack und Ungebür. Ehrenhändel in holsteinischen Quellen" *Kieler Blätter für Volkskunde* XVI (1984): 60; Fuchs, *Um die Ehre*, esp. p. 106.

squeamishness about the use of what Kramer calls "rough insult words."[16] One also sees over time the increased use of "qualified honor insults," where someone (almost always a man) would say "*if* you said this or that, *then* you would be a scoundrel."[17] This formulation could often get one out of a slander accusation in court and therefore was probably claimed after the fact.

The court minutes frequently used the abbreviations s.v. (*salva venia*) and s.h. (*salva honore*), and did so increasingly in the eighteenth century. Both phrases can be translated as "begging your leave." Court secretaries used this abbreviation before writing language they thought might be in poor taste, including crude insults like "dog's cunt," but also scatological language, words for animals (pigs for example), and even clothing considered private. In one case, a secretary used the phrase "his s.v. pants slit," referencing the fly on the front of a man's pants.[18] At other times, scribes avoided writing the offensive words partially or altogether, replacing them with ellipses (...) or with an "etc." This practice is most often seen when reporting the insult "dog's..." or "dog's etc." David Sabean refers to this practice as a kind of "social distancing."[19]

Women were almost exclusively insulted as whores and witches (see Chapter 3 below). These insults, particularly the whore insult, were both broad and dangerous, requiring a response from the insulted party. The whore insult was everywhere and tended to drive out all other issues, making honor conflicts involving women sterile and narrow, at least in the language used. The limited language of insult, in the case of women even more than with men, also creates a further challenge to the historian seeking to understand the context of the conflicts. At times the courts and local officials faced the same problem; if a woman was called a whore, was she in fact being accused of sexual crimes, and if man was a thief, had he really stolen something?

People did sometimes deploy other insults beyond these standard ones. As Kramer writes, "some figured that in some situations, the more the better, and they let loose with a whole cannonade of insults."[20] Jorg Maister's wife (above) was apparently working along those lines. Men were insulted as heretics (*Ketzer*), witch masters (*Hexenmeister*), liars and cheaters, whores' boys, beggars, and vagabonds. Women were wantons, undisciplined, thieves, and lovers of soldiers,

[16] Kramer, "Hohnsprake, Wrakworte, Nachschnack und Ungebür," p. 62. These Latin abbreviations are perhaps best translated by the phrase "begging your leave" or "begging your pardon."

[17] Karl-Sigismund Kramer, "Das Herausfordern aus dem Haus. Lebensbild eines Rechtsbrauches" *Bayerisches Jahrbuch für Volkskunde* (1956): 125.

[18] s.v. and s.h. will appear frequently in the rest of this book. For "s.v. pants slit," see GLAK 61/7602, January 24, 1684, 4r–6v and below, Chapter 4.

[19] David Warren Sabean, "Soziale Distanzierung. Ritualisierte Gestik in deutscher bürokratischer Prosa der frühen Neuzeit" *Historische Anthropologie* 4/2 (1996): 216–33.

[20] Kramer, "Hohnsprake, Wrakworte, Nachschnack und Ungebür," p. 55.

among other things. Most of these invectives were pulled from a widely available trove of insults, but a few seem to have been invented on the spot.[21]

Finally, it should be pointed out that not all insults or verbal attacks that ended up in court were attacks on someone's honor. When a man says he hopes another man will be hit by lightning, is that an attack on the other man's honor? When are menacing words, such as "threatening to burn down the house," also an honor insult? Authorities were concerned with other kinds of words as well—blasphemy, swearing of all kinds, and of course rebellious words directed at the lordship. Obviously the context of the words, not just the words themselves, or even the fact that they were brought to court, is essential to understanding if someone's honor was impugned. And, of course, whether one's honor was at stake in a conflict was itself one of the issues contested in taverns, on the street, and in court.

Varieties of Honor Conflicts

Honor conflicts sometimes began with a simple exchange of insults, without any apparent background conflict. Of course, the combatants may not have mentioned in court other disputes that had led to the exchange of insults, or the court scribe may not have recorded those issues in his minutes. But, at times anyway, insults were themselves the issue. A tavern discussion in Owingen in October 1695 illustrates how sensitive people were to insults and, at the same time, how casually they could be used.[22] Hans Reither and several other men were discussing cattle diseases over wine, and Reither claimed he could cure another man's cow overnight. Baltes Madler exclaimed, "anyone who could do that would have to be a *Hexenmeister* (a master of witches)." Reither took exception and brought charges in the *Oberamtsgericht* at Salem. Madler explained in court that "he did not mean it badly, he had said this without thinking." In the court, the two men "showed good friendship," probably shaking hands, and the case was dismissed.[23]

A failure to respect the normal customs of tavern sociability could easily cause offence. In July 1656, Georg Mendl had toasted Stossel Rueff, but Rueff then "not only did not return the toast, but without giving any reason, insulted [Mendl] as a scoundrel and a scoundrel's child." Rueff denied the insults at first, but after several witnesses testified, he "began to creep toward the cross," and finally admitted his guilt, apologized, and accepted his fine.[24]

[21] See Kramer, "Hohnsprake, Wrakworte, Nachschnack und Ungebür," for a wide listing of insults used in northern Germany.

[22] Ann Goldberg, *Honor, Politics, and the Law in Imperial Germany* (Cambridge, 2010), p. 1. "Germans had long been a thin-skinned people."

[23] GLAK 61/13337, pp. 103–4. [24] HStAS B486/Bd 13, p. 113r.

Taverns were a common place for casual exchanges of insults. In Rot an der Rot, the innkeeper was fined in September 1667 for saying that one of his customers "lies like a scoundrel."[25] A few weeks later in the same tavern, the *Amman* from Hirschbronn called a man a scoundrel, causing that man's son to return the insults and hit him. Both men were fined.[26]

> Hans Rueff, the son of the *Amman* from Kirchdorf, not long ago, while drunk, had attacked his [own] father, insulting him and causing great annoyance, so first he is ordered to apologize to his father, and he is also condemned to three days and nights in the tower.[27]

While we might speculate that there were father/son issues in the background of Hans' outburst, this case came to court like many others, as a simple case of insults thrown around the tavern under the influence of alcohol. It would be possible to present an almost endless number of these tavern cases. Here is a 1661 case that can stand in for many others: "Hans Recher from Mühlberg insulted Hans Miller of Haslach, without any reason, as a dog's etc. and hit him in the throat."[28]

People were explicit about the honor implications of even the most casually uttered insults. The *Amman* (and innkeeper) in Staad filed a slander case when Matthiss Nessler called his wife a whore. Nessler admitted to the charge, but said that the complainant and his wife had given him reason for the words and in particular they had given him a slap (*Maultaschen*) and a shove. The *Amman* responded "such words deserve a slap."[29] And, of course, women exchanged insults as well. In November 1674 Maria Baumerin called Elisabeth Fluxin "a s.h. whore and witch" and also slapped her. Fluxin "asks that the authorities [*Obrigkeit*] help her, [for] she wants to get back her good name, and demands an apology, and wants the *Obrigkeit* to punish [Baumerin] for the blow." She won her case; Baumerin was fined and ordered to apologize. "The insults are removed and the parties reconciled by the *Obrigkeit*."[30]

Certain physical actions could also lead to an exchange of insults and (usually) blows. Slapping, as we have seen, often accompanied insults and was considered damaging to one's honor. Knocking off (or pulling down) another man's hat was another calculated insult, aimed at provoking a confrontation.[31] In September

[25] HStAS B486/Bd 14, p. 79r. [26] HStAS B486/Bd 14, p. 84r.

[27] HStAS B486/Bd 14, p. 101r.

[28] HStAS B486/Bd 13, p. 270v. The Rot court handled multiple cases like this at the same time in the November 22, 1660 session, in a formulaic fashion: HStAS B486/Bd 13, p. 263r–v.

[29] GLAK 61/7599, pp. 108–9. [30] GLAK 61/7600, November 10, 1674.

[31] In the 1970s I saw "Wild Bill" Hagy, a self-appointed cheerleader for the Baltimore Orioles in Section 34 of Baltimore's old Memorial Stadium, take a Yankees hat off a man's head and throw it off the upper deck, to the cheers of Orioles' fans. In the beginning of chapter 1 of *Moby Dick*, Ishmael says: "and especially whenever my hypos get such an upper hand of me, that it requires a strong moral

1672, Martin Wieler took Stoffel Scherer's hat off his head and threw it into a garden. Wieler's son followed this up by slapping Scherer as well.[32] In 1714, Conrad Negelin, a servant, was walking with a boy and took the boy's hat, then returned it, saying "he would like to give you a gift today." The boy was insulted, and called Negelin a "dog's...," to which Negelin responded by slapping him. The boy's father also considered this an insult and physically assaulted Negelin a few days later.[33] These kinds of belittling actions were common and strike us as familiar to this day.

The interplay between strong feelings about honor and a readiness to resort to violence can be seen in the confrontation between Bernhard Stampfer and Johannes Leib at the parish festival in Neufrach in the summer of 1702. "The complainant sadly [*wehmütig*] said that he had been peacefully drinking at the parish festival in Neufrach when the defendant came to his table and brought another (glass of wine), to which he [Leib] answered, I already have my own wine. The defendant [Stampfer] immediately called him a dog's..., without any reason. To this, the complainant [Leib] answered, if he is a dog's..., then he [Stampfer] is two of them." The two men came immediately to blows and continued to fight outside the tavern. Leib became so enraged that he reportedly said "if I only had a knife, I would stab the heretic." Witnesses confirmed the story, with one testifying that Leib beat Stampfer about the head with his fists so badly that Stampfer went in and out of consciousness and people feared for his life.[34]

Layers of honor are in evidence here. Stampfer was insulted that Leib did not accept his offer of a drink, and Leib may have been offended by the implication that he could not afford his own wine.[35] The conflict quickly escalated to verbal insults and physical violence. Violating behavioral norms in the tavern was common, since the boundary lines between friendly joshing and insult were often blurred by alcohol. Did Martin Guldenfuess intend to insult Görd Jacob when he repeatedly touched Jacob's hat in the servants' *Stube* at Mainau? Jacob thought so and told Guldenfuess "he needs to leave him in peace or else he will punch him in the mouth." Not surprisingly, Guldenfuess "daringly" tugged on the hat one more time, leading to a full-blown brawl.[36]

Even disputes over games could end up in court. The innkeeper's wife in Zell called a neighbor a witch in a dispute over a bowling match, to which her opponent responded in kind. Both women's husbands were then punished for building bowling alleys on their properties.[37] Despite the disapproval of the authorities,

principle to prevent me from deliberately stepping into the street, and methodically knocking people's hats off—then, I account it high time to get to sea as soon as I can."

[32] GLAK 61/7600, December 3, 1672.

[33] GLAK 61/7606, pp. 53r–53v.

[34] GLAK 61/13344, pp. 252–5.

[35] Ann Tlusty, *Bacchus and Civic Order. The Culture of Drink in Early Modern Germany* (Charlottesville, 2001), especially on the tradition of drinking toasts. Also, Kümin, *Drinking Matters*.

[36] GLAK 61/7600, May 3, 1673 (*stet*, it was probably June).

[37] HStAS B486/Bd 18, p. 113r.

bowling seems to have been common.[38] In Dingelsdorf in June 1710, a bowling match became the setting for a quickly escalating honor conflict. Mattheus Hotz testified that Leopold Hirscher had played badly and that Hotz, as the winner, did not owe any wine, which was clearly the stakes in the game. Hirscher, however, refused to share the wine with Hotz, who of course objected, demanding Hirscher pay for his round. Hirscher got angry, stating "whoever he [Hotz] thinks he is, he does not have as much money as he [Hirscher] does, at which point he slammed a 1 *Gulden* piece on the table," going on further to accuse Hotz of stealing grain from his own mother. Hirscher stated that he too had been insulted, since Hotz apparently claimed to be "better," for he, unlike Hirscher, was a guildsman. Perhaps reflecting his sense of status, Hotz challenged Hirscher to a duel with pistols or swords.[39] Here we see two men bending or breaking the social rules around both bowling and drinking, probably intentionally to provoke a conflict, which then escalated to issues of status and honor that needed to be resolved in court.

A bowling match would, on the surface, seem to be a relatively peaceful social interaction.[40] But, as we have seen, people gambled on these matches, raising the stakes. More often, men (perhaps exclusively men) gambled on dice. In January 1668, Peter Matzne, the schoolteacher in Rot, physically assaulted a Jew from Erolzheim because he would not give him (or perhaps show him) the dice they were using. The (unnamed) Jew fled, but Matzne pursued him and the Jew ended up insulting a man who tried to break up the fight.[41] In July 1713, the innkeeper's wife in Dingelsdorf, Maria Anna Harderin, complained about four men who came to her tavern after the parish festival (*Kirmesse*) in a neighboring village. Harderin testified that "they gambled there until the middle of the night and when she asked them to call it a night, Leopold Hirsch attacked her with s.v. whore and many other hard insult words, which she cannot allow to sit [on her] and she asks them [the court] to help her get her good name back." Hirsch claimed Harderin had insulted him first, but witnesses contradicted him and he was fined.[42]

Artisans had social traditions that revolved around drinking and a high sensitivity to slights to their honor, a combination that could lead to insults and conflicts.[43] Journeymen could come together at taverns, adding the elements of regional and religious differences to the occasion. In October 1681, three journeymen carpenters and a journeyman glazier spent three days together drinking

[38] On bowling: Toni Drexler, ed. *Kellnerin, a Maß. Das Wirtshaus—die weltliche Mitte des Dorfes* (Jexhof, 1997), pp. 38–9.

[39] GLAK 61/7606, pp. 37r–38r.

[40] Another bowling dispute: GLAK 61/13334, p. 106.

[41] HStAS B486/Bd 14, pp. 96v–97r. It is possible that the Jew was a peddler. See a case from 1713 where a group of young men beat a Jewish peddler. GLAK 61/5174, p. 35.

[42] GLAK 61/7606, p. 32v.

[43] Tlusty, *Bacchus and Civic Order*, esp. ch. 8. There is further discussion of artisans in Chapters 1, 4, and 5.

at the tavern at Rot.[44] When one of them, a man from Württemberg, was ready to leave, the men got heated. The Württemberger complained that the others were not "honorable companions" because they would not accompany him on his road to his next destination. This led to a drawing of daggers and a fight. Perhaps more dramatically, a Lutheran butcher from nearby Memmingen insulted the Virgin Mary in the tavern in Berkheim in 1663.[45] When he stated, in this Catholic village, that "Martin Luther is much better than our Lady," a brawl immediately ensued.

More established men were particularly sensitive to slights to their status and thus their honor. In March 1709, Martin Steegmeyer learned that the local *Gemeinde* (commune), where he held a position on the council, was having a *Trunck* (i.e., a drinking event) that he had not been told about. Steegmeyer made a dramatic entry at the gathering, shouting insults and slamming his fists on the table, sending cups and glasses flying. He then compounded his insulting behavior by demanding his fair share of the wine (two quarts), which he wanted to take and drink alone at home. One of the men there, Johannes Hurber, took particular offense and grabbed Steegmeyer by the hair. Steegmeyer of course felt his honor insulted by being left out of the event—when he arrived, he reminded the others of his elected position in the commune—while his behavior insulted the honor of the other men present.[46]

A final example shows the interplay of youthful socializing, casual assaults on honor, and the honor of established men and families. In July 1710, Andreas Rosenhardt brought a complaint about a dispute involving his son:

> As the young men were dancing this past Sunday in the Kändtlin [a tavern] in Hinderhausen young Caspar Weber stated that he had an honorable father, who had died honorably, and Rosenhardt's son should show him the same [respect] out of friendship. Then he insulted [Rosenhardt] as a dog's . . .
>
> He [Rosenhardt senior] cannot let this go by and he humbly demands that Caspar Weber be told to do what he should do about this injustice.
>
> The defendant answers, he was disgruntled that the young Rosenhardt was not willing to drink toasts with him and he [Rosenhardt] took off his hat before him to ridicule him. He denied that he had demanded respect . . .

[44] HStAS B486/Bd 15, pp. 29v–30r.

[45] HStAS B486/Bd 13, p. 333r. See also Jacques-Louis Ménétra, *Journal of My Life*, ed. Daniel Roche (New York, 1986).

[46] GLAK 61/13346, pp. 357–60. See also Gerd Schwerhoff, "Das Gelage. Institutionelle Ordnungsarrangements und Machtkämpfe im frühneuzeitlichen Wirtshaus" in Gert Melville, ed. *Das Sichtbare und das Unsichtbare der Macht: Institutionelle Prozesse in Antike, Mittelalter und Neuzeit* (Köln, 2005), esp. p. 165 on drinking alone.

Witnesses all agreed that Weber was the instigator, and he was fined.[47] What was behind this altercation, other than drinking and posturing among a group of young people that included young women, is impossible to know. Perhaps nothing, but Rosenhardt senior felt the words traded among young people at a dance required judicial action to restore *his* honor as the head of his family.

A concern with, even a fixation on, honor was necessary for people to function effectively in rural society. A reputation as an honorable man—a *Biedermann*—was essential for propertied men to be able to buy and sell livestock and land, borrow money, sell produce, or make use of communal pastures and woods. For artisans, honor meant producing quality products while meeting the moral and behavioral requirements of the guild. Any insult or accusation that questioned a man's honesty required a response.

But honor was not just a possession of men with property, nor were they only ones to deploy the language of honor. Poor people, including poor women, servants, apprentices, and farm laborers, also defended their honor, often in court and even against their employers and their more powerful neighbors. Importantly, the courts often supported these people, evidence of the complex role of systems of justice in this society.

The importance of honor for a man's ability to operate in a rural community was clear to everyone. In January 1702, Simon Schneider and Matheus Enders brought a slander suit because a certain Bartl Straub had called them "scoundrels and thieves," without stating any reason for the use of these routine insults. As a result, Schneider and Enders were not admitted to meetings of the commune and to the rights that went with being a citizen.[48] Straub admitted to using these insults against Schneider, since Schneider was avoiding paying off a debt. Straub was fined 1fl. and the court restored Schneider and Enders' honor, and presumably they were also readmitted to the commune. The potential consequences of a casually uttered insult were serious.

Accusations of stealing could easily damage someone's honor, confirming the common insult of "you are a thief." In August 1704, Hansjerg Storck brought a complaint against one of his neighbors, Wolfgang Wagner. Storck testified that Wagner had accused Storck's boy (*Bueb*) of stealing a barrel of wine from the communal wine cellar.[49] This accusation, according to Storck, had caused "a great outcry" in the *Gemeinde* and was bad for the boy's honor, and presumably the father's as well. He stated, as was common in these cases, that Wagner needed to prove this charge or give satisfaction.

Wagner's testimony put a new twist on this story. He said that he, and two others, had helped Hansjerg's brother, Lorenz Storck, put a barrel full of wine into the

[47] GLAK 61/7606, pp. 42r–42v. [48] GLAK 61/13344, pp. 8–9.

[49] GLAK 61/13344, pp. 346–9. Storck's "boy" is presumably his son, but we cannot be sure how old he was. The word *Bub* could designate any unmarried young male.

cellar. Lorenz first testified that he did not know what had happened to the wine, but, on further consideration, came clean. Lorenz had taken the wine himself, took it out on the lake, and drank it.[50] For having initially lied to the court, Lorenz was fined a hefty 10fl. "We have given him the money fine, although he deserves more, only so as to protect his good name and not prevent further good luck." The court also restored Hansjerg and his son's honor and concluded with a snarky (and somewhat obscure) comment that Lorenz would need to find a way to make this up to his brother.

This case shows how significant accusations of stealing were in these face-to-face communities. It also shows how a court case could veer off in unexpected directions, in this case implicating a witness, the brother of the complainant. It also illuminates the role of the *Oberamtsgericht* in Salem. The court was sensitive to the consequences of a stealing conviction, and in this case a perjury conviction, and allowed Lorenz Storck to pay a fine and avoid the more humiliating punishments of imprisonment or the stocks. Why the court was concerned to protect his honor and "luck" is not clear. Perhaps they felt that the conflict was now really within the family and Lorenz would face consequences there. Courts did generally prefer to avoid long-term damage to people's honor, at least in the case of established citizens, which Lorenz seems to have been. Unfortunately, we know nothing about the relative power of the Storck brothers or their place in the community, information which might put this case into a deeper context.[51]

Honor disputes that came out of generic exchanges of insults or out of violations of social behavior, for example in the tavern, were usually disputes between people of similar social status. Honor cases that resulted from accusations of theft were more often adjudicated between people of differing social status, with poorer and less powerful people using the court to defend their honor.[52] It also appears that the number of these cases, often with women filing slander charges, increased in the period after 1710, reflecting growing economic conflict at the village level.

Some people appear multiple times as complainants or defendants in such cases. In July 1673, Conrad Bonawer from Allmannsdorf charged Maria Sulgerin with falsely spreading a story that he had stolen a fish, a pike in fact. Sulgerin testified that she had seen Bonawer with a fish and some others had told her it was a pike. Bonawer, however, was able to prove that he had been bringing some meat to be salted, not fish. Sulgerin was fined and told by the court "once again to keep her mouth better under control."[53] The court's irritation with Maria Sulgerin may have stemmed from an earlier case, from June 1672. In that case, she had been

[50] This was the big lake, Lake Constance, the *Bodensee*.

[51] Sreenivasan, *The Peasants of Ottobeuren*, and Sabean, *Property, Production, and Family in Neckarhausen*, have been able to do this in their studies.

[52] Klaus Schreiner and Gerd Schwerhoff, eds. *Verletzte Ehre. Ehrkonflikte in Gesellschaften des Mittelalters und der Frühen Neuzeit* (Köln, 1995), pp. 13–14.

[53] GLAK 61/7600, July 1, 1673.

spreading rumors that Andreas Bonawer's wife had stolen some linen, a story initially started by a maid. In that case, nothing was proven, and the court lamented that "such a case is only women's gossip and complete nonsense [*lauter lari fari*] without any proof."[54] In this case, the court at Mainau dismissed "women's gossip" (*Weibergeschwätz*), but, as we will see, more often they heard out complaints by women.

Courts almost always "officially" removed all insults to honor at the end of court cases. They ordered parties to apologize and quite often exhorted them to let bygones be bygones, to let these disputes go. Still, old accusations and a reputation for dishonorable behavior could haunt people. Jacob Golter went to court in May 1712 to ask for the restoration of his honor, after Jacob Miller's wife had accused him of stealing two hens, an accusation that had left him "defamed before the whole commune."[55] Miller's wife said she had not meant to cause Golter trouble, but it was true that three years before he had stolen two hens from her. Golter denied this charge and predictably argued, "this is an old issue and if she had a complaint, why didn't she go to the authorities then?" The court demanded Frau Miller bring evidence, or stop making accusations. Golter continued to suffer from an unproven charge from several years before and probably had not heard the end of the case.

In the early eighteenth century, increasing numbers of women were found defending their honor against accusations of petty theft. In 1710, the wife of Johann Brunner the *Krautschneider* (the "cabbage cutter," probably a small farmer or cottager) fought successfully against a rumor she had emptied a fruit tree.[56] In June 1713 Francisca Brunnerin filed suit against her neighbor for accusing her of stealing. The neighbor admitted she had no proof that Francisca had stolen wood and grass, but nastily testified "as long as Francisca has bordered on their property, much has disappeared, and she saw from the footprints that is was a barefooted woman, but she cannot however prove that the complainant (Francisca) had done it."[57] In August 1713, Joseph Merzer complained that several neighbors had accused his daughter of stealing half a pig and some silver from the smith. The defendants admitted to having no proof.[58]

The outcome of a slander suit about stealing, as in other issues that came to court, was not guaranteed and could backfire on the complainant. This is what happened to Clemens Messmer's wife (Messmerin in the records) in August 1711

[54] GLAK 61/7600, June 11, 1672. There were many Bonawers (Bonauers) in this region, so one cannot assume that Conrad and Andreas were related. On gossip, Pia Holenstein and Norbert Schindler, "Geschwätzgeschichte(n). Ein Kulturhistorischer Plädoyer für die Rehabilitierung der unkontrollierter Rede" in Richard van Dülmen, ed. *Dynamik der Tradition* (Frankfurt, 1992); David Warren Sabean, "Village Court Protocols and Memory" in Heinrich Richard Schmidt, André Holenstein, and Andreas Würgler, eds. *Gemeinde, Reformation, und Widerstand*; Sabean, *Power in the Blood*, pp. 147–9, 195–7.

[55] GLAK 61/7606, 1712, p. 22r.

[56] GLAK 61/7606, 1710, pp. 55r–55v.

[57] GLAK 61/7606, 1713, p. 27v.

[58] GLAK 61/7606, 1713, pp. 35r–35v.

when she brought charges of slander against Simon Mundhas' wife, claiming Mundhastin had accused her of stealing some cloth and called her a witch.[59] The defendant denied the insult, but admitted to commenting on the stolen cloth. She also brought up some old accusations that the Messmers had stolen flour, bread, hay, and other things when they were living in the Dafingers' house. Witnesses testified that Mundhastin had never insulted Messmerin, and the Messmers were required to pay court costs and reimburse the Mundhas couple for lost work.

The conflict between these two couples raises several questions. Clemens Messmer was also in court the same day as his wife's case, defending himself from a charge of stealing chickens and responding to the accusation with a barrage of insults against the accuser. Did his case affect the case between the two wives? Furthermore, neither family appears well off, and the Messmers had probably been servants when they had "lived at the Dafingers"; in 1711 both men appear to have been fishermen. Accusations of theft against servants were common, as they have been throughout history, and they could easily lead to dismissal.[60] Certainly servants fought an uphill battle defending their honor in courts where the juries were made up of landed farmers, but their cases did come to these courts and they sometimes won them too.

Tensions around economic transactions and debts could also become honor cases, as a demand for payment or an accusation of dishonesty in a sale of livestock or property were also attacks on someone's honor. Although written records of these transactions were increasingly documented in the archives of these courts, much economic activity was still based on verbal commitments. Disputes over the payment (or non-payment) of debts were common, since much economic activity was driven by credit. Peasants took on debt to finance inheritances, since in some places one sibling had to buy out other siblings to keep a farm intact.[61] Others took on debt to finance the purchase of land or livestock, and poorer people had to borrow to get through periods of bad harvests or unemployment.[62]

An attempt by a creditor to collect a debt, particularly if the attempt was made in a public way or a public place, could quickly lead to a burst of insults from the debtor. This sort of escalation is not surprising, since a demand for payment implied that the debtor was not upholding his end of a bargain and therefore was not a *Biedermann*. Benedict Benz, a big farmer in Unteropfingen, attacked Georg König in his own house over a debt that König characterized as small and well

[59] GLAK 61/7606, 1711, pp. 54v–55r, 58v. This case was resolved over several sessions.

[60] Renate Dürr, "Die Ehre der Mägde zwischen Selbstdefinition und Fremdbestimmung" in Sibylle Backman et al., eds. *Ehrkonzepte in der Frühen Neuzeit. Identitäten und Abgrenzungen* (Berlin, 1998): 170–84.

[61] Sreenivasan, *The Peasants of Ottobeuren*, esp. chs 4, 5, and 6.

[62] Sheilagh Ogilvie, Markus Küpker, and Janine Maegraith, "Household Debt in Early Modern Germany" *Journal of Economic History* 72 (2012): 134–67.

documented. Benz called König a dog and a scoundrel for demanding payment. The *Oberamtsgericht* in Rot fined Benz for the insults.[63]

In a May 1710 case involving two less well-off parties than Benz and König, Agatha Bremin sued for payment of a debt of 11 *Gulden* owed to her by Micheal Wilhelm from Dingelsdorf.[64] Wilhelm had initially responded to this demand with insults, but in court said that due to the wretched times (*Ellende Zeiten*) he could only pay after the harvest, presumably in the fall of that year. Bremin said she needed to be paid right away, otherwise she would lose her house. The court was skeptical of Wilhelm's claim of poverty, since he had been taxed for a decent wine harvest the previous year. He was jailed for the insults and ordered to pay the debt.

Perhaps Maria Mayerin, an innkeeper in Staad, was a tad insensitive when she demanded payment of a 1 *Gulden* debt owed to her by Caspar Hamman during Hamman's wedding. Several days later, Hamman stormed into her tavern, calling her "an adulterous whore and witch."[65] Hamman did not deny making the insults, was ordered to apologize, and was fined. Did Mayerin really figure the wedding was a good venue to pressure Hamman for payment, or was this a calculated insult, as Hamman clearly thought? I suspect the latter, given the small size of the debt and the fact that a wedding was a moment when a young man staked out his place as a full adult member of the community. Probably a debt to an innkeeper, no matter how small, was not good for the new husband's reputation.

A 1673 dispute adjudicated before the village court in Rotteln demonstrates again how the "rhetoric of honor" could cause a rapid escalation of common property disputes. "Little Hans" Meyer brought a complaint that Ulrich Scheübli had beaten him bloody and torn his beard the previous year during a meeting of the commune, in a dispute over a burned hedgerow.[66] According to Meyer, Scheübli called him (among other things) a "fat pig" and he demanded satisfaction, "since these insults do not just injure his reputation and honor, but also [that of] his late parents in their graves." Scheübli testified that Meyer gave as good as he got, also beating him, and saying that he, Scheübli, "was good for nothing and from the devil." Scheübli claimed that he had not insulted Meyer or his parents, but he had heard from others that Meyer had attacked his honor. After further denials by both sides, the court ruled that the insults were erased and passed the case on to a higher jurisdiction for adjudication of the violence that had occurred. No mention of the burnt hedgerow appears in the court's decision making—issues of honor took precedence and drove underlying disputes into the background.

[63] HStAS B486/Bd 15, pp. 157r–157v. 1684, 13 March. Benz also called König a *Kretel*. I do not know what that means.

[64] GLAK 61/7606, 1710, pp. 30r–30v.

[65] GLAK 61/7602, November 29, 1687.

[66] GLAK 61/6958, November 23, 1673.

People of all social classes defended their honor, including servants and farm-workers. Servants were willing to speak out against their "betters," at least on some occasions. In September 1677, Hans Meyer, a *Knecht* (farm laborer), met Hans Messmer's daughter-in-law in the fields of Rotteln.[67] Meyer told the young woman that he had heard that she was going to send away her maid and if she was, "she lies like a witch." Messmer filed a slander suit against Meyer, who apologized and claimed he had not meant to insult Messmer's daughter-in-law. Messmer's response was rather conciliatory, stating that if the court found that no one's honor had been impugned, he would accept the ruling. In the end, the court did fine Meyer and restored the Messmer family honor. We do not know why Meyer felt he could use such language in such a calculated way. After all, he did not claim any mitigating factor, anger or drinking being the usual excuses. Perhaps Meyer had family in the region that gave him some protection, or perhaps he felt less compunction insulting a woman. Finally, what was his relationship with the maid that caused him to interfere in this issue?

Families did in fact come to the defense of one of their own who was in service. In February 1704, Valentin Bronner from Altenbeuren filed suit in the name of his sister, Caecillia Bronnerin, against her master, Sebastian Biller from Neufrach.[68] Bronner stated that Biller had accused Caecillia of stealing a calf and had withheld her pay, and Caecillia's brother demanded Biller prove the charge, or restore her honor, presumably by paying her. Biller declined to do this, saying that he had no money and appealed for patience. Bronner responded "he would just be happy if the defendant would just stop yelling at his sister." This solution satisfied all parties, including the court.

Some employees very confidently defended their rights. This was particularly the case for skilled workers of various kinds who worked for the large monasteries of the region.[69] Claus Sprägele filed a complaint at the court in Rot that the monastery's *Hofmeister* (the chief operating officer, we might say) had said that Sprägele had claimed pay for six days when he had not worked.[70] Sprägele considered this an affront to his honor and provided witnesses to support his case. He petitioned "that the *Hofmeister* be ordered to provide him with a reference and the restoration of his honorable name." The Rot *Oberamtsgericht* agreed, telling the Hofmeister "he should speak more carefully on issues that he cannot prove and should not go so far, for this might put his [own] honor at risk." There were clearly practical considerations at work here, as Sprägele needed a reference to be

[67] GLAK 61/6958, September 4, 1677. [68] GLAK 61/13344, pp. 304–5.

[69] These monasteries, including Salem and Rot an der Rot whose court records I am using, were engaged in major building projects, particularly after about 1690. This meant there were many laborers, artisans, and other workers living and working at the monasteries, both permanently and temporarily.

[70] HStAS B486/Bd 14, pp. 111r–v, July 3, 1668.

able to work elsewhere, but both parties (and the court) saw the issue in terms of personal honor.

In August 1696 Regina Voglerin appeared before the court in Salem and testified that "her master Johannes Riggler...had harshly insulted her, stating he did not need such a lazy whore, and now that she wants to leave his service, he refuses to pay her the salary she is owed."[71] Riggler admitted that he had insulted her because of indolence and because she was always talking back to him. He "however did not mean to say anything dishonoring about her," and he did not think these words justified her leaving his service before her commitment had run out. The court attempted to split the difference, ordering Voglerin to remain in service, but stating that if something like this happened again, she might well be justified in leaving.

A case from 1705 probably speaks for itself.[72]

> Issac Jacob from Allmannsdorf brings a complaint against his maid Ursula Kesserin from Immenstaad, that, when he corrects one or the other of her mistakes or punishes her or uses insulting speech, she disparages his house so much, that he is ashamed. He asks that she be punished as she deserves.
>
> Since it is clear from the answers, testimony, and counter-testimony, that both sides have gone too far, even the complainant has been ruled excessive and he should pay a fine of 1 pound. The maid should do penance for her bad mouth by pronouncing her guilt loudly in the courtyard.

Jacob, the master, was fined. Kesserin, the maid, was subjected to a shaming punishment. But both parties were considered guilty, a further indication that servants could find a sympathetic hearing in these local courts.

Women and men had to defend their honor against attacks on their sexual behavior. As we will see in the next chapter, attacks on women's honor almost always came to be subsumed under an attack on women's sexual behavior. Men were sometimes the beneficiaries of social practices and legal systems that overlooked sexual improprieties, particularly for powerful men involved with powerless women like servants. But, in rural communities, men's honor was damaged by public adultery (or rumors of adultery) or by being known as a cuckold. Accusations of adultery, or the spreading of rumors about sexual improprieties, required men to defend their honor.[73]

As Rainer Walz points out, official (and Church) regulations of proper sexual behavior differed in some ways from community expectations, particularly in the

[71] GLAK 61/13337, pp. 340–1. [72] GLAK 61/7604, p. 190r.

[73] See Lyndal Roper, *Oedipus and the Devil. Witchcraft, Religion, and Sexuality in Early Modern Europe* (New York,1994), ch. 5.

area of pre-marital sex.[74] For example, couples guilty of "getting pregnant too early" were fined by courts, but this issue was rarely used by the common folk to impugn someone's honor. Walz is also correct that people could deploy the authorities' moral code in a conflict with a neighbor, particularly a conflict that went to court. And since issues like adultery undermined family structures and threatened both patriarchy and the authority and status of wives, they were regularly referenced in disputes.

Artisans were particularly concerned with sexual honor, something that has been studied in cities and towns.[75] In June 1661, group of journeymen carpenters were drinking in the tavern in the village of Berkheim when one of them, Michael Ertlin, called his fellow carpenter Valentin Widner an adulterer and a *Hexenmeister* (master of witches).[76] Widner said that he needed his honor repaired, for otherwise the carpenters would refuse to work with him and he would lose a future position in the city of Memmingen. The court seemed aware of the stakes involved and sided with Widner, throwing Ertlin into the jail until he apologized. Of course, here as in many other honor disputes, something else may have caused this dispute, but the use of the insult "adulterer" (*Ehebrecher*) struck home.

A 1718 case from the village court at Wollmatingen seems quite specific and may reference a real suspicion of adultery. Johannes Stockher accused Ulrich Weltin of slander for saying that Stockher "had a whore here in the region."[77] Weltin offered no proof and was told that if he could not produce evidence, he would be required to apologize for the slanderous talk. Other uses of the insult "adulterer" may reference all kinds of questionable sexual behavior rather than actual marital infidelity.

In July 1672, Bartle Theyer escorted Michael Sulger's wife home from a wedding. When, sometime after 11 p.m., Sulger found them together in the *Stube*, he insulted Theyer as an adulterer.[78] Sulger said he used this insult "because it is not the practice to spend time with a married woman at that time and hour." Threyer defended himself, saying he had only spent "a half a quarter hour" there and had left without giving any reason for the accusation. He and his mother had escorted Frau Sulger home, "as if he were her cousin," after her husband had beaten her at the wedding reception. Threyer had not been among the men who had attacked Sulger in reaction to his hitting his wife, although he had also expressed his displeasure when Sulger shoved his wife out of her chair.

There was a lot happening in this case beyond the insult of adulterer. Threyer got his apology, although he had to pay a fine for visiting a woman in her house at

[74] Walz, "Agonale Kommunikation," pp. 243–4.
[75] Tlusty, *Bacchus and Civic Order*, esp. ch. 8.
[76] HStAS B486/Bd 13, 276v–277r.
[77] GLAK 61/13268, p. 191r. *eine Hueren im landt habe.*
[78] GLAK 61/7600, 1672, 30 July. The *Stube* was the parlor, the room where one entertained guests.

that hour, so it is not clear if his name was fully cleared. Perhaps not, since he told the court that he wanted to come back and prove that they had returned from the wedding at nine in the evening, rather than after eleven. If proven, this would clear the fine and fully restore his honor. Why did Sulger, the husband, take this case to court? Did he perhaps hope to restore some of his own lost honor after his behavior at the wedding? If so, it is hard to imagine that the publicity around the court case did anything to improve his reputation.

A 1714 case shows how difficult it is to know if the insult "adulterer" was just a generic insult, a kind of male equivalent of "whore." On this occasion, Mathis Manz was on his way home from a tavern when Johannes Schlegel's wife called him an "adulterous scoundrel," adding that she should file charges with the court at Heiligenberg [since] "he deserves to hang."[79] Manz struck her with his walking stick and Johannes Schlegel then threw Manz to the ground. The Schlegels claimed that Manz had started the confrontation by calling Frau Schlegel a "debt maker," presumably a spendthrift. Frau Schlegel also insulted a bystander who called for peace. The Schlegels were punished, with a fine for Johannes and the stocks for his wife.

There is nothing in the court record that indicates that Frau Schlegel was really accusing Manz of adultery. There is some indication of an underlying conflict, perhaps over the debts Manz referenced. Frau Schlegel also told the witness/bystander that "this issue was, by the devil, not in the least any of his business." In any case the insult was considered damaging, and Manz felt he needed to respond.

Women who worked in taverns and inns were always sexually suspect, particularly maids and servants, but the innkeeper's wife (the *Wirtin*) as well. The innkeeper, the *Wirt*, also had to be on the lookout for rumors and reports of sexual impropriety on his part. Johannes Wilhelm, the *Wirt* in Weildorf, insulted and physically attacked a neighbor who had said, in public, that Wilhelm "had more to do with the maid than with his wife."[80] The maid testified that she had had no relations with the *Wirt* and that the previous maid was the one who had been spreading this story. Clearly the accusation of sexual relations with a servant at the inn was considered a threat to Wilhelm's honor. Whether the accusation was true, we will never know. The court considered it "dangerous rumor mongering."

Other sexual attacks were probably more serious than a "simple" charge of adultery. One variation on the adultery charge was to accuse a man of having illegitimate children. In May 1718, Hans Conrad Manz, the *Amman* in Ermattingen, filed a slander complaint against Magdalena Greüssin, who had said he had two illegitimate children.[81] The case was complicated by the fact that Manz had wanted to marry Greüssin, who had then asked another woman if the rumor

[79] GLAK 61/7606, pp. 40r–40v. The Lordship of Heiligenberg held high justice in this area, and Heiligenberg courts were the ones that could bring the death penalty.

[80] GLAK 61/13346, pp. 272–3, May 19, 1708.

[81] GLAK 61/13268, pp. 192r–193r.

of illegitimate children was true. In the end, Manz got what he wanted, a restoration of his honor by the court. There is no information about the success or failure of his marriage suit.

Another variation on this theme is the insult that a man is not in fact the father of his wife's children, that he is a cuckold. Andreas Sprenger's wife said just this about Johannes Eschenbacher and named the *Knecht* (servant) Michel Rotenhäusler as the father of Eschenbacher's wife's children.[82] Eschenbacher demanded redress, saying he could not allow this insult "to sit on him." Sprengerin tried to explain away her allegation by saying she had heard it from a "small child" and in any case "she had not thought that this was a big deal." The court, however, did think it was a serious issue, required her to apologize, and as punishment for her "shameless mouth" she was put in the stocks during mass the following Sunday.

In a similar vein, Mathias Dilger said that Hans Jerg Knoll, the journeyman shoemaker, was the father of his master's wife's child.[83] Knoll filed a slander suit, denying that he was the father or that he had "whored with the shoemaker's wife." The defendant claimed to be just reporting what he had heard. A witness testified "that the people…had been speaking about the shoemaker's child, which is actually of both genders [*beederley geschlechts seye*], at which Mathias Dilger had said, he guesses it therefore has two fathers, and so it was said that the shoemaker's wife must have whored with the Swabian [i.e., Knoll]." Dilger was heavily fined for the attack on the shoemaker's honor.

Other serious attacks on a man's sexual honor were possible, though not frequent.

> Master Andreas Hasselberger, the smith in Wollmatingen, appeared on this date at the Chancellery here and files a complaint against the old Sennin in Dettingen, with the name of Magdalena Letsaüffin, that she has greatly injured him, saying publicly to other people that he had been imprisoned at Reichenau because he had improper relations with his daughter. He asks that the defendant be appropriately punished and that she should apologize and publicly retract the accusation of supposed crimes of which he is innocent.[84]

Hasselberger may not have been reassured that the court heard testimony from "the old Sennin" and several other women. The story was traced to a "beggar woman" who, months before, claimed to have heard about the smith from her brother, who was a beadle in Reichenau. Sadly for the historian, and perhaps for Hasselberger as well, the court records do not record an outcome for this case. This rumor was a serious threat to Hasselberger's honor, and the court investigation showed that it was widely known. What was worse for Hasselberger, the

[82] GLAK 61/7602, November 4, 1686. [83] GLAK 61/133346, pp. 420–1, November 16, 1709.
[84] GLAK 61/7604, pp. 139–41, February 1, 1703. The case was heard at the court in Mainau.

authorities decided the rumor was worth investigating further, rather than just punishing the gossiping women and protecting the smith's honor.

Attacks on male sexual honor almost always focused on the proper behavior of the *Hausvater*, the head of household. Adultery, incest, or a failure to keep the household in line all called a man's honor into question. On the other hand, sexual activity before marriage was punished in other ways and did not impugn a man's honor. Furthermore, it was women who most often attacked men as adulterers and as fathers of illegitimate children. In some cases, it seems that women were defending other women, perhaps a wronged wife, by publicizing stories about a man's infidelity. Perhaps women spoke about dishonorable male sexual behavior because they were hyperaware of these issues from their own experience. More speculatively perhaps, were women impugning *male* sexual honor to highlight that the rhetoric of honor, backed up by the legal system, made *female* honor almost exclusively about sexuality?[85]

The Innkeeper, the Innkeeper's Wife, and the Widow

On July 17, 1684, the *Oberamtsgericht* in Rot spent much of the day hearing testimony in a case that pitted the innkeeper in Zell, Hans Petscher, against Regina Eisnerin.[86] Petscher brought the case, accusing Eisnerin of slandering him by publicly accusing him of an inappropriate relationship with a widow, an accusation that caused conflict in his marriage. The widow, Georg Sommer's wife, known as Horerin, was staying in Zell with her blind and aged mother. Petscher asked the court that "the accused present evidence for this public accusation [*Beschreiung*], or if this is not available, that, in addition to compensation for all costs and damages, the *Obrigkeit* will help in the restoration of his honorable name." This was a common opening for these kinds of slander cases.

Eisnerin did not deny the basic charge. She had said, in front of Petscher's tavern, that the *Wirt* had visited Horerin in her house. Eisnerin went further: "she had reproached Horerin herself, and is of the opinion, and believes it too, that Horerin is happy to see the *Wirt*, and the *Wirt* on his part [is happy to see] her. To this Horerin only answered, she, [Eisnerin] should go ahead and talk, so that she can refute what she says in the future."

In her testimony, Horerin explained that she had heard these stories, but there was no proof. Asked by the court where the rumors had come from, she said that

[85] See especially Gowing, *Domestic Dangers*. Ann Goldberg argues that women in Imperial Germany could manipulate the language of sexual honor to their benefit. Goldberg, *Honor, Politics, and the Law*. See also Dinges, "'Weiblichkeit' in 'Männlichkeitsritualen'" and "Ehre und Geschlecht in der Frühen Neuzeit" in Backman, eds. *Ehrkonzepte*.

[86] HStAS B486/Bd 15, pp. 172r–175r. The court heard only two other cases that day, a dispute over the sale of a cow and the punishment of an innkeeper for illegal wine sales. Eisnerin was the wife of Hans Pitschen, a name quite similar to that of the complainant in this case.

the previous winter she was often at the tavern, helping with the cleaning, baking, and other work. At times she had also stayed overnight there, but she had always slept with the servant, Anna Maria Josephin. Josephin confirmed this in her testimony, adding that she had never seen anything untoward between the *Wirt* and the widow.

Testimony from Catherina Locherin, a shepherdess, revealed more about how suspicions about the *Wirt* and the widow had spread in the village. Locherin claimed to have seen Petscher touch and "lie on" Horerin during an event at the tavern. Locherin testified that Petcher's wife, Anna, had told her "that during this past cold winter Horerin could have gone home at night and slept with her old blind mother." Locherin had been threatened by Petscher's two sisters, and she told them that she would not spread these stories any more in Zell, but if called to the court in Rot, she would reveal all she had heard from the *Wirtin*.

The third witness was Maria Petscherin, the innkeeper's sister. She was the one who had told Petscher about the stories/rumors/accusations that were circulating in the village. She had also seen the ways this issue was affecting her brother's marriage. That situation was not improved by Franz Rehm, a young man who had helped with some farm work on the inn's property and had stayed for dinner. Over dinner he told the innkeeper's wife, Anna, that the knife the *Wirt* was using had been given him by Horerin's elderly mother, Lisabeth, with the implication that Petscher had been at Horerin's house. He went on to say about the *Wirt* and the widow: "he is surely in love with her." Maria reported that Anna did not take this conversation well. But, Rehm was a bad witness when he came before the court, and the court dismissed his testimony as riddled with contradictions and not worth taking seriously.

We see here the interplay of the discourse of honor, the spread of stories and rumors, and the legal effort to determine what "really happened." It seems likely that nothing, or nothing much, had happened between the *Wirt* and the widow, but enough circumstantial evidence was publicly known to raise suspicions. Petscher's sister was convinced that several women were intentionally spreading false rumors and the court agreed. For innkeeper Petscher, though, this was ultimately about two things: his honor and his marriage. He could defend the first in court and in public, but of course we do not know if the "great tension and discord" (as he said) in his house could be repaired.

In any case, Petscher had some clout in Zell. The *Amman* testified on his behalf and the court ruled forcefully in his favor. All those who had spoken against him, Eiserin, Locherin, and Rehm, were punished, the women with the stocks and Rehm with a prison sentence. Eiserin had to pay all the court costs as well. In this case, the court was an effective place for Petscher to defend his honor and, by contrast, not a good place for Locherin to tell her truth, despite her earlier threat to Petscher's sisters to tell all when she was called to Rot. Yes, the courts sometimes defended the weak against the powerful, but not in this case.

This case reveals some common ways in which honor, conflict, and peacekeeping worked in rural communities. One of these is the importance of publicity for an insult to truly damage someone's honor. Martin Dinges has written that "without publicity, there is no honor," and the corollary is that damage to honor had to be repaired in public.[87] Courts knew this and required public apologies from people convicted of slander.

* * *

Honor was at the center of conflicts in rural society. In important ways it functioned like identity functions in the modern western world by defining the place of every person in society.[88] Everyone had honor, whether rich or poor, powerful or powerless, and everyone needed to defend that honor. It was a characteristic that adhered to the individual, but it also had a family component, and it was threatened in all kinds of social interactions. Malcolm Greenshields adds a further element, pointing out that "...physical and mental boundaries were closely allied, combined into what I have called elsewhere 'physic property,' as a sense of oneself that included both inner and outer territory, both honor and space, subject to violation."[89] A peasant's honor was impugned when physical boundaries were violated, in the fields or in the tavern, with important implications for one's social status.

Spaces were important in other ways. As we will see, taverns were the main center of communication in most villages, particularly as churches were increasingly controlled and disciplined spaces and thus less active as centers of sociability. It was often at the tavern where stories were told and spread and where rumors brought in from elsewhere were amplified and became more dangerous. Furthermore, the role of rumor, particularly rumors told by women, often denigrated as *Weibergeschwätz* (women's prattle), was almost ubiquitous in this world, a source of power for women and dangerous to everyone.[90] Gossip and rumors were integral to the sharing of information in these communities.

And of course honor was gendered. Women and men defended their honor in many of the same ways. They countered insults with insults of their own, they demanded satisfaction from their opponents, they turned, often very quickly, to violence, and they sometimes brought slander suits to the local courts. Many of the issues that led to honor conflicts were the same for men and women as well, such as accusations of stealing or demands for the payment of a debt. But women's honor was also qualitatively different because of the ubiquity of the insults of whore and witch.

[87] Quoted in Michael Frank, "Ehre und Gewalt im Dorf der Frühen Neuzeit. Das Beispiel Heiden (Grafschaft Lippe) im 17. und 18. Jahrhundert" in Schreiner and Schwerhoff, eds. *Verletzte Ehre*, p. 323.

[88] I am indebted to Peter Wallace for this insight.

[89] Greenshields, *An Economy of Violence in Early Modern France*, p. 75.

[90] On taverns, see especially Chapter 4. On publicity, rumor, and gossip, see Chapter 5.

3

"You are a whore and a witch" Women's Honor in German Villages

It is a truism to say that honor was deeply gendered in early modern society, indeed in any society. Martin Dinges' studies of honor conflicts in eighteenth-century Paris emphasize the gender differences in the causes of honor conflicts, the nature of insults, the progression of conflicts, and the kinds of public spaces where these conflicts were carried out.[1] German villages differed in significant ways from the working-class neighborhoods of Paris studied by Dinges, but the essential idea, that "gender is fundamental for honor and its violation," was of course true there as well.[2]

We also have to be careful to avoid a simplistic application of ideas about women's honor developed by anthropologists of Mediterranean societies to other parts of Europe. Women's honor in Germany, and also in England and France, was always first and foremost sexual honor.[3] But this was not the world of passive women whose honor needed to be defended by their fathers and brothers, as studies of Italian and Spanish elites have emphasized.[4] German rural women were active in defending their own and their families' honor, including stepping up to defend their husbands at times. Women fought more often with words than with fists, and they did so in public, but more often on the streets than in the tavern. They also regularly filed slander suits in court and testified on their own behalf. Issues of sexual honor were most often at stake, but women also had to face the ominous witch insult throughout this period.

The standard insults were whore and witch. Whore was a ubiquitous insult and used in almost all cases of slander that came to court. Often the word *Hur* was used as a kind of all-purpose insult of women, indicating a lack of

[1] Dinges, "'Weiblichkeit' in 'Männlichkeitsritualen.'"

[2] Martin Dinges, "Die Ehre als Thema der historische Anthropologie" in Schreiner and Schwerhoff, eds. *Verletzte Ehre*, p. 48. See also Susanna Burghartz, "Geschlecht-Körper-Ehre. Überlegungen zur weiblichen Ehre in der Frühen Neuzeit am Beispiel der Basler Ehegerichtsprotokolle" in Schreiner and Schwerhoff, eds. *Verletzte Ehre*, pp. 214–34; Martin Dinges, "Ehre und Geschlecht in der frühen Neuzeit" in Martin Backmann and Sibylle Backmann, eds. *Ehrkonzepte in der Frühen Neuzeit. Identitäten und Abgrenzungen* (Berlin, Boston, 1998), pp. 123–47.

[3] Dinges, "Die Ehre als Thema der historische Anthropologie," pp. 54–5. For England, Gowing, *Domestic Dangers*.

[4] Recent studies have presented a more nuanced understanding of the function of honor and gender in Mediterranean and Latin American societies as well. For one example, see Taylor, *Honor and Violence*.

Keeping the Peace in the Village: Conflict and Peacemaking in Germany, 1650–1750. Marc R. Forster, Oxford University Press. © Marc R. Forster 2024. DOI: 10.1093/oso/9780198898474.003.0004

trustworthiness or an unwillingness to obey social rules and fulfill proper roles in the family and the community. At other times, insults referenced specific examples of sexual impropriety, requiring a strong response from the insulted woman. The use of whore as an insult highlights a tension between the routine use of certain words—a cultural style available to everyone—and the particular context when the insult was used.[5]

The frequent use of whore as an insult of course contributed to the construction of gender in early modern German villages, as it did in other places and other times. Laura Gowing's *Domestic Dangers* shows how slander cases in English courts perpetuated and reinforced a popular view of women's honor as defined by a woman's "sexual probity." In England, as in Germany, whore was the insult of choice against women used by men and women. "The sexual insult of women absorbed and refracted every kind of female transgression," and "the word 'whore' stood for a whole way of defining women."[6] Dinges' study of honor conflicts in eighteenth-century Paris lists "*putain*" and "*garce*," both words for whore or prostitute, as the top insults used against working-class women.[7] Parisian women of course fought to defend their sexual honor, more violently and less often in court than English women.

The focus on female sexual honor continued into the modern period in Germany. Ann Goldberg's study of honor in Wilhelmine Germany points to the emphasis on women's domestic and sexual virtues. "Above all, a woman's honor was composed of her sexual chastity and modesty."[8] Goldberg makes direct connections between slander suits filed by women in the late nineteenth century to those filed in Gowing's England and in early modern Germany. "One senses a similar, sexualized rhetoric of abuse in daily life among the small-town and city working-class and petit bourgeois women who made up the bulk of women's honor suits in the *Kaiserreich*."[9] Women used courts in all these periods and places to defend their honor.

Women were also insulted as witches in early modern Germany. Not as ubiquitous as whore, nevertheless people used the word "witch" frequently. This was, of course, a dangerous insult, especially in the seventeenth century, when women were still being arrested, tortured, convicted, and executed as witches. As we will see, women and their families were quick to file slander charges when they were called witches. Although most witch insults were in a way casual or routine, some did reference behaviors that smacked of malefice or sorcery, raising the stakes for all parties.

[5] Krug-Richter, "Von nackten Hummeln und Schandpflasten," esp. pp. 269–90.
[6] Gowing, *Domestic Dangers*, esp. pp. 118, 138.
[7] Dinges, "'Weiblichkeit' in 'Männlichkeitsritualen.'"
[8] Goldberg, *Honor, Politics, and the Law*, esp. pp. 66–73. Quote p. 66.
[9] Goldberg, *Honor, Politics, and the Law*, p. 72.

Female Sexuality

The basic insults used against women, whore and witch, were both terms that referenced sexual behavior. Women could and did go to court to defend their honor, usually demanding, just as men did, that the defendants either prove their accusation or take the dishonoring insult back. In a typical case, this one from September 1674, Maria Leherin won a slander case against Ulrich Sprenger, who had called her a "frivolous soldier's whore." Her honor was officially restored by the court.[10] Parents could also bring cases to restore the honor of a daughter, as Madlena Weberin did in July 1676, charging Thomas Baumann with calling her daughter Madlena Morgin a "known and used up whore,"[11] Baumann claimed his brother had had relations with the daughter when serving in her father's house, but he could not prove his case. Baumann, unusually for a man, was given a shaming punishment when he was sentenced to stand before the church door during mass and the sermon, and then made to apologize to the *Mädle* (the girl) before the whole community. In another case, two young male servants in the tavern in Rot were punished for calling the maid there a whore, although in that case it is not clear who brought the charges.[12]

After about 1700 more women came to court to defend their honor. For example, in 1702 Agatha Moserin from Owingen filed a slander suit against the innkeeper there for calling her a whore and a thief.[13] It appears that Moserin worked at the inn and the innkeeper had used these insults after hearing that Sebastian Enders, who had been courting Agatha, claimed to have eight children scattered around the region. Apparently extrapolating from Sebastian's "dissolute behavior," the innkeeper assumed that Moserin's "virginity is nothing to admire." The court restored Moserin's honor and fined Enders for insulting her and, one might hope, for bragging about his sexual conquests. Similarly, in 1706, a bride was forced to defend her honor after a wedding guest called her a whore.[14]

Not all women were successful with slander suits. Magdalena Hügin wanted her honor restored after an altercation at a tavern where a soldier threw her to the ground and jumped on her. She testified that she swore at him and he left her alone, but a witness, Johannes Küenzle, claimed that the soldier "had done something that is not proper to her." Küenzle denied saying anything to dishonor Hügin, and in this case the court told her she would have to bring more evidence to get a favorable ruling.[15] Finally, these slander cases could backfire. When Maria Golterin, a servant, demanded that a neighbor woman apologize for calling her

[10] GLAK 61/7600, September 15, 1674. Accusations of "soldiers' whore" were common wherever soldiers were quartered. See also GLAK 61/7606, 1713, pp. 9r–9v.

[11] GLAK 61/7600, July 4, 1676, *ein offentlich und s.h. abgeridtene huor seye.*

[12] HStAS B486/Bd 15, p. 157v. March 13, 1684.

[13] GLAK 61/13344, pp. 11–12, 18–19.

[14] GLAK 61/13346, p. 88.

[15] GLAK 61/13344, pp. 337–8. June 21, 1704.

an adulteress, other women testified that Golterin had had improper relations with soldiers when serving in the city of Constance.[16] The court not only ruled against Golterin; it also punished her with the stocks for her earlier "improper" behavior with the soldiers.

Several servants/maids were involved in the above cases. Of course, female servants were particularly vulnerable to accusations of sexual impropriety and often the object of strict discipline from courts. Renate Dürr argues that maids in cities were less protected by courts than other women there and, in particular, that they had little chance of turning premarital sex into a marriage. Maids in rural communities were somewhat less vulnerable however, perhaps because they could be protected by their family of origin. In an important insight, Dürr points to "the contradictions between the view of others of the honor of maids and their own self-awareness."[17]

Servants could and did win cases and restore their honor, even in disputes with their employers, an indication of their "self-awareness." In December 1701, Elizabeth Klingenbergerin received an apology and her honor was restored after her mistress had called her an adulteress and thief.[18] The court in Mainau was irritated by the case, calling it an "unnecessary women's conflict," and refusing to rule on a dispute about the possible theft of a ring belonging to one of the children in the house. The court also did not take seriously that the mistress was insulted by Elizabeth's snarky comment that she had a child every year.

Elizabeth Klingenbergerin's family of origin was referenced in the above case, giving her a social status beyond being a servant. The importance of family support can also be seen in the 1702 case of Sara Beitzerin, "born in Buxheim, at this time serving at the house of Jacob Bidtman in Aichelberg."[19] Sara claimed she had been slandered by Georg Reister, a fellow servant with whom she had previously worked. Reister had said in the tavern in Berkheim that Sara "had not behaved properly and out of bad intent had drunk out of an [animals' feeding] trough." Reister had repeated this story before the parish priest (who seems to have tried to quash this tale) and had told Sara he would stand by the story in court as well. When confronted in the *Canzley* at Rot by Sara, her father, and the *Amman* from Aichelberg, Georg changed his story, admitting he had not seen her drink from the trough and had made up the story. Reister was ordered to apologize to Beitzerin the following Sunday in front of the church immediately after mass.

The twist on the story is that another man, Thomas Pendt, was sentenced to a prison term for having visited Sara Beitzerin at night over a period of two years. The court in Rot explicitly said it made no judgment about the validity of the

[16] GLAK 61/7606, p. 23r. April 18, 1714.
[17] Renate Dürr, "Die Ehre der Mägde," quote p. 184.
[18] GLAK 61/7604, pp. 107–9. The sources identify Elizabeth's family of origin.
[19] HStAS B486/Bd 18, pp. 4r–5r. *sich nit wohl gehalten, und zu einem bösen intent hin aus einem schleüff trog getrunckhen.*

marriage promise between Pendt and Beitzerin and that the case would have to be adjudicated in the ecclesiastical court. The marriage case and the slander case against Georg Reister, however, were not unrelated. Sara and her father were trying to clear her name in preparation for the case that might bring her a marriage. We do not know if Pendt was fighting to avoid this marriage, nor do we know if Sara had in fact misbehaved as a servant in Aichelberg. But it appears her family was helping her to restore any damaged honor as she found herself a husband and established an honorable place in the community.

It was not unusual for women to explicitly talk about the importance of honor, which they recognized was primarily sexual. In June 1686, a group of eight *Mädlein* (unmarried young women or girls) badly beat Maria Wilhelmin in the tavern at Dettingen—so badly that she passed out several times.[20] Maria and her husband, Balthes Conrad, filed charges against the young women for assault and for attacking her honor. The defendants explained their attack as a defense of their honor. Wilhelmin had said "they are all whores forever and she cannot recognize them as anything but whores." The young women continued: "In response, they had attacked her, in order to rescue their honor and their status as virgins [*Jungfrawen*], they treated her to some blows and some hairpulling. They hope they did not behave too badly in this, but they were attempting to rescue (*verhelfen*) their damaged reputation."

If female honor centered around sexuality, it was also threatened by family tensions. Maria Wilhelmin (Balthes Conrad's wife), the same person who was beaten by the eight young women, had previously had a detailed conversation about honor with a female acquaintance by the name of Apel (no last name given) during a ferryboat ride across Lake Constance.[21] According to Wilhelmin, Apel said that she [Wilhelmin] was trying to take Apel's brother's property away. Apel testified to another conversation, in which she brought up the Conrad brother's upcoming marriage.

> The witness [Apel] said that she has heard that [Maria Wilhelmin's] brother will be marrying her father's maid. She thinks this is a good thing since the maid has a good reputation. To this Balthes' wife said yes, an honorable name is a good thing, because the accused [Apel] had wanted to take her [good name] away, when...[Apel] and her family had called her [Wilhelmin] a s.v. whore and witch. Yes, [Apel] replied, that happened about a year ago when people were saying that sort of thing after the court had decided, not without good reason, that the [Conrad's] maid was to be sent out of the territory.[22]

[20] GLAK 61/7602, June 22, 1686. [21] GLAK 61/7602, April 14, 1685, pp. 38r–39r.
[22] The maid had been convicted of stealing wine. GLAK 61/7602, December 9, 1684, 30r–v.

Apel went on to say that Wilhelmin responded to this by saying "by 100,000 sacraments, her maid was treated unjustly." Not surprisingly, Wilhelmin disputed this testimony, stating that Apel had begun the cycle of insults. The court came to no decision, stating it needed to hear from witnesses. Wilhelmin, however, was warned to control her temper and stop talking about the old case of the maid. This warning did not have a lasting effect, since a year later Maria Wilhelmin decided to call the eight young women "whores forever" in a tavern on a feast day.

This case shows the mix of issues that constituted disputes over honor. Basic to women's honor is sexual honor, discussed here in reference to the maid who was marrying into the Conrad family. The routine insult hurled at a woman—"you are a whore and a witch"—was also used here. Then we also see the role of family, as Frau Conrad's honor was called into question by the arrest and exile of a maid in her household. Finally, there are references to the role of rumor—"people were saying that sort of thing"—in impugning someone's honor.

A 1674 case from the village of Dettingen is a typical case and shows the self-confidence of rural women's response to being called a whore.[23] Maria Lehrin brought a slander charge against Ulrich Sprenger, stating he had called her a "frivolous soldier's whore" and that she "is in no way guilty of such a vice." Sprenger admitted he had said this and that he had no evidence and said that he was only passing on something he had been told. The Mainau court ruled in Lehrin's favor. "The defendant has precisely proved nothing, and asks for forgiveness." Lehrin's honor was officially restored. It was a simple case; it reflects a social reality when men casually called women whores, but also a situation in which women could and did use the courts to defend themselves. Perhaps, on balance, courts operated for the benefit of the wealthy and powerful, of men and *Hausväter*, but not so much so that women, servants, and other subalterns did not attempt to seek justice there as well.

The Fate of Johanna Silberin, Wirtin in Mimmenhausen

In the early 1690s, Johanna Silberin was the *Wirtin*, that is the wife of the innkeeper, in the large village of Mimmenhausen near the monastery of Salem.[24] Between 1696 and 1698, Silberin appeared at least six times before one of the two courts at Salem.[25] In all these cases, Silberin and her husband came into conflict

[23] GLAK 61/7600, September 15, 1674.

[24] Parts of the following section appeared in: Marc R. Forster, "Women, Conflict, and Peacemaking in German Villages" in Amy E. Leonard and David M. Whitford, eds. *Embodiment, Identity, and Gender in the Early Modern Age* (Abingdon, 2021), pp. 159–69. Used with permission.

[25] GLAK 61/13337, pp. 169, 245. It is not clear how long Silberin's husband, Simon Strigel, kept the inn. Valentin Hagenbach, one of Silberin's opponents in court in 1696, was the innkeeper, *Amtmann*, and *Stabhalter* (an administrative position) in Mimmenhausen from about 1700 through the 1730s. GLAK 62/19821, GLAK 98/3142.

with their neighbors (and with each other). Furthermore, it is clear that these neighbors, men and women, considered Silberin a difficult woman of questionable moral character. In her case one can see clearly the significance placed on the twin issues—publicity and sexuality—that came to the forefront in all cases of slander involving women.

Silberin first appears in the records of the *Oberamtsgericht* at Salem on February 22, 1696, as the complainant.[26] She accused another woman, Catherina Messmerin, of slander, saying Messmerin had publicly called her a *Luoder*, a wicked or debauched person. Messmerin admitted using this word, "stating, if she (Silberin) were an honorable person, she would not have a camisole made for her [purchased for her?] by the soldiers in the camp." Furthermore, Messmerin said, the *Wirtin* had called her a whore. Silberin testified that this latter accusation was true, since Messmerin, a servant, had arrived in Mimmenhausen pregnant. Messmerin admitted this as well but testified "she had only said that she was pregnant so that she could get a husband, it was not true, she had done nothing with the fellow" (*sie habe auch nichts mit dem Kerl gehabt*). Pressed by the court, which was not convinced by this story, Messmerin (apparently successfully) hit a different emotional register. "She responded very mournfully and with tears in her eyes, that she is an ignorant girl and had not thought through what she was saying. Despite what she had said, she is innocent and a virgin."[27] The court ruled in favor of Silberin, requiring Messmerin to apologize and telling both women, under threat of more serious punishment, "to use such words more carefully in the future."

This case involved a dispute between women. Silberin, the wife of the innkeeper, was using the court to defend her honor, with some success. As we have seen, this was a risky strategy, as testimony in these local courts was fairly freewheeling and the behavior and reputation of the complainant was always fair game. What stands out about these cases is that two issues, women's sexuality and issues of publicity, were central to both the way people used courts and the way courts thought about their work. Almost every dispute involving women, and certainly every dispute involving slander, referenced sexuality. At the same time, women's words were powerful, especially if delivered in a public setting.[28]

In May 1696, Silberin again appeared in court, this time as the defendant.[29] Early one morning, she had confronted Catherina Hagenbacherin, the servant (*Dienstmädel*) and cousin of Valentin Hagenbach. "Who said you, Hagenbacherin, could cut grass there, to which she answered her employer told to do this, to

[26] GLAK 61/13337, pp. 169–71. [27] GLAK 61/13337, p. 171.

[28] Compare Gowing, *Domestic Dangers*; Martin Ingram, "Ridings, Rough Music, and the Reform of Popular Culture in Early Modern England" *Past and Present* 105 (1984): 79–113; Merry Wiesner-Hanks, *Women and Gender in Early Modern Europe*, 3rd Edition (New York: Cambridge University Press, 2008).

[29] GLAK 61/13337, pp. 245–50. "*ich will die schon Zech machen.*"

which the *Wirtin* said further, your cousin is doing this to me, he wants to take the field from me, come here I want to let you have it. At this point, she [Silberin] began to hit her hard." The maid fled, but she admitted in court to calling Silberin a "soldier's whore" one time, although Silberin testified that Hagenbacherin had called her a *Stutten* (a bawd) at least twelve times, while Hagenbacherin said Silberin had called *her* a whore. The court ruled against Silberin this time, fining her 1 *Gulden*, a substantial fine. In the final decision, the court stated that in the future Silberin should "contain her unnecessary slander and fighting and should seek to maintain peaceful behavior, if she ever were to seek help from the lordship when her honor or good name are injured."

A year later, in June 1697, Silberin came into conflict in a similar way with another woman, this time Barbara Steüerin, not a maid but a person of some status in the village.[30] Silberin brought a charge of slander against Steüerin in a dispute that began with a conflict between their husbands over a debt. While the husbands appear in the records as co-complaint and co-defendant, they neither testified nor appear in the records after that. Although Silberin was the complainant, the case came to revolve around her sexual honor. Steüerin's initial insult echoed earlier slander—"[Silberin] had a whore's child (*hueren Khind*) from a Corporal" and, furthermore, Steüerin said Silberin had confided to her that she was passing the child off as her husband's. Steüerin also reported that Silberin, hearing that she, Barbara, was going regularly to a chapel to pray, had said "she wished that the thunder (sic) would strike Barbara in the chapel." Silberin denied all of this, but the court was now interested in learning more about her behavior and, what was dangerous for her, about her reputation in the village. Her attempt to use the court to quash gossip about her seems to have backfired.

Several other women were called to testify about Silberin's relationship with the soldiers. One, Magdalena Huerzen, gave a virtuoso performance of how to slander someone without explicitly doing so.

> The corporal was often at the *Wirtin's* [tavern], by day and night, and drank and ate. Whether he paid, she did not know. People say that she [Silberin] often went to Bermatingen because of the corporal (*dem Corporal zu lieb*) and that the Corporal had taken her to and from Markdorf on a horse. Now if this is true, she does not know. This much she knows, that the *Wirtin* often went to Markdorf. She has actually not seen anything improper (*unrechts*) from the *Wirtin*, but she has been seen walking together with the corporal (*aber sye seye dem corporal zu Steeg undt weg zu lieb geloffen*), the Wirtin has not shared with her with all she

[30] GLAK 61/13340, pp. 71–4, 81–4, 89. I believe Steüerin was married to the *Amtmann*. A Barbara Steuerin appears in the minutes of the Oberamtsgericht Salem in 1695, accused of socializing with soldiers at the tavern in Mimmenhausen. GLAK 61/13337, pp. 130–2.

> [shared] with Barbara Steüerin, so she does not know what they [the Corporal and Silberin] had with each other...[31]

Then the court investigated a purported exchange of letters between Silberin and the Corporal. Magdalena Knechtin admitted that she had written one or two letters for Silberin to send to the Corporal. She claimed that she could not remember the content, since this had happened three years earlier. Still, under questioning she was quite specific: "...this much she knows, that Johanna reported to the Corporal, that the Mimmenhausener were opening their snouts (*Mäuler*) as if [there were a relationship] between her and the Corporal, [and] he should come and shut people's snouts." Knechtin also pointed out that Silberin had come regularly to her house to learn to read and write, and this had led to the rumor that she was writing all the time to the Corporal, which was not true.[32] The court did not come to a decision, but rather asked for more information in order to find out if the rumors about Silberin's adultery, which had spread to the whole *Herrschaft* (lordship), were true.

One is tempted to look behind the testimony about Silberin's relationship with the soldiers for something we might call the "real" issues. After all, there were property disputes here over the use of fields and the payment of debts. There is an implication of family conflicts and the idea that Silberin might be doing a poor job managing the tavern by giving free food and drink to the soldiers. These issues are there in the record, and we know that courts adjudicated such issues when the parties were men. But the testimony of the parties, most of them women, led the court to focus on Silberin's sexual behavior, not property issues. Silberin was herself adept at deploying the language of sexual honor and dishonor to attack her enemies, but this language was also hard to control.

In March 1698, Silberin was again in front of the Salem *Gericht*, this time as the defendant, along with her husband, Simon Strigel.[33] The plaintiff, Barbara Bommerin, accused Strigel of slander, for calling her an adulterer (*eine Ehevertrennerin*) for having taken money from a Swiss soldier. Bommerin, in a classic fashion, stated that she was not an adulterer, but "the defendant's wife certainly was," an accusation she followed with details of Silberin's relations with the soldiers stationed in nearby Owingen. Bommerin listed in detail clothing items, a ring, and a book she said Silberin had received as gifts. In a seemingly random aside, Bommerin testified that Strigel had accused her of ruining a tree and stealing some ducks. Perhaps this was the "real" issue that triggered the clashing charges of moral turpitude?

[31] GLAK 61/13340, p. 82. [32] GLAK 61/13340, p. 83.
[33] GLAK 61/13340, pp. 172–7. In March 1698, Silberin was also charged in a similar case by another woman, Anna Lieberin. GLAK 61/13340, pp. 177–8.

Strigel did not appear to answer the charges, but Silberin did. She claimed that it was Bommerin who had tried to lead her astray and had encouraged her to leave her husband, whom Bommerin regularly badmouthed as a heretic and a scoundrel (*Schurke*). Silberin admitted to taking clothes from the soldiers one time, at Bommerin's house, encouraged by Bommerin. Bommerin denied these charges and said that Silberin had borrowed nine *Gulden*, which she took to Bergetreute (a local shrine) "to have prayers said for her husband's death (*Ihren Mann todt betten lassen*)."[34] The court responded to all of this with skepticism:

> It appears from the complaint and answers, that both sides are not worth much, with each one helping and encouraging the other to do bad, and also trying to scare the other, both should be "stretched." Then they should be turned over to the *Herrschaft* for further punishment.

Barbara Bommerin and Johanna Silberin seemed to have known each other well. Bommerin's critical comments about Silberin's husband may have referred to a court case from several years earlier (November–December 1696).[35] In that case, the complainant had been Silberin's husband, Simon Strigel, who had gotten into a fight with two men on the road from Markdorf to Mimmenhausen. The two men, Michael Brunner and David Hausen, had intervened when Strigel, "because of a quarrel, was disciplining [his wife] with blows." Hausen testified that Strigel had called the men "whore's boys" (*hueren bueben*) when Silberin had called out to them for help. Hausen also commented that Silberin's "wicked life is known," implying perhaps that she deserved the blows from her husband.

Silberin's testimony took a different tack. When the two men came to defend her,

> ...her husband told them it was no one else's business if he is hitting his wife. Then the two men had asked her what the reason was for the blows, she said she does not know what goes on in the man's head. [However], he had reproached her that she surely knows other whore's birds she would like to go with. The men asked if he meant them, but Simon said he had not named them. To this the men said, she should not go with the man, he is a rogue, a scoundrel, a puker (*Kotzer*), and a s.v. dog's etc., [and] he could kill her.

Strigel fled from the two men, injuring himself in the process. Brunner and Hausen, Silberin's erstwhile defenders, were sentenced to eight and six hours in

[34] GLAK 61/13340, p. 176. *streckhen* = stretched, but I do not know if the reference is to the stocks or torture on the rack.
[35] GLAK 61/13337, pp. 395–9, 408–11, 417–18.

the stocks and Silberin to three hours, although her punishment was converted to a money fine.

Johanna Silberin was becoming, among other things, the victim of a more efficient and activist court system in the territory of Salem.[36] In April 1698, referencing all the cases discussed above, the court convicted Silberin, along with two other women involved in court cases with Silberin, Barbara Bommerin and Anna Lieberin, of solicitation and public scandal. The court focused on Silberin, citing her stealing of a book, her exchange of gifts with the soldiers, and her keeping company with the soldiers in a way that was inappropriate for a respectable wife as clear evidence of her "debauched life." Bommerin and Lieberin were given light sentences of three hours each in the stocks. Silberin was considered the ringleader and deserving of an exemplary punishment. She received a sentence of six years' exile from the territory. This was a major and severe punishment and very unusual for a person of property and status. It is impossible to determine if this punishment was actually enforced, or if it was perhaps converted to a money fine.[37]

A straightforward analysis of these court cases might suggest that Johanna Silberin was a combative woman who made enemies among the other women in Mimmenhausen and even in the wider region. As the wife of a tavern keeper, she helped run the tavern, which gave her the power that came from access to gossip and stories exchanged in the tavern. It also brought her into contact with travelers and other strangers, particularly the soldiers stationed nearby. Just like all women who worked in taverns, her sexual morality was always suspect. Even her husband came to suspect her of adultery or even of running a prostitution ring, or at least that is what he is reported to have said. So, in this interpretation Johanna was guilty of violating gender norms and was punished.

But the story is not that simple. Did Simon Strigel really think his wife was a whore? Or did he resort to the standard language of sexual insult as well as physical violence when angry with his wife? And, as we have seen in this case, and as was true in all slander cases involving women, the accusation of whore (and often witch) was quite literally ubiquitous.[38] And, attacks on a woman's sexual honor were powerful in multiple ways. They reflected on the whole family, calling into question a family's ability to function within a community, to buy and sell property, to exchange favors, and to live cooperatively with neighbors.

Johanna Silberin, and the women she engaged with in court, knew that these words—whore and witch—had power, and they hurled them at each other, in the streets and in court. Silberin also believed that the court at Salem could be used to defend her honor and to denigrate others. And the court basically agreed, seeing

[36] GLAK 61/13340, pp. 193ff.

[37] Servants and vagrants were expelled from the territory at times, but Silberin was a person of status and her husband was a citizen, so her expulsion was unusual. See Jason Coy, *Strangers and Misfits: Banishment, Social Control, and Authority in Early Modern Europe* (Leiden, 2008).

[38] The use of the insult "witch" could be, of course, especially dangerous. See below.

its role as one of regulating and controlling gossip and attacks on honor, as one way of maintaining peace and order in the lordship.[39] Silberin, however, used the court too often and exposed herself to counter charges too frequently. It is an indication of the willingness of this court to regulate local society (and the growing professionalization of its staff) that court officials went back into their records to investigate Silberin and eventually punish her severely. Here we have a court operating in an administrative fashion that was becoming the norm even in tiny German states. In fact, because Salem's jurisdiction was so small, Salem officials surely recognized Johanna Silberin when she appeared in court.

Finally, the case of Johanna Silberin reflects that central tension about gender relations in the countryside. As Martin Ingram has written about English country women:

> A variety of sources testify that, in practice, the balance of authority between husbands and wives in marriage varied considerably. Equally it is plain that strong, active, able wives were often prized, despite the fact that the behaviour of such wives was unlikely to conform exactly to the stereotype of female virtue.[40]

Merry Wiesner-Hanks puts the same issue in a slightly different frame. "A woman's labor, rather than her father's occupation or wealth, determined her value as a marriage partner, giving her more power within the family and in the community at large."[41]

By all accounts, Joanna Silberin worked hard and was powerful in her community. She was a strong, active wife. Perhaps she was also able, although her misjudgments about how and when to go to court may call that into question. Was the beating she took from her husband an effort on his part to assert his authority when she questioned it? Were her dealings with the nearby soldiers part of an effort to make money off of them, leading to jealousy from other women and perhaps suspicion from her husband? The people of Mimmenhausen did not say this in court or in the public conversations they testified about. Unfortunately, we cannot know what they "really thought," for here we come up again against the usual way of attacking women. Silberin's enemies, no matter what their quarrel with her might have been, could only call her a whore. The use of the language of sexual honor then created a community-wide reputation that was spread and reinforced by further gossip. Silberin's often heavy-handed efforts to change that reputation failed.

[39] See, for example, Holenstein, "*Gute Policey" und lokale Gesellschaft*.

[40] Ingram, "Ridings, Rough Music, and the Reform of Popular Culture" *Past and Present* 105 (1984): 97.

[41] Merry Wiesner-Hanks, *Women and Gender in Early Modern Europe*, 3rd edition (New York, 2008), p. 113.

So, we will probably never know what "really happened" and if Johanna Silberin had an affair with one or more of the soldiers, or if she and the other women ran a prostitution ring to serve the soldiers. The language of sexual honor so pervaded this society that it both created gender relations and reinforced them in ways that clashed with, and distorted, the realities of a world where "strong, active, able wives were prized."

The Witch Accusation

Calling a woman a witch was a standard insult, usually deployed in tandem with whore: "you are a whore and a witch." But the witch insult could also be an accusation, and a dangerous accusation as well, even as the number of actual witch trials and executions declined after about 1670.[42] The word *Hexe* (witch) appears regularly in the court records, and its use always activated this tension between an insult to someone's honor and the accusation of actual witchcraft, from the 1650s into the first several decades of the eighteenth century. As a consequence, women (and their families) felt they had to respond forcefully to the witch insult and treat it as an especially dangerous kind of slander.

The number of witch trials certainly declined between "the last witch of Langenburg," executed in 1672 in the County of Hohenlohe-Langenburg (masterfully analyzed by Thomas Robisheaux), and the mid-eighteenth-century execution of Catherina Schmid, a resident of Alleshausen, a village not far from Mainau, Rot, and Salem, described by Lyndal Roper.[43] And maybe in most cases the decline in actual trials reduced the phrase "you are a witch" to the level of "just" an insult after about 1700, but the accusation remained a serious threat to a woman's honor, and in rare cases might still land a woman in prison and in the torture chamber.[44]

The casual use of *Hexe* as an insult echoed across the period. In January 1661, Hans Lang from Herdern, "pickled in wine" at the tavern, let loose a string of insults against three other men, finishing his tirade by calling the daughter of one

[42] H. C. Erik Midelfort, *Witch Hunting in Southwestern Germany, 1562–1684: The Social and Intellectual Foundations* (Stanford, 1972); Robisheaux, *The Last Witch of Langenburg*; Gudrun Gersmann, "Gehe hin und vertheidige dich! Injurieklagen als Mittel der Abwehr von Hexerei Verdächtigungen—ein Fallbeispiel aus dem Fürstbistum Münster" in Backman, ed. *Ehrkonzepte*, pp. 237–66; Laura Kounine, "The Witch on Trial. Narratives of Conflict and Community in Early Modern Germany" in Stephen Cummin and Laura Kounine, eds. *Cultures of Conflict Resolution in Early Modern Europe* (Farnham, 2016).

[43] Midelfort, *Witch Hunting in Southwestern Germany*, esp. Appendix, pp. 199–203; Robisheaux, *The Last Witch of Langenburg*; Lyndal Roper, *Witch Craze. Terror and Fantasy in Baroque Germany* (New Haven, 2004), ch. 10.

[44] Men were occasionally insulted as *Hexenmeister* (master of witches) or as sorcerers, but these insults were rare.

of them a "witch whore."[45] A few years later, Andres Meyer, a weaver, also from Herdern, struck one of his neighbors after his opponent called his wife a witch.[46] In both these cases, conflicts among men included insults about wives and daughters. More often the insult was exchanged between women, as in a 1683 exchange of words between Verena Scheüblin and Anna Baumgartnerin.[47] Anna had said that Verena had vomited at Adam Müller's recent wedding, to which Verena responded, "whoever said that about her, she lies like a witch, because it is not true." By the time this case was heard by the village court at Thengen, the parties had forgiven each other, and the court stated that everyone's honor was restored. A case like this seems to indicate that the witch insult was often treated much like the other basic insults of scoundrel, thief, and whore.

There are many more examples of women insulting each other as witches. Like other insults, it was often deployed as part of a larger conflict. When Felix Klingenberger's wife caught the son of Rohm's wife stealing vegetables in the summer of 1676, she treated him with rough words.[48] Rohm's wife then stormed into the Klingenberger house, insulting her opponent as "a witch, a dissolute fool, and some other things." Rohm's wife testified that Frau Klingenberger had called her children "witches' and thieves' children." There were other conflicts between these two families, since the Rohms, husband and wife, had accused the Klingenbergers of cheating on the tithe, which was also an attack on their honor. Not surprisingly, Frau Rohm referenced this issue when she attacked Frau Klingenberger in her house. She was fined for the insults, but the tithe issue was to be further investigated. This case is another example of the witch insult functioning as part of a normal repertoire of insults embedded in the conflicts of everyday life.

"The complainant (Magtalena Jaugin from Oberuldingen) brought forward that the defendant Winterin and her husband had insulted her as a whore and a witch in a room full of people, and threatened her, (saying) they wanted to put her in the stocks."[49] While putting someone in the stocks was a shaming punishment, it was not something that happened to people convicted of witchcraft, so Winterin was attacking Jaugin's honor, but not accusing her of actually practicing witchcraft. According to the defendant, Salomen Winterin, Jaugin had called her a witch as well. The issue behind this confrontation was Jaugin's purported behavior with some soldiers the previous spring, behavior that had earned her, and several other young women, a lecture from the parish priest from the pulpit. The court investigated this case further, and several women were punished with the stocks for partying with the soldiers.[50] Jaugin's slander charge had backfired.

In 1710, Johan Galley the Elder proved himself a difficult member of the community, particularly around a dispute over his obligation to pay for *Rebstecken*

[45] GLAK 61/6958, January 16, 1663, *in Wein füechte.*
[46] GLAK 61/6958, June 17, 1676.
[47] GLAK 61/6958, October 16, 1683.
[48] GLAK 61/7603, 53r–54r.
[49] GLAK 61/13340, p. 216. August 16, 1698.
[50] GLAK 61/13340, pp. 223–4.

(stakes for vines), as recorded in the *Stecken Register*.[51] When the *Amman*'s daughter requested that he pay, he called her a witch and her father a scoundrel. Witnesses were not sure if he insulted the *Amman*'s daughter conditionally ("if she says that he owes for the *Stecken*, she lies like a witch") or directly. He also called her a *Lusch*, perhaps meaning a greedy person.[52] Galley then insulted Carl Baumann in front of the whole commune, saying that Baumann did not care for his vineyard properly, a charge that was disproved by the testimony of four impartial observers who inspected the vineyard.[53] The witch insult, which initially caused a court case, was only a small aspect of Galley's conflicts with his neighbors and the local officials.

Also in 1710, Ephrosine Hingerbihlerin, a Swiss servant in Staad, was insulted by a local woman (referred to only as Sulgerin) at a *Kunckelstube*, an evening gathering of women where sewing and other handicrafts were practiced.[54] Sulgerin's performance was an impressive display of imaginative insults, in which "witch" was just one smear among many. "She is a cursed Swiss, the bull on the mountain was her father, and she (Sulgerin) incessantly intoned whore and witch over her." As is often the case in these court records, witnesses were not clear on exactly what had been said. One said Sulgerin was not happy that Hingerbihlerin had been invited to this event, saying "her mouth is like that of a Rohnhauser bull that has mouth blisters."[55] Another quoted Sulgerin as saying "she should go back to her witch-ridden Switerland (*hexen Schweitzerland*), the bull from Rohenhausen is her father, a louse her mother." The reason for Sulgerin's focus on the bull is unclear, but it does not seem to be a reference to any actual practice of malefice by the maid.[56] Despite her imaginative use of insults, Sulgerin insulted the Swiss maid as a witch in a very generic and routine fashion.[57]

Local courts sometimes grew impatient with these exchanges of insults, whether it was a witch insult or some other set of slurs. In just one example, from 1702, the court in Mainau called a slander case "an unnecessary dispute," despite the fact that the two parties had deployed a robust set of insults, including

[51] GLAK 61/7606, 1710, pp. 58r–58v.

[52] GLAK 61/7606, 1710, pp. 59v–60v. It is interesting that the *Amman* sent his daughter to demand the stakes from Galley.

[53] GLAK 61/7606, 1710, pp. 59v–60v.

[54] GLAK 61/7606, pp. 63r, 64r. Known as Spinnstuben in other places. Kunkelstube seems to be a particularly Swabian word. Foundational article: Hans Medick, "Spinnstuben auf dem Dorf. Jugendliche Sexualkultur und Feierabendbrauch in der ländlichen Gesellschaft der Frühen Neuzeit" in G. Huck, ed. *Sozialgeschichte der Freizeit. Untersuchungen zum Wandel der Alltagskultur in Deutschland* (Wuppertal 1980), pp. 19–49.

[55] This reference is obscure and my translation speculative. See *Schweizerisches idiotikon: Wörterbuch der schweizerdeutschen sprache*, Volume 5, pp. 203–4. Accessed online.

[56] Accusations of witchcraft often included the cursing of livestock, so perhaps that explains the focus on the bull.

[57] There are other cases where the witch insult is routinely used in a non-specific way. GLAK 61/7606, 1711, pp. 54r, 54v; GLAK 61/7606, 1712, 18v.

scoundrel, thief, liar, whore, and witch, as part of a property dispute.[58] But the witch insult could not be ignored, and the potential for it to become a dangerous accusation was always present.

Even a passing reference to "real" witchcraft or to witch trials raised the stakes of this insult. In 1686 Mathias Waldpardt's wife called Ursula Bonawerin a witch, adding, "no one ever decided to put her [as opposed to Bonawerin] before the executioner."[59] Not surprisingly, Ursula stated she "could not allow these kinds of insults to sit on her" and filed a slander suit. The reference to the executioner or hangman, the person who tortured suspected witches, was a particularly insulting attack. In this case, the defendant was probably not suggesting that Bonawerin should be tried as a witch, but was referring to Bonawerin's earlier conviction for stealing. Frau Waldpardt clearly did not think that she deserved to be charged with slander by Ursula, a convicted thief. But the court did in fact fine her.[60]

If Frau Walpardt was perhaps slyly implying that Bonawerin should be investigated as a witch, Mathias Thumb's wife went a step further in 1686.[61] The Thumbs' cows had strayed onto the Hans Meyers' property and damaged some fruit trees. Hans Meyer's wife drove the cows from her field, prompting Frau Thumb to insult her as a witch, "with the accusation that no one other than the complainant (Frau Meyer) had bewitched her calves." The Meyerin responded by calling Frau Thumb "a marker mover" (a *Marckhtenrukherin*), accusing the Thumbs of moving boundary markers, a serious charge and an insult itself. The court ordered the charge of moving the marker to be further investigated and fined the Thumbin for the witch insult.[62]

By the later seventeenth century, local courts generally did not want witchcraft accusations to go too far, as everyone was aware of the socially damaging nature of witch hunts and witch trials. As a result, lower courts worked hard to reach a resolution of the case before it was sent to a criminal court for adjudication. In the above cases, the court decisions never treated the use of the word "witch" as anything except an insult. They responded with fines and required apologies, as they did in other honor cases.

In a 1662 case, Anna Riedlerin and her husband Jacob Harder brought a complaint against some youths in their village of Oberndorf, because the young people had been saying that Anna had put a curse on a horse.[63] It turns out that this discussion had taken place among a group of boys and girls, aged eight to

[58] GLAK 61/7604, pp. 159–60. [59] GLAK 61/7602, October 19, 1686.

[60] There was also a dispute between the two husbands, which was brought up during this hearing and was adjudicated several weeks later.

[61] GLAK 61/7602, February 23, 1686.

[62] Women's names can be confusing in the court records. Officially, their names were their birth name, with their father's last name with the feminine "-in" added. Hence, Johanna Silberin. At other times, women were referred to by their husband's name in the feminine form, as in this case, "the Thumbin."

[63] GLAK 61/7599, July 1, 1662, pp. 49–52.

nineteen. The story is somewhat jumbled, but the children had discussed how the horse could have gotten sick, and they had speculated that it had been cursed by a witch. One youth, Martin Ried, 18 years old, stated that the curse must have come from a house near the owner of the horse, an idea he claimed to have heard over dinner with his father and sister. Apparently, some people in the village hesitated to take their animals on the path by Riedlerin's house, though they did not explicitly accuse her of witchcraft. The children were not as circumspect and jumped to the conclusion that Martin was referring to Riedlerin. The court was clearly uninterested in considering whether Riedlerin had actually used sorcery to injure the horse. Instead, the court quashed the discussion immediately. "There is nothing else to be found except that this was pure youth and children's talk. The parties should apologize to Harder and his good wife... that they did not mean what they said. And, for their well-earned punishment, they should be beaten with rods. And that was what happened."

Maria Wagnerin faced a full-blown accusation of witchcraft in 1702.[64] Anna Winterin said Wagnerin was a witch who had "killed the servant and the maid and lamed a bull." Anna Winterin, however, was "a small girl," and her accusation carried no weight. The court took the witch insult seriously enough that the gatekeeper at Salem was ordered "to punish her [Anna] with a rod to good effect."[65]

Even in 1695, an insult could become an accusation, perhaps not easily given the skeptical attitude of local courts toward witch-hunting, but nevertheless in a way that was dangerous for women. Maria Müllerin from Owingen sued Peter Kayser for slander because of a detailed witch accusation Keyser made in the tavern in Owingen during Carnival time that year. It is worth listening to Maria's words.[66]

> The complainant [Maria Müllerin] testified that the defendant [Peter Kayser], whom she had never met, which others can vouch for, came into her house before *Fastnacht* and took her keys with him to the tavern, and there denounced her as if she were imprisoned for witchcraft. In the presence of the parish priest and the *Wirtin* he told how he had shot a bird, which had let these very keys fall to the earth. He further said that if the complainant is not a witch, then all the holy sacraments he has taken and will take in the future would be lost to him.
>
> These insults have hurt her deep in the heart and have been brought to the mouths of others and spread around, so she begs the *Herrschaft* for help and that the defendant be ordered to give her back her honor and be punished as he deserves.

[64] GLAK 61/13344, pp. 329–30. [65] *mit der ruether empfindlich abstraffen.*
[66] GLAK 61/13338, pp. 106–7. GLAK 61/13337, pp. 250–2.

Neither the Salem *Oberamtsgericht* nor the *Oberamt* in Nellenburg, which held higher jurisdiction in Owingen, had any interest in Kayser's fantasies, despite the fact that he held an official position as the *Jäger* (supervisor of the hunt) in Bonndorf. Kayser was run to earth by both courts and ordered to apologize to Müllerin and pay a fine. Here again, the courts did not investigate the explicit witchcraft charge, but they did take the damage such an accusation could do very seriously.

The Schön Girls and the Cooked Mouse

> Hans Schön's wife from Berkhen (Berkheim) filed a complaint that people have been spreading the story everywhere (*hin und wider aussschreye*), that one time her daughters, without clothes, cooked a mouse, and after they stirred it with a rake handle and tasted some of it, the mouse jumped out and onto the stove and then out of the house. [But] no one can prove the smallest misbehavior based on the truth about her daughters.[67]

This case from 1684 was of course about a witchcraft accusation. A story of naked girls cooking and eating a mouse, and holding a rake, that closely resembles a broomstick, touched on many witch stereotypes. The Rot court moved to get to the bottom of the story, but showed no inclination to investigate the Schön daughters' behavior. Instead, a large number of defendants, six named witnesses, and "others" were called in an attempt to trace the origin of these rumors. The source of the story appears to have been Georg Kirchenmayer's wife, who passed the story on to several other women, their daughters, and their maids, "so that it spread everywhere and became a widespread outcry or rumor (*Geschrey*)."[68]

Frau Kirchenmayer, however, had not made this story up out of the blue. Her husband Georg had come home from the *Brandweinhaus* (the schnapps bar) quite drunk and told a story involving a cooked mouse, which he had heard from the Kugelmayer's son. This young man admitted to telling a story at the bar.

> When he was a servant in Rot, he one time was late in the barn and saw the cowherd, a maid, cooking a mouse, [although] after that she did nothing to it or with it. He has no idea how, *ex post facto*, the story was attached to Schön's

[67] All primary source references in this section are from HStAS B486/Band 15, 184v–186r. Hans Schön was the long serving innkeeper (*Wirt*) in Berkheim. He appears below in Chapters 4 and 6. He was reported to have been on his deathbed in April 1684, so it is unclear if he was still alive at the time of this case.

[68] Note that an outcry was more serious than a rumor, and really required a response. See Sabean, "Village Court Protocols and Memory."

> daughters, he had never said a word about them. Kirchenmayer or his wife must have, out of limited understanding, fed the story, and, by adding circumstances and facts, put this serious accusation on Hans Schön's daughters.

The court took a strong stance and punished all the parties who had spread this rumor. A whole group was ordered to publicly apologize in order to restore the daughters' honor. Kirchenmayer was sentenced to time in the tower, and his wife and one other woman were to be put in the stocks. Kirchenmayer's wife, however, was also to be led, in stocks, to both Bachen and Berkheim. There she was to be paraded in front of the villagers, and the *Amtmänner* were to tell the people how "completely irresponsible it was to spread these rumors about the completely innocent daughters of Hans Schön and that an injustice had been done to them before God and the people."

The court at Rot, like all the other lower courts in the region, defended girls or young women accused of witchcraft, or, perhaps less altruistically, the court worked to head off an outbreak of witchcraft accusations. Although there were no witch trials in the region in this period, the fear of accusations of witchcraft is apparent in court records well into the eighteenth century.[69] It is also apparent that the court took such rumor-mongering very seriously, since the punishment of Frau Kirchenmayer was quite exceptional.

* * *

The witchcraft insult was of course a threat to individual women and their families. It was also a threat to peace and order in the wider community. Under normal circumstances, local officials and local courts were well aware of the danger of a witch hunt and did everything they could to prevent an insult from becoming an accusation. By the first decades of the eighteenth century, this effort appears to have led to a kind of domestication of the witch insult. It was now just one insult in the repertoire of insults that could be deployed.

In a sense, the witch insult was a particularly dramatic example of the danger honor conflicts posed for peace in the community. A high sensitivity to insult often brought mundane daily tensions to a boiling point. Tensions around a small debt, for example, were unlikely to result in serious conflict, but if a person's honor was impugned, another level of conflict was triggered. As we have seen, honor conflicts were always tied to the social, economic, or political conflicts of daily life. Honor was thus everywhere and had an ambiguous impact on social peace. If honor often exacerbated existing conflicts, honor could also displace and even disguise serious social tensions by making conflicts primarily personal and individual.[70]

[69] Robisheaux, *The Last Witch of Langenburg*.
[70] Dinges, "Die Ehre als Thema der historische Anthropologie," p. 54.

When people—women as well as men—brought honor conflicts to a court, they were looking for (another) way to end a dispute. Perhaps other solutions—mediation, negotiation, violence—had previously failed, or perhaps they considered the court a better option in that particular case. Courts almost invariably had the same goal: to bring honor disputes to an end and to prevent them from becoming, or continuing to be, long-lasting conflicts or feuds. This juridification of honor seems significant, even if we cannot be sure what percentage of disputes ended up in court. On the one hand, we clearly see people trying to use the court to their benefit. On the other hand, one can see courts imposing the authorities' priorities on rural people, but inconsistently and erratically. The courts in these small territories were generally part of the world they judged, not above or separate from them.

No doubt some people carefully calculated their needs before filing a slander suit, or fighting such a suit. But the court records give a strong sense of the feelings and the emotions of the litigants. The complainants especially had deep personal reasons for going to court to defend their honor, one might say a psychological need for resolution. Did this compulsion help bring peace, or did it provide the conditions for ongoing social conflict? Perhaps both, but the balance of these desires contributed to the creation of a fairly stable system of conflict resolution.

4
Conflicts in Public Spaces
The Tavern

Taverns, Courts, and Churches

The conflicts that appear in the court records were by definition public quarrels. The parties were willing to testify about them in court in front of local officials and often juries of their peers. Many of the conflicts originated in taverns, where honor and reputation were on public display, and where the lubrication provided by alcohol brought the conflicts of everyday life into the open. In the tavern, emotions were high, language was uncontrolled and often insulting, and violence bubbled just below the surface. And taverns were, in the view of government officials then and of some scholars even now, places of conflict, symbolic of the violent and dangerous culture of the common folk.[1]

Courts, by contrast, represented order and discipline and the desire for peace.[2] They were, in theory at least, orderly spaces where decisions were made and peace was restored. The regular appeal for peace at the end of cases and the statement that the court had "restored the parties' honor" reflected this way of thinking. The court minutes themselves, which laid out in a tidy fashion complaint and response, testimony and counter-testimony, in clearly official German (with smatterings of Latin when the secretary wanted to show off), convey a sense of discipline and structure.[3] Of course this impression is misleading, and courts were surely places where voices were raised and lively exchanges took place in the earthy dialect of the region; at times this language does seep into the protocols.

The contrast between taverns and courts should not be overstated. Brawls did not occur every day in taverns, even if they were regular occurrences. Furthermore, taverns were often sites of negotiation, mediation, and reconciliation. Property

[1] Tlusty, *Bacchus and Civic Order*; Kümin, *Drinking Matters*; Renate Dürr and Gerd Schwerhoff, eds. *Kirchen, Märkte und Tavernen. Erfahrungs- und Handlungsräume in der Frühen Neuzeit* (Frankfurt, 2005).

[2] Arnold Beuke, "In guter Zier und Kurzweil bey der Naßen angetastet. Aspekte des Konfliktaustrags in der Frühen Neuzeit" in Barbara Krug-Richter and Ruth-Elizabeth Mohrmann, eds. Praktiken des Konfliktaustrags in der Frühen Neuzeit (Münster, 2004), p. 133; Regina Schäfer, "Frieden durch Recht. Zur Funktion des Dorfgerichts in der Gemeinde" in Olive Auge and Kurt Andermann, eds. *Dorf und Gemeinde. Grundstrukuren der ländlichen Gesellschaft in Spätmittelalter und Früheneuzeit* (Ostfildern, 2012), esp. p. 69.

[3] Sabean, "Village Court Protocols and Memory"; Sabean, "Peasant Voices and Bureaucratic Texts."

Keeping the Peace in the Village: Conflict and Peacemaking in Germany, 1650–1750. Marc R. Forster,
Oxford University Press. © Marc R. Forster 2024. DOI: 10.1093/oso/9780198898474.003.0005

transactions, marriage negotiations, and loan agreements were discussed there and sealed with a drink. Communal councils, the *Gemeinden*, often met in taverns and discussed local affairs. At the same time, court decisions did not always bring peace, and the defeated party might well carry resentments into the future. The entreaties that courts made for peace and reconciliation reflected a pragmatic understanding that a legal decision did not necessarily mean an end to a conflict.

An examination of the locations of disputes deepens our understanding of how the system of conflict resolution functioned. Specific spaces provided opportunity for conflict and framed what was considered appropriate and what constituted transgressive behavior; they could also be spaces for public reconciliation.[4] Spaces also determined how public a dispute was, and the nature and extent of publicity often determined the severity of a conflict. The parties to a dispute were highly sensitive to their audience and the consequences of widespread discussion of a case. Courts were also aware of these issues, often hoping to lower tensions by characterizing rumors and gossip as "simply women's gossip" and demanding that parties curb their tongues. Perhaps some gossip could be dismissed in this way, but, as we have seen in honor disputes, gossip (*Geschwätz*), rumors, and what David Sabean has called the village *Sage*, or communal knowledge, were integral aspects of the conflicts of rural life.[5]

Churches and taverns have often been compared as public spaces and are probably the best-known (and best-studied) spaces in early modern villages.[6] They were increasingly regulated over the course of the early modern period. Church reformers were intent on cleansing churches of "profane" activities, and worked, with considerable success, at making church services more somber and disciplined occasions. In this process, the boundary between church and street was reinforced. Where people, particularly men, had traditionally moved in and out of the church during services, they were now expected to stay indoors, more often than not seated in the newly constructed pews. As John Bossy has pointed out, the Tridentine Church was intent on narrowing the role of the parish church and limiting its interactions with everyday life.[7]

[4] Susanne Rau, "Orte der Gastlichkeit—Orte der Kommunikation. Aspekte der Raumkonstitution von Herbergen in einer frühneuzeitlichen Stadt" in Dürr and Schwerhoff, eds. *Kirchen, Märkte, Tavernen*; Marion Füssell and Stephanie Rüther, "Einleitung" in Christoph Dartmann, Marion Füssell, and Stephanie Rüther, eds. *Raum und Konflikt. Zur symbolischen Konstituierung gesellschaftlicher Ordnung im Mittelalter und in Früher Neuzeit* (Münster, 2004): 9–17.

[5] Sabean *Power in the Blood*, pp. 195–6. See also Holenstein and Schindler, "Geschwätzgeschichte(n)."

[6] Marc R. Forster, "Space, Gender, and Honor in Village Taverns" in Marc R. Forster and Maren Möhring, eds. *Public Eating, Public Drinking. Places of Consumption from Early Modern to Postmodern Times* (Food and History 7/2, 2010), 15–29.

[7] John Bossy, *Christianity in the West, 1400–1700* (Oxford, 1985) and *Peace in the Post-Reformation* (Cambridge, 2012).

The partial closing off of the church from secular life made taverns more important in village life. They were harder to regulate than churches and remained the quintessential setting for the drama of everyday life. Efforts by the authorities to make tavernkeepers enforce codes of behavior and speech in their own establishments inevitably failed. In Wollmatingen, for example, the local *Wirt* was regularly fined for keeping his inn open too late in the evening.[8] Tavern brawls occurred frequently, particularly since taverns were not only male dominated, but also the setting for property and livestock sales and a variety of other economic activities. Marriage agreements were signed in inns and weddings were celebrated there. The consumption of alcohol of course heightened emotions.

Hans Schön the Innkeeper and Hans Pfalzer, Amman and Drinker

By the late seventeenth century there was at least one tavern in every village in Southwest Germany.[9] Taverns and inns performed many functions in the countryside. They were centers of sociability, communications nodes, meeting places for business, and stages for local politics, social conflicts, and even rebellion. Not surprisingly, the local courts of the smaller principalities, like the monasteries of Salem and Rot an der Rot, handled a steady flow of court cases involving disputes in and around taverns. In fact, it appears that a majority of cases involving conflicts between villagers originated in taverns. Several aspects of these cases stand out. As we have seen, law cases remind us how village taverns, like their counterparts in cities, were theaters where notions of (primarily) male honor were played out. More indirectly, the archives show that while taverns tied villages to the outside world, they were even more important for local communication.

Scholars have emphasized how the meaning of spaces, including taverns, in villages was defined by how those spaces were used.[10] While this seems like an obvious point, it is useful to examine several individuals in action in taverns. Rural taverns welcomed customers from all social groups, with perhaps the exception of the poorest residents. The tavernkeeper, the *Wirt*, was an important man in any community, partly because a tavern was potentially a very profitable enterprise and because it required considerable capital to start up. Furthermore, a tavernkeeper had a semi-official position that required him to exercise oversight

[8] GLAK 61/13268, pp. 3, 6, 9, 184r, 185r.

[9] This was the case in other regions as well, for example in Bavaria: Drexler, ed. *Kellnerin, a Maß*, pp. 8–9; Kümin, *Drinking Matters* for Switzerland.

[10] Rau, "Orte der Gastlichkeit—Orte der Kommunikation," and Susanne Rau, "Das Wirtshaus. Zur Konstitution eines öffentlichen Raumes in der Frühen Neuzeit" in Carolina Emmelius et al., eds. *Offen und Verborgen. Vorstellungen und Praktiken des Öffentlichen und Privaten in Mittelalter und Früher Neuzeit* (Göttingen, 2004).

over the goings-on in his establishment. At the center of gossip, rumor, and communication, the *Wirt* had considerable power, as did his wife.

In the 1650s, Hans Schön was the tavernkeeper, the *Taffern Wirt*, in the village of Berkheim. Berkheim lies between Biberach and Memmingen in the valley of the Iller, right on the major road that ran between Kempten to the south and Ulm to the north. The village was partly under the jurisdiction of the Premonstratensian Abbey of Rot an der Rot, and partly under that of the Benedictine monks at Ochsenhausen. Schön leased his inn from the monks at Rot, to whom he paid an annual fee and taxes on each measure of wine and beer sold. By all indications, Schön was a man of some substance in Berkheim. The inn also seems to have stayed in the family; in the 1730s and 1740s a Frederick Schön was innkeeper in Berkheim.[11]

For at least a decade Schön appeared regularly at the sessions of the local court presided over by officials from the monastery, often in conflict with Hans Pfalzer, the headman, or *Amman*, of Berkheim.[12] Schön's appearances at court are not surprising, since innkeepers were frequently witnesses to (and sometimes participants in) honor conflicts, verbal disputes, and drunken brawls that loomed large in the work of these *Niedergerichte*. The business of providing drink, food, and lodging was also of interest to the authorities, and they regulated it carefully, keeping a close eye on all innkeepers.

Hans Pfalzer represents another group of men who were frequently present in taverns, the wealthier big farmers, or *Bauern*, who controlled large farms and often many of the political positions in the village. In Bavarian villages they were given the best seats in the tavern, at the *Ofatisch*, the table closest to the oven.[13] Taverns, like the parish church, were public spaces and open to everyone, but, also like the church, seating (or standing) arrangements reflected social and economic status and were often a source of tension and conflict. Pfalzer, as we will see, was a frequent tavern customer, particularly in the tavern in his home village of Berkheim, run by Hans Schön.

The conflicts between Schön and Pfalzer were particular to their situations and personalities, but tension between tavernkeepers and local officials like the *Amman* were common. After all, the *Amman* was supposed to keep an eye on the tavern and oversee the collection of taxes and fees from the Wirt. We first encounter Schön and Pfalzer in December 1653, in a dispute over Pfalzer's duty to inspect the innkeeper's wine cellar in his role as wine inspector (*Weinspener*). On this occasion, Schön was fined a small amount for protesting the inspections too vociferously. Schön admitted objecting to the inspections, but claimed he only became abusive when the *Amman* asserted that the wine the innkeeper was selling was of poor quality and that Schön was overcharging his customers. Schön

[11] HStAS B487/Bd 138 (Rot Rechnungen).

[12] HStAS. B488/Bd 13.

[13] Drexler, ed. *Kellnerin, a Maß*, pp. 26–7.

claimed to have been poorly used: "It hurt me most of all that the *Amman* reproached me publicly in front of the people."[14]

A year later, during the post-harvest period as well, Pfalzer once again appeared to inspect the inn's cellars, and once again there was trouble. Schön was quoted as saying "he should not have the power to go into his [Schön's] cellar." Furthermore, according to the innkeeper the *Amman* did not come back up from the cellar until he had tasted not one *Mass* (½ a liter) of wine, but rather six. Pfalzer, he claimed, was "now in a state of complete drunkenness (*in voller weiss*)" and, in his drunken state, wanted to set the tax rate. Despite the fact that Schön was in other legal trouble at this court session, the judge did not fine him for this altercation.[15] Did monastic officials know something about the drinking habits of the *Amman* of Berkheim?

Perhaps being wine inspector was not a good job for Pfalzer, for he seemed to enjoy his wine rather more than was a good for him. In early March 1656, Pfalzer was drinking together with Hans Erma, the baker, and both their wives in Schön's tavern. The men's drinking got them into an ugly altercation with their wives. According to the court minutes, "while drinking, the men behaved in an unseemly manner, and the women attacked (*überfallen*) both men, one giving the *Amman* some serious blows, the other throwing the beer mug in the baker's face." There were witnesses to this scandal, "foreign people" (*frembden leüthen*), which, as the judges opined, meant "that people from all around would surely be talking about it." The court ordered Schön to work harder to prevent such altercations, but, rather surprisingly, did not level any fines on the parties.[16]

By May 1656, the court was starting to side with Schön, the innkeeper, against Pfalzer, despite the *Amman*'s status as a local official. On this occasion, Pfalzer and five other men complained in court that their honor had been damaged by the innkeeper's attack on their tobacco smoking. Schön had certainly been intentionally insulting: "*pfui, wie stinken die schelmen* (pfui, how these scoundrels stink)." He compounded the insult by repeating it the next morning, when he could no longer claim that he was under the influence of his own wine. The court, recognizing that Schön's use of the term *Schelm* was an attack on the other men's honor, ordered the innkeeper to apologize. Pfalzer and the other men, although they were the original complainants, were fined for drinking and smoking too much and for staying too late at the inn, and all parties were required to apologize.[17] Perhaps it was not very safe to throw around complaints in court. Or perhaps the complainants felt that the innkeeper's apology was worth the fine!

By the summer of 1656, the relationship between Pfalzer and Schön had clearly degenerated into a feud. Both appeared in court in August of that year because of

[14] HStAS B488/Bd 13, pp. 9r–v.
[15] HStAS B488/Bd 13, p. 53r.
[16] HStAS B486/Bd 13, p. 101r.
[17] HStAS B486/Bd 13, pp. 110r–v.

a heated exchange of insults that led to a fight, apparently in the inn itself.[18] Schön called Pfalzer an *Aufklauber*, a term that meant that the *Amman* was a person who listened to everything others said and noted it down, usually in negative ways, as a kind of tattletale.[19] Pfalzer responded with the standard insult, calling Schön a *Schelm*, which led directly to a physical confrontation, with the innkeeper the aggressor. As the court minutes state: "it did not end with this, but the *Amman* called Schön the son of a whore etc. and Schön called the *Amman* a murderer." Both men were fined, and Pfalzer was ordered to stay out of the inn, except "when business took place" there.[20]

Both men next appear separately from each other in the records. In November 1656, Schön was fined for buying "foreign wine" during the *Seefahrt* to the *Bodensee* and selling it without permission.[21] The *Seefahrt* was an annual trip to vineyards along the shores of Lake Constance, where the Upper Swabian monasteries had property. Farmers and tavernkeepers were required to provide transport to bring the *Seewein* from the Bodensee to the monasteries' cellars. On this trip, Pfalzer, drunk, had traded insults with the Ochsenhausen *Amman* of Berkheim, at which point the court assumed that Pfalzer was at fault, noting his long-standing feud with Schön.[22]

Pfalzer's reputation with the court and with his lords at Rot got worse in 1657, when Schön again filed a complaint against the *Amman*:

> He [Pfalzer] was, as always, in the inn, day and night, and with kindness is not to be gotten out of there even long after he should have gone home. He also insulted him [Schön], by calling him, begging your leave, a dog's etc. and saying that the night watchman did not have the power to throw the *Amman* out of the inn.

Pfalzer then went on to threaten the watchman, and the other guests, with fines or other official acts. The abbot himself intervened in the case, stating that "as long as he [Pfalzer] is *Amman*, he will neglect his domestic affairs [*nur hinder sich hauset*]." Partly for the good of his wife and children, he was to be removed from his office, and the abbot advised him "that from now on he should be more moderate in going to the inn and in drinking."[23]

Pfalzer reached a new low in June 1658. On Ascension Day he was once again drunk in the inn at Berkheim, where he insulted an official of a neighboring

[18] HStAS B486/Bd 13, pp. 112v–113r.

[19] *Schwäbishes Wörterbuch*: *Aufklauben*: To take the words of others painfully at face value, or to pay attention to and note down what others say. (1. *Worte anderer peinlich genau nehmen; alles übelnehmen*. 2. *Worte anderer aufpassen und sich notieren*).

[20] HStAS B486/Bd 13, pp. 114r–v. [21] HStAS B486/Bd 13, p. 122r.

[22] HStAS B486/Bd 13, p. 159r. Both Rot and Ochsenhausen had seigneurial rights in Berkheim where there were two *Amtmanner*, one from each monastery. There were also two taverns, one owned by Rot and one owned by Ochsenhausen. The lordship of the village belonged to Rot.

[23] HStAS B486/Bd 13, pp. 160r–v.

nobleman. The reaction of the court was severe. "This [episode] has convinced everyone, since he has for many years drunk too much and in various inns has spoken too much," that he should be seriously punished. As a result, Pfalzer was removed from the Berkheim *Gericht* (i.e., the local communal government) and was sentenced to eight days of bread and water in the tower, presumably at Rot itself.[24] Several days later, a group of local officials, including Schön and the new *Amman* in Berkheim, interceded on Pfalzer's behalf, reducing his punishment to one day in the tower, "in consideration of his poor wife and children."[25] Still, the former *Amman* had apparently not learned his lesson, or, put differently, the sad story continued, and Pfalzer was fined again in November 1658 for going into a *Wirtshaus*.[26]

Pfalzer continued to frequent taverns, including Schön's tavern. In July 1662 he was sentenced to three days in jail for "spending 14 days, from one midnight to the next, in the tavern here (in Rot)."[27] Schön was fined for allowing him to spend all that time in the tavern, one must assume, drinking. In September Pfalzer was back in Schön's tavern, drinking at a wedding, despite being forbidden from entering a tavern.[28] He also got into one more dispute with Schön, in November 1663. The conflict began in Schön's tavern, and the innkeeper was the aggressor.[29] He called Pfalzer a "whore's boy, a fart, and a perjurer." Several days later, Schön attacked Pfalzer on the street, scratching his face and throwing him to the ground. Schön spent a day in jail and bought off the rest of his prison term with a hefty fine. Pfalzer spent three hours in jail for responding to the attack by throwing a stone at Schön and pulling his beard.

Pfalzer makes a final appearance in the records in May 1667.[30]

> Hans Pfalzer has misbehaved continuously for eight days in the taverns, also with his children, whom he [has] increasingly plagued with curses and swearing. He should be put in the tower for a day and a night, and tomorrow should be put on the *Lumpen Taffel* here (in Rot) and in Berkheim.

The *Lumpen Tafel* was a board in the tavern where those who were not allowed into the tavern were listed. This kind of ostracization was viewed as a desperate measure by the courts, deeply dishonoring, and is very rare in the records.[31]

What about his old nemesis, the innkeeper, Hans Schön? He was still fined almost every year for selling wine that had not been properly examined, or wine

[24] HStAS B486/Bd 13, pp. 197v–198v.
[25] HStAS B486/Bd 13, p. 200r.
[26] HStAS B486/Bd 13, p. 213r.
[27] HStAS B486/Bd 13, p. 301v.
[28] HStAS B486/Bd 13, p. 310r.
[29] HStAS B486/Bd 13, p. 327r.
[30] HStAS B486/Bd 14, p. 71r.
[31] Another example of the *Lumpen Tafel*. The *Bader* in Rot was not sober for eight straight days from drinking too much *Branntwein* and as a result is put on the *Lumpen Tafel* at Rot. HStAS B486/Bd 14, pp. 63r, 98v.

that had been bought improperly.[32] These violations brought him into conflict with Pfalzer's successor as *Amman* and others in the village, and such conflicts invariably degenerated into verbal clashes. Perhaps Schön's personality was not quite the best for an innkeeper. One neighbor and customer brought Schön to court because the innkeeper had called him an adulterer, "saying openly that he [the neighbor] had cheated not only on his previous wife, but also on his current wife." For this outburst, which he claimed in court to regret, Schön was fined and told "in the future he should keep his immature mouth better under control."[33]

This admonition seemed to have had little effect on Schön's behavior or his mouth. Schön appeared in court for insults and brawls on multiple occasions in the 1650 and 1660s.[34] In February 1667 he was again in court, having insulted the groom during his wedding reception, held in Schön's tavern.[35] For unknown reasons, Schön kept trying to provoke the groom into a fight, until Schön was thrown out of his own tavern. Again, Schön paid a fine to avoid prison time, an indication that his tavern was prosperous and he had the resources to avoid the more humiliating punishments. It is telling that the prison at Rot was referred to as "the tower," but also as "the fools house," *das Narrenhaus*, a place where drunks could dry out. Interestingly, Schön's lack of discretion, a failing in a business where one learned much about one's neighbors, did not prevent him from carrying on as innkeeper, until his death sometime after April 1684.[36]

The story of the two Hanses illuminates many issues about taverns. A moralizing discourse would probably emphasize the temptation the tavern offered to Pfalzer, a man given to drinking heavily, quite possibly an alcoholic.[37] Pfalzer lost his position as *Amman*, was reprimanded multiple times, and found himself on the *Lumpen Tafel*, all marks of a decline in status in the community. Yet at times his peers, including Schön, appealed to have his punishments reduced and his status (at least partly) restored.

The conflict between Schön and Pfalzer began around the supervision of taverns, and Schön bristled at the inspections of his wine cellar. He also regularly circumvented the regulations around purchasing and selling wine and was, at least sometimes, caught doing so. These violations did not cost him his license, and one has the impression that he considered the fines the cost of running a profitable business. Business seems to have been good for Schön, and he was

[32] HStAS B486/Bd 13, pp. 178r–v, 213v.

[33] HStAS B486/Bd 13, pp. 220v–221r. "*Voriges*" = previous wife. She was probably deceased.

[34] HStAS B486/Bd 13, pp. 263r, 271r, 316v.

[35] HStAS B486/Bd 14, pp. 59r–59v.

[36] HStAS B486/Bd 15, p. 166v. He was reported to have been on his deathbed in April 1684. See below, Chapter 6. In September 1684 his wife brought a slander case to the court in Rot and Hans does not appear. But she is not listed as his widow, so perhaps he was still alive. See above Chapter 3 and HStAS B486/Bd 15, pp. 184v–186v.

[37] For an example of this way of understanding taverns, see Christina Claus, "'Alles hat er versoffen'—Der Wirtshaus Besuch und seine Folgen" in Drexler, ed. *Kellnerin, a Maß*, pp. 89–101.

willing to pay some hefty fines that resulted from his regular insulting of customers and his brawls rather than suffer the indignity of spending a night in prison.

One aspect of the supervision of taverns is that the local authorities, as well as the officials at Rot, just down the road, knew what was happening in the tavern at Berkheim. Schön's own behavior got him into regular trouble, certainly a consequence of his combative character, but also simply as a result of running a tavern, where local people and travelers came together. As centers of communication, sociability, and economic activity, taverns played an essential role in villages.[38] Schön's experience reflected this reality as he responded to the regulation of his tavern and participated personally in the conflicts there. If the *Herrschaft* expected him to keep the peace in his tavern by breaking up fights, discouraging excess drinking, and reporting violations of the opening hours, they were surely disappointed. Of course, the goals of tavern regulation were almost always in conflict with the business plan of tavernkeepers and with the role of taverns in village sociability. Taverns were at once places of (often rowdy) sociability and community building, but they were also places where notions of honor and emotional reactions created conditions for conflict and violence.

Taverns and Other Drinking Establishments

Taverns, inns, alehouses, and other similar establishments were categorized together as purveyors of alcoholic beverages, but all these institutions clearly had other functions as well. In the South German lands, large inns or taverns (*Tavernen*), such as the one managed by Hans Schön, were usually leased from the lord and were required to provide beds, stables for horses, and a substantial menu of food for travelers.[39] Travelers, government officials on missions, pilgrims, and merchants and traders of all kinds mingled with local people in such places, trading news of the wider world.

State officials wanted to create a network of inns that would provide for the needs of travelers and merchants and would thus support trade and economic growth. Larger inns did, in fact, serve travelers and provided an important connection between the countryside and the wider world. I argue here, however, that inns and taverns were mostly important as a locus of local communication, as a place where rumors and stories were shared and where local conflicts and disputes were played out in local politics.

[38] Kümin, *Drinking Matters*, esp. ch. 4.

[39] Fabian Brändle, "Public Houses, Clientelism, and Faith: Strategies of Power in Early Modern Toggenburg" in Beat Kümin and B. Ann Tlusty, eds. *The World of the Tavern. Public Houses in Early Modern Europe* (Aldershot, 2002), p. 86.

Nonetheless, taverns did provide links to the wider world. The Abbot of Salem issued an extensive *Wirtschaftsordnung* (Taverns' Ordinance) in 1605, which was renewed with only a few changes in 1668. In addition to the clauses regulating the sale of wine (and of course the taxes owed on each glass served), the ordinance emphasizes that innkeepers should provide high-quality services to their guests. A full-fledged tavern should serve good food, including meat, fish, vegetables, and white bread. "Foreign" guests should be given no reason to complain about the food; the innkeeper should never be caught unprepared, because "a nobleman could arrive at any time." Innkeepers should not hire inexperienced cooks, even if they were their own wives. The beds should have clean linen and an inn should have proper stalls for horses.[40]

The 1668 Ordinance repeats the earlier concern for travelers, or "foreign guests," but adds a new emphasis on fairness in the treatment of guests. All guests were to be treated well. "Both the rich and the poor should be courteously given and served what their money paid for, and they should not be harmed or cheated" (presumably by serving them bad, doctored, or watered drink). All customers were to be "given their penny's worth," and "the food should always be served, as much as possible, fresh, clean, and well-cooked, and there should be no rush in the serving or removal of meals, especially not if it is done to increase your own profit."[41] These regulations were aimed at providing fairly high levels of service at the larger taverns, without eliminating their role in providing drinks and meeting places for local people.

Take the inn at the monastery of Salem. It was particularly busy, because high-ranking travelers, monks, students, and priests stopped there to take advantage of the hospitality of the wealthy Cistercians.[42] Innkeepers served such visitors food at the expense of the abbey, and they kept little chits, or bills, recording who the guests were and what they ate. Most ate a meal, served with a half a *Mass* of wine. On August 15, 1701, for example, a priest from Salzburg was given *Mittagessen* and wine, and the next day a priest from Alsace was given the same. A few days later, two "lay sisters" had a meal there, as did a "Reformed [i.e., Protestant] officer" and a Baron and his wife. The inn at Salem also served local people, especially artisans and farm laborers who worked for the monastery, and the steady flow of visitors must have kept them well informed about developments in the wider world.

If we return to Hans Schön, the innkeeper in Berkheim, we see that, despite the presence of outsiders, his tavern was above all a center of local sociability. In the inn (and at the local church), "specific identities were shaped and community was

[40] Both *Ordnungen* in GLAK 98/3142.
[41] GLAK 98/3142, 1668 Ordinance.
[42] GLAK 62/19821, *Rechnungen* 1700–1.

manifestly formed."[43] The tavern was a place where local people (primarily, but not exclusively, men) told stories about their neighbors, confronted enemies, and developed friendships and alliances. It was also the site where local politics was conducted.

The authorities were intent on regulating taverns, not just to raise money, but also to limit what they considered excessive or dangerous behavior there. For example, in 1615 the Monastery of Rot ordered a limit on wine drinking at weddings and baptisms, restricted the amount of money that could be bet on cards and bowling and forbade boys under 18 from gambling at all, and banned dancing on most feast days.[44] Dancing came to be forbidden on a whole series of holidays. Drinking establishments were to be closed during church services. Tavernkeepers and the guests were expected to report "excessive drinking, drunkenness, illegal gambling, cursing and swearing" to the authorities. A roster of fines for fighting was listed, with fines increasing if weapons were used, if blood was drawn, if bones were broken, or if objects were thrown. The ordinance thus had a paternalistic flavor.

> When the poor subjects come to them [the local authorities] in their official capacity, they should not take them (as has happened up to now) to the tavern, or allow themselves to be taken there. They [the subjects] should not have costs put on them and then, on top of that, be expected to pay for drinks for the *Amtmann* or the beadle [*Bittel*].[45]

This clause gives a sense of the role of the tavern as not just a social setting and a setting for family and communal celebrations, but also as the location for business and administrative meetings. Court records indicate that these regulations were hard to enforce, whether they were paternalistic or disciplinary in nature.

Smaller establishments were more locally focused than the larger taverns. The 1728 "Contract for the *Schenkhaus* (bar, public house) established at the Lower Gate [of the monastery of Rot]" lays out the rules for this new locale.[46] The publican was permitted to serve wine, schnapps, *Kirschwasser* (cherry liquor), and beer. He had to buy the alcohol from the monastery. Guests could sit and could also stay overnight, but this *Schenkhaus* did not have "tavern rights," which meant weddings, gatherings of the commune, guild celebrations, and baptism receptions were not allowed. Unlike in taverns, baking and butchering were not permitted either, although the proprietor could sell bread and meat to his customers, as well

[43] Michael Frank, "Satan's Servant or Authorities' Agent? Publicans in Eighteenth Century Germany" in Kümin and Tlusty, eds. *The World of the Tavern*, p. 42.

[44] HStAS B486/1581, pp. 1r–7v. This ordinance was reissued around 1715, with minor changes: HStAS B486/211.

[45] HStAS B486/1581, p. 5v.

[46] HStAS B487/Bd 138, loose sheets folded into volume.

as tobacco.[47] The monastery, which owned the building, encouraged the renter to build a still for distilling schnapps, which would then allow the monks to raise the rent.

Taverns as Public Spaces: Meetings, Tavern Sociability, Tavern Brawls

Sometime in early 1662, Peter Lutz, a man of about 50, sat in the *Stube* (the main room) of the tavern in Thengen having a drink with his servant and another man, Mathis Meyer.[48] Lutz lived in Thengen, although he was originally from Prulingen, and Meyer was from nearby Stetten. When Jagli Meyer, a big farmer, came into the room the servant said "ah, there comes someone who wants to pay me." Jagli responded by saying, "that could well be the case." The two men then negotiated the servant's pay. Jagli preferred to pay with *Rüben* (turnips probably, though possibly carrots or beets) rather than grain, but the servant responded, "he needs to have bread too." The two men agreed on payment that was half in grain and half in vegetables. The court needed to know about this agreement because the servant had died in the meantime. Lutz admitted that he did not know why Jagli owed his servant money, but was clear about what he had heard.

It is unusual to find such a mundane event in the court records, since of course they more often recorded conflicts than agreements. Here we see the tavern functioning as a place of business and a meeting place. Lutz, a bystander, could testify, some time after the fact, to an oral agreement between two men and the court agreed to enforce the agreement. Lutz also pointed out that there was at least one other witness there, Mathis Meyer, making the agreement even more public.

The physical layout of early modern taverns contributed in obvious ways to their public character. As Beat Kümin has shown, taverns of all kinds in Germany had a large room on the main (or ground) floor, usually known as the *Stube*.[49] Larger taverns would have guest rooms on the second floor and in some cases a smaller room on the main floor for private gatherings. Larger taverns also had outdoor spaces, for dancing and for bowling. Wooden tables, benches, and chairs were the basic furnishings, and most taverns had some sort of oven to keep them somewhat warm in winter.[50]

[47] Tobacco was apparently forbidden in the seventeenth century, but allowed in the eighteenth. See HStAS B487/Bd 13, p. 244r, March 8, 1660. Subjects (*Untertanen*) were forbidden to "drink tobacco." Also p. 305r, October 23, 1662—a man objects that the *Herrschaft* has forbidden tobacco.

[48] GLAK 61/6958, March 21, 1662. Testimony was taken on this day, but it is unclear from the minutes when the events discussed here took place.

[49] Kümin, *Drinking Matters*, pp. 37–49.

[50] Hans Conrad Peyer, *Von der Gastfreundschaft zum Gasthaus. Studien zur Gastlichkeit im Mittelalter* (Hannover, 1987), chapter 3, section 7.

When Martin Lurz sold the tavern in Rot to Johan Wellburger in 1665, he sold a variety of furnishings along with it.[51] These included four chests, seventeen tables of various kinds (*Tische* and *Tafeln*), nineteen large chairs, and five benches. This was a larger tavern, well enough appointed to serve a sizable crowd of customers. It is easy to see why taverns also hosted communal meetings and court sessions. No other building, except the church, had this much space.

As officially public spaces, taverns were open to everyone and regulated as such by the authorities.[52] Conflicts in taverns often occurred precisely because this space was open to all. Groups of people, mostly men, encountered others whom they might not usually interact with. "Foreigners" could be found there, that is, people from other regions, or just people from other villages or towns nearby. Soldiers stationed in the region were a particularly problematic group of outsiders, but Jews and Roma (*Zigeuner*, "gypsies") were not particularly welcome either. Taverns also hosted groups of guildsmen, a notoriously prickly group of men on the lookout for rival artisans. Finally, groups of young people, who came more sporadically into taverns, could clash with the regular customers, who were usually the established farmers in a community.

This combustible public space was made more unstable by the presence of drink. Taverns were, however, also subject to a lot of peacekeeping efforts. When a new innkeeper took over the tavern at Rot in 1706, he was instructed "If any crimes occur he is required, either in person or through his people (*die Seinigen*), to appeal for peace. And by the duty that comes from his oath he must report criminals to the authorities and the *Canzley*; in doing so he should protect no one."[53] The Salem ordinances of 1605 and 1668 regulating taverns have a similar clause, requiring that innkeepers both report crimes and demand peace when trouble broke out in the tavern.[54] The *Wirte*, then, were put in a difficult spot, acting as agents of the authorities, while also functioning as members of the community attempting to keep the peace. On top of that, any good innkeeper knew that some disorder was part of the business, and an overly strict enforcement of the rules might hurt his profits.

Members of the community were also supposed to keep the peace, as we saw in the Rot ordinance of 1610.[55] Bernd Schildt's study of village ordinances from sixteenth-century Thuringia shows that "neighbors" were told to appeal for calm when violence threatened in the tavern, although local officials and the *Wirte*

[51] HStAS B486/Bd 14, p. 15r.

[52] Rau, "Das Wirtshaus"; Susanne Rau, "Ort der Gastlichkeit—Ort der Kommunikation" in Dürr and Schwerhoff, eds. *Kirchen, Märkte und Tavernen*.

[53] HStAS B486/Bd 18, pp. 120r–121v.

[54] GLAK 98/3142. In just one example, the tavernkeeper in Steinbach was warned to make sure that wedding receptions in his tavern did not get unruly. HStAS B486/Bd. 14, p. 24r.

[55] HStAS B486/1581, pp. 1r–7v. Also in 1715 ordinance, HStAS B486/211.

were primarily responsible for keeping the peace.[56] The *Amman* in Tiffingen testified that he demanded peace three times when a brawl broke out during the parish festival in 1669, to no avail.[57] Christoph Hueber, the tavernkeeper in Dingelsdorf, also appealed for peace in his tavern in 1714, but, as he said himself, "the only thanks he got were crude insults."[58]

The response Hueber elicited when he waded into a severe brawl in his tavern was not uncommon. During a 1663 brawl at the tavern in Rot, Bartle Kapfer stated "he would consider anyone who tried to come between them [the combatants], or who called for peace, nothing better than s.v. a scoundrel."[59] Kapfer was fined at the higher rate set for those who rejected a *Friedbott*, a call for peace. There appear to have been more calls for peace in taverns after 1700, but the assumption was always that violence would take place in drinking establishments. Not surprisingly, men in the middle of a fist fight were quite deaf to calls for peace. In the right situation, however, bystanders could and did intervene. After all, Hans Schön was thrown out of his own tavern for misbehaving at a wedding reception. It was in taverns, more than anywhere else in the village, that conflicts played out in front of people. This gave the call for peace more clout, but also made it harder for the conflicting parties to back down.

Early modern rulers (and historians) have tended to focus on tensions and conflicts in taverns and view them as disruptive spaces in cities and rural society. As Beat Kümin points out, the role of taverns was actually complex and ambivalent. He argues, as does Ann Tlusty in her study of taverns in Augsburg, that taverns provided space for sociability, the exchange of news and information, and political functions that could stabilize society as well as disrupt it.[60] For every card game or bowling match that ended in insults and fisticuffs, there must have been many others that brought people together, cemented personal and family ties, and perhaps led to a marriage, business partnership, or other kinds of social, economic, or political cooperation.

We know that taverns hosted important family and community events like weddings.[61] Wedding receptions meant drinking and dancing and they brought whole families into the tavern, including married men and women, single people, and children. Here again, the only other place where such a cross-section of a community came together was the church.[62] In fact, the guests at a wedding might include large numbers of people from outside the community, broadening

[56] Bernd Schildt, "Der Friedensgedanke im frühneuzeitliche Dorfrecht: Das Beispiel Thüringen" *Zeitschrift der Savigny-Stiftung für Rechtsgeschichte*. Germanische Abteilung 107 (1990): esp. p. 210.

[57] GLAK 61/13334, p. 1. [58] GLAK 61/7606, pp. 62v–63r.

[59] HStAS B486/Bd 13, pp. 326r–326v.

[60] Kümin, *Drinking Matters*, pp. 126–30. Tlusty, *Bacchus and Civic Order*, pp. 181–2. Also Schwerhoff, "Die Große Welt im kleinen Raum" in Dürr and Schwerhoff, eds. *Kirchen, Märkte und Tavernen*, pp. 367-75.

[61] Tlusty, *Bacchus and Civic Order*, pp. 174–6.

[62] Rau, "Orte der Gastlichkeit—Orte der Kommunikation," p. 415.

the experience of local people. For young people weddings were of course a chance to look into the marriage market, or to show off their talents. This was the case in Nussdorf in the summer of 1670, when a group of young men performed their *Valet Tanz* (servant's dance) at a wedding.[63] This performance, by a group of servants from the monastery of Salem, required them to organize and pay for musicians in advance.

Young people gathered at the village tavern at other times as well; this was, at the very least, a change from the routine serving of drinks to groups of propertied men playing cards or discussing local politics or rumors. In January 1705 a group of young people, male and female, gathered in the tavern at Staad, "drinking, dancing, and having fun."[64] One of the party, Elisabetha Klingenbergerin, became so drunk that she vomited, causing an exchange of words among the young people. On the Pentecost holiday of 1695, the *Rossbuben* (horseherders) gathered at the inn in Bermatingen.[65] Upon leaving, an exchange of insults and a brawl broke out, with the young men insulting the innkeeper and his maid.

Parish festivals also generated business for village taverns and brought together people from surrounding villages. In attendance at the 1669 church festival in Tüfingen were people from a number of different villages and even several young men from Switzerland, probably servants serving in the region.[66] A large group of men were drinking in the tavern during the Allmannsdorf church festival in 1704, and while some of them got into a fight, others claimed "they were not there, but were instead dancing, and know nothing about what happened."[67]

Carnival—*Fastnacht*—was another occasion that brought large and diverse groups of people into the village tavern. In 1705 the young men in Haslach started a serious enough brawl there that it ended up in court.[68] Seven people were fined for insults and fighting, including the wife of the *Wirtsknecht*, the servant at the inn. The innkeeper was one of the people fined, presumably for failing to keep order when this "*Zank-Rauf und Schlaghandel*" (quarrel, scuffle, and fighting incident) broke out. Here again, the tavern was the setting for conflict in the context of a large gathering of people.

Carnival, parish festivals, holidays, and weddings were all special occasions, days outside the routines of everyday life. People, especially young people, took a certain license on those days and sometimes the resulting disorder ended up in court. Taverns were often the settings for those occasions, but they were also the scene of everyday social life and everyday drinking. As Gerd Schwerhoff has shown, based on sources from early modern Cologne, routine drinking in taverns

[63] GLAK 61/13334, p. 55.
[64] GLAK 61/7604, pp. 182r–182v.
[65] GLAK 61/13337, p. 13.
[66] GLAK 61/13334, pp. 1–2. The conflict broke out over paying for the musicians, who had been hired by the local people. The locals complained that the "foreigners," that is, those from outside the village, did not want to pay their share.
[67] GLAK 61/7604, pp. 166r–166v.
[68] HStASt. B486/Bd 18, p. 90r.

was subject to the rules of custom.[69] The *Gelage*, an occasion of ritualized drinking, created a "ritual drinking community" that set the rules for social interaction in the tavern.[70] "The collective drink (*Gemeinsame Trunk*) and the rituals that accompanied it created peace and built community," Schwerhoff further argues.[71] The traditions of sociability in the village taverns of Southwest Germany were not significantly different from what Schwerhoff describes for Cologne.[72] Men did not come to the tavern to drink alone; they usually drank together in groups of two to four, played cards, and followed the traditions of paying for rounds of drinks—and if they did not pay their share, there could be trouble.[73]

Men could use the tavern as a place to vent their opinions about the authorities. When Jorg Moser griped about taxes in the tavern in Owingen in 1671, it sounded like casual *Stammtisch* talk, the German tradition of discussing politics in a drinking establishment.[74] One witness reported his words to the *Oberamt* at Salem, the lords of Owingen, and Moser's three table companions were called as witnesses. Tellingly, the court reprimanded the innkeeper for failing to report the rebellious words, and other disobedient talk. Fifty years later, Joseph Dudli was also talking tough in the tavern in Dettingen, saying that "it would take many chancellery officials [*Canzleyverwalter*] to make him obey."[75] The investigation of this outburst led to the identification of another man who had also said critical things about the *Herrschaft*. There is little doubt that such talk was, if not common, far from unusual in taverns. "Rebellious words," however, do not appear often in court records, despite the concern the authorities expressed about them.[76] Perhaps social peace was preserved because people could "blow off steam" over a few drinks, but it is also reasonable to argue, as Schwerhoff does, that traditions of tavern sociability were designed to maintain order and peace, even as the danger of conflict and violence was also always present.

Drinking was the everyday activity in taverns and all drinking establishments, but we have seen that people ate, played cards and other games, and discussed all kinds of subjects. Kümin's point that the public house, in its daily activities, was also a communications center should not be forgotten either. Especially in the eighteenth century, growing trade and the advent of postal services made taverns even more important for the exchange of information and the decreasing

[69] Schwerhoff, "Das Gelage" in Melville, ed. *Das Sichtbare und das Unsichtbare der Macht*.

[70] Schwerhoff, "Das Gelage," p. 171.

[71] Schwerhoff, "Das Gelage," p. 173.

[72] The word *Gelage* does not appear in the sources. *Zechen* was the most common word to refer to a group of men drinking together.

[73] See above, Chapter 2, the story of the man who offended another man by refusing a glass of wine. GLAK 61/13344, pp. 252–5. Also, from Chapter 2, the example of the man who wanted to take his wine home and drink alone. GLAK 61/13346, pp. 357–60.

[74] GLAK 61/13334, pp. 111–13.

[75] GLAK 61/7606, pp. 37v–38r, 43r–45v.

[76] Another example, from Wollmatingen in 1679: GLAK 61/13268, p. 25; anti-clerical talk in Dettingen in 1710: GLAK 61/7606, p. 34r–v. Authorities' view: GLAK 98/3142 (Salem Tavern Ordinance), esp. clauses 38 and 39. Bernd Schildt, "Der Friedensgedanke" *Zeitschrift der Savigny-Stiftung für Rechtsgeschichte. Germanische Abteilung* 107 (1990): esp. pp. 204–11.

isolation of rural communities.[77] As we will see, the most important communication role of the tavern was in the spreading of stories, rumors—or public exposure more generally—to neighboring villages and towns and across the region.

Taverns were also linked to the roads and squares in their vicinity. Then, as now, tavernkeepers told combative customers to "take it outside" when they came to blows or appeared about to resort to violence. Furthermore, the practice of "calling someone out" (*herausfordern*) was deeply entrenched in this society.[78] In its purest form, as described by Karl-S Kramer, one "called someone out" of their own house as a form of breaking the peace of the house and insulting one's opponent. This practice could be applied to a tavern if it was being used as refuge by a party in a conflict.

On August 25, 1697, four men were drinking in their home tavern in Nussdorf when they got into an altercation with several outsiders, two men from the neighboring free city of Überlingen.[79] One of the four locals, Conrad Jung, "under false pretenses" knocked one of the Überlinger, Matheus Dechler, to the floor of the inn, leading to an outburst of insults from Dechler. Outnumbered, the Überlinger left, but on the way home they met Matheus Hueter, a servant who was working in Überlingen, and with this reinforcement they decided to return to the inn. They then called the Nussdorfer out, pounding on the doorframe and the door to the tavern. As Kramer points out, attacking doors (and windows) was a calculated violation of *Hausfrieden*, the protected sphere of the house, and was a criminal act.[80]

The Nussdorfer feared that their opponents would break down the door, thus "gaining an advantage," so they went outside. One of the Überlinger, Bartle Bader, attacked Joseph Urnaw, but Urnaw gained the upper hand and threw Bader to the ground. This brought the fight to a dramatic moment, since, according to the testimony of the four Nussdorfer, Bader pulled a knife out of a sack, ready to cut Urnaw's throat. This was a major escalation of a rather typical tavern quarrel that had gone from what was probably an intentional insult (throwing someone to the ground), to verbal insults, to calling out, to fisticuffs. Now outside, perhaps Bader felt it less dangerous to draw a knife. Fortunately for Urnaw, he was able to defend himself and push the knife away, while one of his friends disarmed Bader. This was fortunate for Bader as well, since further violence and any bloodletting (not to mention murder) would have meant serious punishment. Urnaw showed the court the scar from the knife and deposited the knife as evidence. After this, the fight continued, "and each one, as well as he could, defended himself and struck blows."

[77] Wolfgang Behringer, *Im Zeichen des Merkur. Reichspost und Kommunikationsrevolution in der Frühen Neuzeit* (Göttingen, 2003), esp. pp. 72–3 about taverns.

[78] Kramer, "Das Herausfordern aus dem Haus." [79] GLAK 61/13339, pp. 103–5, 106–7.

[80] Kramer, "Das Herausfordern aus dem Haus," pp. 126–9. See below, Chapter 5, for more on "calling out."

In testimony at the Salem *Oberamt* several days later, the Überlinger initially admitted to the insults, the attack on the door, and starting the fight, but said "they know nothing about the knife." Confronted with their accusers, they eventually admitted to bringing out the knife, using drunkenness as an excuse. The Überlinger were convicted of the insults and of starting a "very dangerous brawl," fined heavily, and kept in custody until they paid their fine.

This episode exemplifies the way a tavern provided a setting for violence, even when there was no real underlying conflict, other than an encounter between drinking men. It also shows how clashes often erupted when groups of men from different villages came together in a tavern. These encounters were moments when men from a village might close ranks against outsiders or when they might decide to assert their physical superiority. If other issues, such as conflicts over resources like forests, fishing grounds, or pastures were at stake, conflicts were even more likely.

In the region around Lake Constance (*Bodensee*), there was ongoing tension between fishermen and ferryboat operators from different communities, tensions that were exacerbated by the different jurisdictions in this politically fragmented region. On a winter evening in December 1683, the tavern in the village of Staad, on the shores of the lake, was crowded with groups of men from several different villages and towns.[81] Bad weather meant that a group of men from Bodman could not sail home and they decided to go to the inn to wait for the weather to improve. Another group of men from Sermatingen, across the lake, were also at a table, while a larger group of men from the Imperial city of Überlingen were already ensconced and, according to witnesses, well into a night of drinking.[82]

What transpired appears to be a case of pure provocation on the part of the Überlinger. One of them, Jacob Strehl, came over to the table of the men from Bodman "and said that he had lost a hen, which those from Bodman had stolen, so they were all chicken thieves and should give him his hen back." The Bodmaner denied any knowledge of the hen, at which point the Überlinger attacked their table and a full-scale fight ensued. The combatants ignored first the innkeeper's *Friedbott* (call for peace) and then the *Amman*'s order to stop fighting, which included the threat of a fine. The fighting only stopped when (as witnesses later testified) "during the fight the missing hen fell out of Strehl's, s.v. pants' slit." The somewhat chagrined Überlinger then left the tavern, jumped into their boat, and sailed away, ignoring the *Amman*'s calls to stay and face arrest. One of the Überlinger admitted in court to the insults and the fight, but said he never heard

[81] GLAK 61/7602, January 24, 1684, 4r–6v. The case was heard in court four weeks after the events.

[82] For discussion of drinking groups and drinking rituals: Gudrun Gersmann, "Ort der Kommunication, Ort der Auseinandersetzung" in Eriksson and Krug-Richter, eds. *Streitkulturen*, esp. pp. 250–9; Peter Wettmann-Jungblut, "Gewalt und Gegen-Gewalt. Gewalthandeln, Alkoholkonsum und die Dynamik von Konflikten anhand eines Fallbeispiels aus dem frühneuzeitlichen Schwarzwald" in Eriksson and Krug-Richter, eds. *Streitkulturen*, pp. 17–58. esp. pp. 36–45.

the *Amman*'s order, stating "the wine had a big effect on this situation, since they were all pretty drunk." The court fined the Überlinger, particularly for their disobedience of the *Amman*, although the fines were somewhat reduced out of neighborly respect for the Free City of Überlingen.

Whatever the symbolism of the hen and whatever we make of it falling out of Jacob Strehl's pants, the obvious point is that the confrontation in the tavern was primarily a case of two groups of men exchanging insults as they defended their turf (in this case their table at the inn) and the reputation of their village or town.[83] Perhaps as the residents of a larger and politically independent town, the Überlinger felt or acted superior. There may have been other underlying conflicts, perhaps over fishing rights or rights to run ferries over the Bodensee, for such conflicts appear elsewhere in the Mainau court records from this period. The big lake brought men from communities around it into regular contact, probably more often than in the case of landlocked villages. What we do know for sure is that tavern conflicts between groups of men, fueled by alcohol, were common.

"Foreigners" from further afield could also cause trouble, as well as bring trade and news of the wider world. In October 1669, four travelers, two brothers from Switzerland and two men from nearby Augsburg, shared a table at the inn in the village of Weildorf, near Salem. One of the Swiss men began singing religious songs, no doubt Protestant hymns, which caused the Augsburger to request he stop singing. According to a witness, the Swiss then went on to praise their own country, further asserting that "the Swabians [like the Augsburgers] are a slovenly [*liderliches*] people and (begging your leave), dogs' etc. compared to the Swiss." Not surprisingly, the Swabians called the Swiss out and a brawl ensued, with the deeply insulted Swabians getting the upper hand.[84]

The tavern at the monastery of Salem, as we have already seen, was a lively place where people from far and wide met. In February 1670 a butcher from Constance, a carpenter from Franconia, and a tailor were eating and drinking together at a table.[85] For reasons that are unclear, the carpenter insulted the butcher, then went on to attack his master and other officials at Salem. He demanded that the butcher come outside to fight, which he refused to do. These kinds of conflicts between locals and outsiders probably play an oversized role in the court records. It was sometimes only possible to resolve a dispute with someone from another village or another lordship by bringing them to court. Conflicts between neighbors, as we have already seen with honor conflicts, also regularly played out in taverns, but these disputes were more likely to be solved outside of courts, since the parties regularly interacted in the community.

[83] Perhaps the chicken story started as just a joke, and then was used as an excuse to start a fight. Or perhaps the chicken was a female image, contrasted with the male (and sexually aggressive) rooster?

[84] GLAK 61/13334, p. 8b.

[85] GLAK 61/13334, pp. 24–5.

Even a conflict between people who worked together might be played out in a tavern, where the parties had an audience and possibly support from allies. A 1688 dispute between the smith in Mainau and his two servants spilled over into the tavern.[86] The smith brought charges, saying the servants had come into the shop and thrown tools around the room, then had complained in the presence of several citizens that he had wanted to fire them. The servants also stated (somewhat obscurely) that "his [the smith's] wife is certainly not safe." The two servants testified that this episode went down very differently, that the smith's wife had come into the tavern (where they had only come to smoke a pipe of tobacco) and verbally attacked them. As a result of this insult, they admitted to being angry and went to the workshop and threw the hammer and tongs into the water bucket. They stated that the smith then insulted them and they "similarly, in order to rescue their honor, called him a scoundrel as well." Both parties were concerned with what people in the tavern had heard, the smith that his servants had questioned his treatment of his wife and his employees, and the servants that their honor as responsible workers had been impugned.

As we have seen, when taverns brought larger groups of people together it could bring local conflicts into the open. In 1705, four men, together with their wives, met in the tavern in Staad, on the occasion of the sale of new wine.[87] A dispute among the women led their husbands to start insulting each other. We do not know what the issues were that led the women to start arguing, but the *Amman* reported that the men "each said they were better trained in their craft and more knowledgeable and capable [than the others]." While several of the men heeded the "appeal for peace" of the *Amman* rather than face a fine, one of the men reopened hostilities by saying "you are like gypsy servants [*Zügeiner gesind*], first peaceful, then not peaceful." This was taken as an insult and led to hair pulling and slaps, and one man was thrown out the front door. The court case was brought by the *Amman*, since the men had violated his appeal for peace. A dispute like this, involving eight people, all of whom were from established families, was a public scandal and no doubt reports about it spread widely in the village. Several of the men were used as examples and fined.

As we can see, women were certainly present in village taverns, though clearly not as often as men. On Ash Wednesday 1695, a mixed gender group of eight couples, one single man, and two women alone, all apparently adults, enjoyed several hours of dancing at the Ochsenhausen tavern in the village of Berkheim.[88] Most of the people there were married couples, though the Schwarzbäurin and Sailer's wife came without any accompanying men. In the inn in Rot in 1665, a woman, probably an innocent bystander, was hit by a flying plate.[89] Two women

[86] GLAK 61/7602, June 14, 1688. [87] GLAK 61/7604, pp. 180r–181r.
[88] HStAS B486/346, Extract Protokolle f. 75. [89] HStAS B486/Bd 14, p. 24v.

got into an altercation with their husbands in the inn in Berkheim after a few drinks.[90] In 1669, Ursula Endrassin attacked Georg Kholmann both physically and verbally in the same inn, apparently in retaliation for an insult by Kholmann.[91] The seventeenth-century court records show that the presence of women in taverns was unremarkable.

There is even a sense that women, even single young women, could go to a tavern and behave honorably. Despite the suspicions of the Salem *Oberamt*, the innkeeper at the tavern there testified in January 1698 that Anna Maria Kümmerlein and Agetha Meinerin "had left to go home by closing time [10 p.m.] and had done nothing improper" in his tavern.[92] The *Oberamt* was still concerned and, before letting them go, warned the young women not to spend so much time in the tavern.

It is not unusual to find inns run by women, either as the wife of the innkeeper or as a widow. As we saw in the case of Johanna Silberin, the *Wirtin* was an important figure; like the innkeeper, she had access to a lot of information and gained power from that information. This seems to have been the case with Margaretha Luzin, the wife of the innkeeper and *Gerichtsamman* in Rot. Luzin brought Ursula Endrassin to court in 1662, accusing Ursula of making snide comments about the honor of the *Wirtin*. Endrassin, wife of a smith, was fined by the court for the second time that year for behavior in the tavern (see above).[93] Perhaps because, as an innkeeper, she spent a lot of time in a tavern, Luzin was especially sensitive to the threat to female honor in such places.

Another group of women found in taverns were maids and servants who prepared the food and served the customers. Like all servants, maids in taverns were vulnerable to the advances of their employers. They were also frequently propositioned by the customers and as single women their virtue was called into question as a matter of course. We have seen that these women defended their honor, at times in court, and sometimes the innkeeper defended them as well. Stoffel Messmer and Martin Guldenfuss put the popular view of taverns into words in 1686 when they said that the tavern in Staad was a "whores' and murders' house."[94]

One case from the summer of 1670 probably confirmed to the authorities, and perhaps local people, the sexual promiscuity of tavern maidservants. In a case discussed above, Catherina Dürrin, a tavern servant, admitted to having sex with Jacob Seutern in the tavern at Leutkirch.[95] In court she explicitly listed (or was asked to list) those locations; "the first time at night in the kitchen of the tavern at Leutkirch on top of the oven, the second time in the *Stube* standing, the third and

[90] HStAS B486/Bd 12, p. 101r. [91] HStAS B486/Bd 13, p. 295r.
[92] GLAK 61/13339, p. 180. [93] HStAS B486/Bd 13, pp. 295r–v.
[94] GLAK 61/7602, November 16, 1686. They were fined for insulting the tavern keeper, a woman.
[95] Also discussed in Chapter 1, in relation to the punishment. GLAK 61/13334, p. 55.

fourth time in the kitchen and the *Stube*." Catherina's defense was "that she did not understand what he was doing to her, also did not know what it meant." The *Amman* bringing charges against her did not know who her family was, and it seems that Dürrin may have been a vagabond and was perhaps mentally challenged.

Barbara Friyen was a maid servant in the tavern in Oberuhldingen in 1670 when she and Hans Sager, a miller's servant from Switzerland, were convicted of having sex in the tavern.[96] Several witnesses testified to the act, including a young horseherd (*Rossbub*), who said he saw Barbara move a table close to the oven in the *Stube*, where Sager was sleeping. The *Rossbub*, however, was sleeping under the oven and claimed that the room was dark and that he "had seen nothing."[97] Another maid, Anna Präckin, said she had seen the couple together on other occasions, at the bathhouse and in the tavern, and that on one occasion Hans had his shirt out, Barbara's breast was uncovered, and Hans had said "you women need a kiss to warm you up." Finally, the tavernkeeper testified that another guest, a grain dealer who was also sleeping in the *Stube* that night, had joked in the morning that "something inappropriate was going on behind the oven with your servants... and he had been awakened several times."

Obviously, the tavern's main *Stube* was a public place, and the young couple was sure to be found out. Yet perhaps their apprehension and conviction were not a forgone conclusion; certainly the facts of the case are somewhat unclear. The complaint was brought to the court by two local *Amtmänner*, who had heard rumors and decided to investigate. The young boy sleeping under the oven was reluctant to confirm the story and, while an enthusiastic witness, Anna Präckin did not claim to have seen the young couple in the act. The innkeeper was perhaps concerned about the reputation of his tavern and limited his testimony to reporting the joking comments of the grain dealer. Barbara Friyen pointedly denied having sex with Sager on a table in the *Stube*, saying instead that they had been intimate in her bed. Sager, for his part, initially denied the charge, finally admitting that he had "behaved dishonorably with her" only once. They were both given a stiff fine and put in the stocks.

Of course, cases in these courts did not require clear proof of a misdeed, and rumors and hearsay were always admissible. Courts regularly investigated the reputation of defendants, particularly around sexual crimes, as we saw in the cases involving Johanna Silberin. In this context, the tavern was a particularly suspicious location. Barbara's insistence that the sex took place in her bed seems to indicate that the location mattered and that her reputation would be further tarnished by sexual activity in the dark *Stube* of a tavern. Moreover, Hans was an

[96] GLAK 61/13334, pp. 25–6.

[97] This case also highlights the privileged place of sight in court cases. What witnesses saw was considered more important than what they heard in a case like this. Words, however, were also of great significance, as we have seen in the honor cases. It was what people said that generally led to honor disputes.

outsider and a person of low status, a servant from Switzerland. Would the case have even reached the court if the parties had been the children of local propertied farmers? As it was, the reputation of the tavern was at stake, since the grain merchant was making jokes, and the reputation of Salem, as the lords of the village, also needed to be defended.

Another case from 1670 demonstrates the vulnerability of maidservants in taverns, but also serves as a reminder that female servants were vulnerable in other settings as well. In this case, Anna Röcklin, a 19-year-old servant at the tavern in Oberuhldingen, filed charges against Jacob Gerstler, a Jew from Wangen who had been a guest at the tavern.[98] Anna testified that Gerstler left the guest room on the first floor and, around midnight, came up the stairs and went into the room where the two female servants, Anna and Barbara Schröfferin, were sleeping. He asked if he could stay with them, touched and kissed Barbara, who said she defended herself. Anna ran out of the room and fetched the innkeeper's wife who came in with a light. At this point, as Anna testified, "the Jew quickly retreated back down the stairs to the guest room."

The next day, when the other maids and the innkeeper and his wife were all out of the house, Gerstler again harassed Röcklin, both trying to touch her and offering her money, saying that no one was there and no one would know anything. Anna insisted that she rejected his offer and firmly defended herself, responding to his proposition by answering "he has his own wife, he should stick with her (*soll mit ihr zuhalten*)," to which he said, "yes, he has a wife, but she is not here." Anna was rescued by some passing girls who heard her screaming and again Gerstler fled. Gerstler was fined one *Gulden* and also had to pay some damages.

There are several lessons from this case. Once again, it shows how taverns brought together people from different places and communities. The maids were physically vulnerable and sexually suspect, as evidenced by Gerstler's entering the maids' bedroom and his offer to pay Anna, presumably for sexual favors. Of course, Gerstler (referred to only as "the Jew" throughout the court minutes) was also vulnerable, and Anna Röcklin felt she could bring charges against him. These kinds of charges, by women sexually harassed by men, while not unknown, are rare in the records. The court's decision was also somewhat ambiguous, since the one *Gulden* fine was not particularly large, leaving the impression that the court did not consider this a particularly serious crime. Gerstler, unlike the young couple in the previous case, was not given a shaming punishment.[99]

* * *

[98] GLAK 61/13334, pp. 44–6.

[99] I suspect that there were jurisdictional conflicts here too and that perhaps the Salem *Oberamtsgericht* could not put a Jew who was under the jurisdiction of the Imperial City of Ulm in the stocks. Also, there was no real point to make to the community by putting an outsider like Gerstler in the stocks in front of the parish church. The fine of one *Gulden* was quite a bit less than six *Gulden* the young couple in the previous case paid.

A village tavern was then a kind of hothouse for conflicts. It was a place where locals and outsiders interacted, always a combustible situation. It was also a place where larger groups of people, especially young people, came together on feast days and other holidays. Importantly, conflicts that erupted there always had an audience, making it the center of communication of all kinds. But the tavern was not the only space for conflict. As I have described above, the tradition of calling people out—*herausfordern*—brought tavern conflicts into the streets and squares outside.[100] Other spaces, the church, the streets, the fields, and private houses, were all settings for conflicts and those spaces all influenced how they were carried out, publicized, and resolved.

[100] Other examples: HStAS. B486/Bd 13, pp. 271r, 326r–326v.

5
Conflicts in Public Spaces
The Church, the Street, the Fields, the Road

Taverns and courts were just two of the public spaces where conflicts played out and peace was made. Importantly, both courts and taverns were primarily, although not exclusively, male spaces. Conflicts involving women (as well as young people and children) were more likely to play out in other spaces, such as the village streets, squares, pathways, and fields. In fact, any village space where people congregated could be the setting for disputes, especially the church and the square in front of the church, as well as the mill, the bakehouse, the bathhouse, or the well or watercourse where women did laundry. After about 1700, more prosperous villages built *Amtshäuser* or *Rathäuser*, village and town halls, which were locations for communal meetings and another setting for conflict and reconciliation. While someone's house was increasingly understood to be a private and protected space, the density of villages meant that private houses too had a public character, for people heard and saw what happened there and also went in and out of each other's houses.[1]

The interactions of daily life were revealed in concrete places, and those settings profoundly affected the nature of those interactions. The settings for conflicts and reconciliation can be analyzed along a spectrum of how controlled that space was. Courts were tightly controlled spaces, increasingly governed by written rules and procedure, even if village courts like the one at Wollmatingen still functioned on the basis of custom. Taverns were less regulated, but there too behavior was subject to rules and regulations. Furthermore, tavern conflicts were quite ritualized, usually following a predictable pattern. The spaces examined in the present chapter were less controlled and predictable. Conflicts on the streets, in public squares, even in houses, could develop in a lot of different ways. Fields and the paths through them, and especially roads outside of villages, were even more uncontrolled and also potentially more dangerous to passersby.

Different spaces were also populated by different groups of people. Courts and taverns were predominantly, but by no means exclusively, male spaces. The public

[1] Joachim Eibach, "Das offene Haus. Kommunikative Praxis im sozialen Nahraum der europäischen Frühen Neuzeit" *Zeitschrift für Historische Forschung* 38 (2011): 621–64. Arnold Beuke, "In guter Zier und Kurzweil bey der Naßen angetastet" in Krug-Richter and Mohrmann, eds. *Praktiken des Konfliktaustrags in der Frühen Neuzeit*, pp. 141–2.

Keeping the Peace in the Village: Conflict and Peacemaking in Germany, 1650–1750. Marc R. Forster, Oxford University Press. © Marc R. Forster 2024. DOI: 10.1093/oso/9780198898474.003.0006

spaces of villages and small towns were much more diverse, often dominated by people who appeared less often in courts and taverns, particularly women and young people. Young people were especially active in these spaces, often setting the tone for public behavior on holidays and Sundays. Women, too, often initiated public interactions in the streets and in the fields, making the interactions in these spaces more varied and less predictable.

Village Spaces

One consequence of the increased regulation of behavior in and around churches promulgated by the Tridentine Church was that misbehavior during services could end up in court. Parish churches certainly remained places where all members of the community came together each week, even as new modes of behavior took hold.[2] What took place before, during, and after services was widely known in the village and thus had a special significance.

Conflicts over seats in the parish church became common after the Thirty Years' War, as seats and pews were being installed. Before the seventeenth century, most people stood in church. These disputes could end up in court, and plaintiffs asked courts to formulate rules for possession of chairs. A 1672 case from the village of Allmannsdorf is a typical example of these disputes.[3] Appelonia Röschin and Madlena Weberin filed a complaint that Jacob Ocklin and Caspar Forster wanted to remove them from their seats in the church, which the two women said they had inherited from their mothers. Since these seats were on the female side of the church, the two men were acting in the name of their wives and daughters. Ocklin and Forster claimed that they should have the chairs since they had "come down to them from their ancestors." The court ordered a compromise. Röschin and Weberin were to remain in possession of their chairs and three more chairs could be put in the same area. If the older women, the wives, were not present, the eldest daughters could use the chairs, but the total number of seats could only be five.

A 1685 dispute, also in Allmannsdorf, had a similar feel to it. Martin Waldparth filed suit in the name of his wife, with the goal of preventing Jacob Sulger's wife from removing his wife from the chair "where her mother and grandmother, and also she [had sat] for over 50 years."[4] Furthermore, the chair was in the section for the fishermen's wives, while Sulger was a farmer, and so his wife was not eligible to sit there. On the previous feast day, Sulger's wife had refused to allow

[2] Marc R. Forster, *Catholic Revival in the Age of the Baroque: Religious Identity in Southwest Germany, 1550–1750* (Cambridge, 2001); Bossy, *Christianity in the West*. The feminization of the church in the eighteenth century probably meant men were less present, at least outside of Sundays.

[3] GLAK 61/7600, August 11, 1672.

[4] GLAK 61/7602, p. 54r.

Waldparth's wife to sit, had insulted her as a witch, and had shoved her. Sulgerin claimed her grandmother had had the chair made before leaving for Constance, presumably fifty years earlier during the Thirty Years' War. The court ruled for the complainant, saying Sulgerin had no claim after so many years.

We know that conflicts over seats, and even over places to stand in church, were usually disputes over precedence and status. In the cases above we cannot be sure of the relative status of the women involved, although one might imagine that in both cases the women were defending their position against either new residents or newly wealthy families. The assumption was that seats were inherited, so they were treated as a form of private property. Emotions could be high in these disputes as insulting words were said and physical altercations erupted.

Insults and violence like that perpetrated by Sulgerin were unusual inside churches. Elizabeth Bernhartin did call another woman a witch in the parish church in Mimmenhausen in 1702.[5] In 1669 two men got into a physical confrontation right after taking communion in the church at Rot.[6] But most disruptions inside churches seem to have been caused by younger people. Thomas Stauck, a farmhand, threw "coins" fashioned from nails from the balcony down on the women below.[7] In 1712, the *Aufseher* (supervisor) at the parish church in Allmannsdorf reprimanded a boy for talking and otherwise misbehaving during the sermon, leading to a confrontation with an older man who took exception to the *Aufseher*'s "rude" treatment of the boy.[8] When Stophel Rays drew a gallows on two other men's backs during church services, he claimed he had done so "thoughtlessly."[9] His victims felt otherwise, and successfully filed a slander suit against him at the *Oberamtsgericht* in Mainau.

Churches were partially pacified in this period. Women and young people occasionally came into conflict there, but men generally did not. The fact that church services brought people together did mean that conflicts occurred as people left church. In March 1685, as they were leaving church, one man asked another when he was going to pay off a debt, to which the purported debtor replied, "he owes him nothing more."[10] The creditor struck his opponent in the face. Disputes outside the church were similar to other village conflicts, involving honor disputes, property conflicts, or other vaguely defined issues.[11] Like the tavern, the very public nature of the space in front of the church doors raised the stakes of such conflicts and made the need for a public resolution more pressing.

Processions and local pilgrimages (*Wallfahrten*) were integral parts of religious and community life in these Catholic villages. Parishioners were required to

[5] GLAK 61/13344, p. 371. [6] HStAS B486/Bd 14, p. 112r.
[7] HStAS B486/Bd 13, p. 232r. [8] GLAK 61/7606, pp. 1v–2r.
[9] GLAK 61/7600, September 9, 1672. It is not clear if he actually drew the gallows in ink or perhaps chalk, or just outlined them with his finger.
[10] GLAK 61/7602, March 13, 1685. [11] GLAK 61/13344, p. 417; GLAK 61/7606, p. 43v.

attend, giving these events a role in community life akin to Sunday services. But pilgrimages were hard to supervise and were opportunities for gossip and storytelling, for young folk to mingle and flirt, and for local conflicts to come to the surface.[12] In the early eighteenth century, the communal procession to Wollmatingen seems to have been particularly rowdy. In 1704, Johannes Bronner and Michael Waldbarth from Egg got into a fight after leaving the procession and going to the tavern in Wollmatingen.[13] In 1712, four boys (*Bueben*) from Allmannsdorf got drunk during the journey and ended up fighting each other on the way home.[14] And, in 1727, two men from Oberndorf and Litzelstetten fought with a local man from Wollmatingen.[15] The Wollmatingen *Wallfahrt* was a large event, with groups coming from many parishes in the region to the village. The potential for conflict was then fueled by rivalries between people from different villages and by neighbors and families spending long days together on the road. Men, in particular, also drank during and after the procession, bringing customers to the tavern in Wollmatingen, but also increasing the possibility for conflict.

Villagers clashed on the streets, and these confrontations were almost as public as those in taverns. Witnesses testified to what they had seen and heard, and the parties talked about how insults used on the street, that is, publicly and openly, required a response. Conflicts on the streets, even more often than those behind the doors of the tavern, could also lead to an "appeal for peace" from passersby or a local official like the *Amtmann*. The streets could provide a big audience for conflicts, for children, young people, and women were more likely to be there than in the tavern.

Streets within a town or a village often functioned as extensions of neighboring buildings. This situation was most obvious in the case of taverns, since fights spilled out into the streets when the parties were told to "take it outside" or when drunken men made their way home through the streets. If the crowded space outside the parish church could be the stage for a confrontation, so could the square outside the tavern. Furthermore, the boundary between the house and the street was fluid, despite the theoretical dividing line of the threshold.[16] People came into their neighbors' houses, sometimes uninvited, people could talk to each other through doors and windows, and dense settlement greatly limited privacy. Many people also shared houses with grown children or retired parents, and it was not unusual for heirs to divide a house, usually building a dividing wall. In these situations, the possibility of family conflict was heightened.

Conflicts in villages, then, moved through interconnected spaces, bringing quarrels into the open and communicating the conflicts to widening audiences.

[12] Authorities tried to control behavior on processions, doubling fines for fights: GLAK 61/7604, pp. 89r–90r.

[13] GLAK 61/7604, p. 176v.

[14] GLAK 61/7606, p. 2r.

[15] GLAK 61/13268, p. 321r.

[16] Eibach, "Das offene Haus," pp. 621–64; Kramer, "Das Herausfordern aus dem Haus."

We see, for example, exchanges of insults between men in the tavern spill over into fisticuffs on the village streets. After Jerg Messmer insulted and threw a glass of wine in the face of Joseph Beumer in the tavern in Buggensegel in 1709, he called on Beumer to come out and fight him in the square.[17] Beumer refused and stayed in the tavern until he thought Messmer had left. But Messmer jumped him on the square and beat him up. Something similar happened in Neufrach in 1706, when Gabriel Wilhelm followed Hans Georg Baumann out of the tavern and started a fight.[18] These examples could be multiplied many times over.

Parish festivals were centered on taverns, but they certainly took place out in the streets as well, particularly since one tradition was dancing in front of the inn or on a large public square.[19] At the Owingen *Kirchweih* in 1706, three men dragged Johan Kayster out of the tavern by his hair and beat him bloody, in revenge for insults thrown out in the tavern.[20] Alcohol of course made men particularly belligerent at parish festivals, as at the Owingen *Kirchweih* in 1709, when two men beat up the "watch," local men hired to keep order during the festival.[21]

Events at the 1714 parish festival in Dingelsdorf exemplify how conflicts could move from place to place, thereby drawing more men into the dispute.[22] The conflict began with Thomas Schulter calling Sebastian Spindler a "dog's etc." during the public dance, apparently because of a conflict over a woman. Spindler testified that Schulter then attacked him physically in the tavern, beating him "unnecessarily hard" and bloodying him before bystanders intervened and broke the fight up. At this point, two other men, Joseph Schrof and Jacob Huober, entered the fray, as did Spindler's brother.

What happened next was disputed by the parties. Spindler said he refused to fight his three enemies and headed home. He stated further that Huober and Schrof followed him and beat him so badly he feared for his life. Huober told a different story and portrayed himself as the peacemaker in the original conflict. According to Huober, it was Spindler who called him out and offered to fight on the square, which Huober refused to do, despite Spindler saying "then he, Huober, is not man enough." According to Huober, he and Schrof encountered Spindler later on the streets and asked him why he had insulted them, leading to another fight. Huober claimed again that he was the peacemaker, saying "if he had not gotten in the middle, it could have been much worse."

A witness, Jacob Landuss, testified that he had not seen the initial confrontation at the dance, but did see the conflict in the tavern and had intervened and

[17] GLAK 61/13346, pp. 337–40. [18] GLAK 61/13346, pp. 41–2.

[19] This was a favorite subject for painters. *Kermesse*, by Martin van Cleve, for example (https://en.wikipedia.org/wiki/Kermesse_(festival), and also one by David Teniers the Younger. Perhaps most famous is Pieter Bruegel the Elder's 1567 painting *The Peasant Dance*, which may depict a Kermess or a wedding.

[20] GLAK 61/13346, pp. 62–3. [21] GLAK 61/13346, pp. 400–2.

[22] GLAK 61/7606, pp. 40v–41v.

sent the Spindler brothers out of the *Stube*. Unfortunately, Landuss testified, after a short time the brothers returned to the tavern and the conflict proceeded as Spindler had laid it out. The dance, the tavern, the square in front of the tavern, and the streets of Dingelsdorf were all settings for this conflict involving at least five men, as well as Landuss and perhaps some others as peacemakers. In certain ways, this conflict looks a lot like the standard honor conflicts we have already seen, but by moving around Dingelsdorf the dispute took on a different character. Removed from the more ritualized setting (or stage) of the tavern, it seems to have become more dangerous, as Spindler himself recognized. "Had he not fended off the last blow from Huober, he might have actually been murdered."[23]

Women were more likely to confront a neighbor on the streets than in a tavern or in front of the church. A routine conflict on the streets of Staad reached the *Oberamtsgericht* in Mainau in 1712.[24] Magdalena Schrofin testified that she passed Christina Schonin on the street and Schonin, "without any cause, called after her, saying you should thank God, you loudmouth, you known witch." Schrofin responded in kind, calling Schonin "an old witch." By 1712, the witch insult had lost much of its power, so the court restored both women's damaged honor, but imposed no punishments. This conflict and the court case between women played out without any participation of husbands, fathers, or other male relatives.

What happened on the streets of course drew people out of their houses as well. When two groups of young men insulted each other and brawled on the streets of Dingelsdorf in September 1675, several men came out of their homes to call for peace.[25] Perhaps it was a warm night and windows were open, because the peacemakers clearly heard the exchange of insults on the street. Andres Dembler testified that he heard from his room that Johan Harter had told his opponent (a visitor from another village) that "the Litzelstettener are all whore's boys." Dembler also detailed how the fight moved through the village, from the street in front of his house to the square. Jacob Linse testified that "terrible tumult, cursing, and swearing" brought him and several other men out into the streets to demand peace. One of the brawlers was heard to say "they will have to wait on their peace," and it was this refusal to abide by the call for peace that led the court to fine three of the fighters.

A fight in 1703 between Joseph Weltin "the younger," the local barber, and Joseph Romer, a tailor, further highlights this focus on peace and quiet.[26] The two men had encountered each other outside a drinking establishment (*Schenkhaus*). When Romer said, "who is there," Weltin said "a good friend," to which Romer

[23] Kümin, *Drinking Matters*, uses the metaphor of the tavern as a stage, as does Tlusty, *Bacchus and Civic Order*.

[24] GLAK 7607, pp. 18v–19r.

[25] GLAK 7600, September 28, 1675.

[26] GLAK 61/13268, 80–1.

responded "he did not see it the same way, since the barber was going around outside the house with his coat inside out." Weltin's fashion statement was apparently taken as an insult in this brief confrontation.[27] Now both men were insulted, and Weltin escalated the conflict by standing in front of Romer's house and calling him out. When Romer's elderly mother called down from an upstairs window asking for "quiet and peace" (*ruhe und friden*), Weltin called her an old witch and threw a rock at her. When Romer came to the door, he was hit by another rock that drew blood, so he pulled a knife and cut Weltin's skull and armpit. When the *Jäger*, a local official, arrived intending to end the "tumult," Weltin hit him with several stones, before fleeing the scene. The court took a dim view of these proceedings, fining both men and ordering Weltin to pay the medical costs of the *Jäger*.

This bloody confrontation had elements of both an honor conflict and a more general disturbance of the peace. The old woman's call for quiet and peace echoed the court's concern for public order and the calls for peace in other conflicts, all of which were becoming more apparent in the period after the Thirty Years' War. Villagers shared this desire for peace and acted to limit violence.[28] In conflicts between close neighbors, tensions could become long-standing feuds, as interactions between neighbors were ongoing. In the case of neighboring houses and properties, these conflicts also often involved wayward farm animals and disputed field boundaries.

In the late 1660s, Jacob Peitschern seems to have been a difficult neighbor in the village of Berg.[29] He had a long feud with his direct neighbor, Ulrich Schöllhorn, who in June 1669 grabbed Peitschern by the throat and threw him to the ground. Another neighbor, Jacob Rieger, pulled them apart, but Peitschern started arguing with him as well, at which point Rieger hit Peitschern over the head with a stick. The *Oberamtsgericht* in Rot fined Schöllhorn and Rieger for the violence, but also stated "since Peitschern behaves shamefully with his neighbors, he was reprimanded very seriously."

In August of 1669, Schöllhorn and Peitschern were back in court, with Schöllhorn filing a complaint that Peitschern was illegally grazing horses and cattle. When asked about it, Peitschern had immediately become combative, threatening to drive Schöllhorn from the village.[30] Interestingly, the *Oberamt* sent a servant of the court (an *Amtsknecht*) to interview Peitschern in his house and to repeat the admonition that he should behave more peaceably with his neighbors.[31] Peitschern did not seem happy to have a representative of the lordship in his

[27] Why the inside-out coat constituted an insult is obscure.

[28] Schildt, "Der Friedensgedanke."

[29] HStAS B486/Bd 14, pp. 144r.

[30] HStAS B486/Bd 14, pp. 145r–146v.

[31] This is the only example I have found of the court sending someone out to a village to interview the parties. Usually, the local *Amtmann* was the person who did this. The courts did sometimes appoint "impartial people" to gather evidence on the spot, particularly about boundary disputes.

house and refused to come down the stairs to meet him. The *Amtsknecht*, however, went up to his room to see him and was treated to an extensive tirade about Peitschern's woes. Complaining that his wife and his father-in-law badgered him regularly, he said that they made him feel unwanted in his own house. Although his mother tried to remind him to keep quiet and keep the peace, she also needed to "shut her mouth" more. Peitschern was even "coarser" in speaking about his neighbors, saying they made all kinds of false accusations about him and that Schöllhorn was trying to steal away his wife. When he repeated these opinions, and more, before the *Oberamt* in Rot, he was sentenced to eight days in the tower, so he could think over his "immodest and angry disturbances and his coarse and repeated failures."

These kinds of conflicts among neighbors played out along property boundaries, in the street, and in houses. Here, again, the locations where the conflicts occurred affected their progress and outcome. One senses Peitschern's feeling that he was trapped, in his house by his unsupportive family, and in the village by his obstreperous neighbors. Even his lords, at the monastery of Rot, seemed to be out to get him, sending a court official into his house. We could see him as a difficult and unhappy person; perhaps he was also the victim of the pressure of social discipline imposed by the community and backed up by the authorities. Alternately, perhaps Peitschern was one of the many immigrants who moved into these villages in the aftermath of the Thirty Years' War and either did not understand local traditions or was not welcomed by his neighbors. It is also possible that he married into the village, hinted at in his discussion of relations with his wife and her family.

Conflicts occurred inside houses as well. The most extreme conflicts involved a neighbor entering the house uninvited to confront a resident. House invasions of this kind were very serious violations of community standards as well as the law.[32] This happened in 1706 in Weildorf when, despite an official warning to "keep the peace and quiet," Barthel Scheidegen's wife came into Catherina Amännin's house and called her a witch.[33] After 11 p.m. in February 1672, Martin Rauber forced his way into Joss Rauber's house.[34] The court minutes do not explain if these men were related, but Martin became belligerent when Joss's wife asked him to leave, taking him by the arm, and leading him to the front door. Martin pushed her—saying she had been quite "abrasive" with him and he needed to defend himself—and she fell to the floor, hurting her arm. In one more example, in 1721 Matthias Schroff chased Dominico Brandt through the streets of Dettingen.[35] Brandt took refuge in the house of a local official, the *Jäger*, but Schroff came into the house anyway. In these cases, the courts levied higher fines and punishments for house

[32] Eibach, "Das offene Haus"; Kramer, "Das Herausfordern aus dem Haus."
[33] GLAK 61/13346, p. 34. [34] GLAK 61/7600, February 22, 1672.
[35] GLAK 61/7607, pp. 24r–24v.

invasions, which were considered by definition violations of the peace. In the case above, Schroff was explicitly reprimanded for chasing Brandt into the house. Catherina Amännin testified that her opponent "came into the house at night without knocking...," clearly a violation of community standards.

The village court in Wollmatingen generally punished people severely for invading the house of an enemy in order to confront them. Joseph Bächlin, a smith, came into Peter Merckh's house during the midday meal in June 1716, started a dispute, drew his sword, cursed, and threw things around the room.[36] Bächlin had previously been found guilty in another fight and as a repeat offender was sentenced this time to fourteen days of labor service. The court said this punishment was milder than it might have been, "out of respect for Bächlin's elderly father."

An episode from Sierenmoss in August 1685 shows the high level of sensitivity people had about people coming into their houses and gives some indication of what people considered proper behavior.[37] Hans Jerg Markh told how two men, Carl Röschen and Johannes Sonntag, showed up at his house at night, which made him suspicious, and he brought a complaint to the court, asking "what was the reason for this visit." Sonntag replied he had come with Röschen and had no intention of coming into the house unless invited in. "He came in with good manners (*in gueter Manier*); he has no dispute with the complainant (Markh), and considers him an honorable man." The court absolved Sonntag of any guilt, but Markh had clearly thought something was fishy—*verdächtig*, suspicious, was the word he used—about this late-night visit. Sonntag's use of the phrase "good manners" (*gute Manier*) also lays out a behavioral expectation shared by others. This phrase appears elsewhere in the sources, sometimes meaning that a person behaved *unmanierlich*, that is, badly or with bad manners.[38]

The tradition and the rituals of "calling someone out" (*herausfordern*) both highlighted and blurred the divide between houses and streets.[39] Standing outside of a neighbor's house, a man demanded that his opponent come out, usually to fight. "Calling someone out" challenged another man's honor of course, but Kramer, who has studied this phenomenon, argues that this practice was primarily a violation of the *Hausfrieden*, the protected space of the house. An escalation of this practice was to attack doors and windows, and in the extreme threatening, or even attempting, the destruction of the house. Kramer's study is based primarily on urban sources, and he insists on the centrality of the "peace of the house" in early modern society. The rural communities studied here had a weaker sense

[36] GLAK 61/13268, June 13, 1716, May 16, 1716. [37] GLAK 61/7602, pp. 56v–57r.

[38] GLAK 61/13268, December 7, 1709 (Wollmatingen); GLAK 61/7606, pp. 1v–2r. Compare the discussion of treating people *Con buona maniera* in the Roman countryside: Castiglione, *Patrons and Adversaries*, p. 144.

[39] Kramer, "Das Herausfordern aus dem Haus."

of the divide between house and street; or perhaps the street impinged on the house more easily in a village than in a city.

Calling people out also brought conflicts out of the house and back into the streets. When Jacob Steegmeyer came to Michael Wüest's house in Mittelstenweiler in June 1703, he claimed he behaved with good manners ("*mit guter Manier*").[40] But when he asked Wüest whether he had been near his cherry tree, Wüest responded with insults. Wüest testified however that Steegmeyer had opened the confrontation with insults, and after an exchange of words he called Wüest out of the house. According to witnesses, the two men then continued their dispute in the street and on the square, airing a variety of conflicts over trees, field boundaries, and long-standing insults before coming to blows.

In 1661, Jacob Usel and Maria Sautterin called Georg Bolter Jung out of his house in Allmannsdorf "at night and in the fog."[41] This was an episode in a long-standing feud, involving accusations of theft against Jung and insults between Sautterin and Jung's wife. Usel defended the calling out, saying it happened "as everyone does it." However, calling someone out "at night and in the fog" was not proper, even if calling out in general was normal and apparently common. Similarly, Johannes Schlegel called Georg Golter out at night in Allmannsdorf in 1685.[42] Golter accepted the invitation, and a brawl took place in the street, involving Golter's son and a servant of Schlegel's, as well as the two main combatants.

According to Kramer, the penultimate stage of a conflict involving *Herausforderung* was an attack on the doors and windows of the house.[43] This is what happened in Wollmatingen in 1725 when Joseph Ritter broke down the door of Peter Merchken's house, earning himself a three-day work punishment.[44] Similarly, two men smashed in the windows of Hans Keller's house in 1706.[45] They excused themselves by stating they were very drunk, but also admitted they had "a little hate" for Keller and the other big farmers. The court at Salem was not pleased with this whiff of class conflict in their testimony and fined the guilty men harshly.

Calling people out of their houses and into the streets of the village brought a dispute out of a primarily private context into the public space. Conflicts in fields and gardens were usually less public and thus less dangerous to the parties' honor, but also harder to resolve, since there were usually no witnesses to what was said and done. At the same time, emotions could run high in the fields, which were the source of most people's livelihood and also the places where differences in wealth might be most apparent. When, for example, a wealthy farmer let his herd of cows wander into a field, the damage they did might be a disaster for a small property holder.

[40] GLAK 61/13344, pp. 235–40.
[41] GLAK 61/7599, pp. 11–14.
[42] GLAK 61/7602, pp. 52r–52v.
[43] Kramer, "Das Herausfordern aus dem Haus," pp. 126–9.
[44] GLAK 61/13268, p. 314r.
[45] GLAK 61/13346, pp. 126–8.

Conflicts in the fields also highlight the importance of boundaries of all kinds, as we have already seen in the issue of home invasions. The defense of boundaries was part of defending one's honor and one's family's honor, as Malcolm Greenshields astutely points out in his study of violence in Auvergne. Men and women worked close to one another in neighboring fields, and thus "the fields were more public than one might think. Borders were important and all too easy to violate."[46]

Sometimes it was simply the damage done to a field that caused conflict, as happened in 1704, when Michael Küenle's cows wandered into Georg Fimpern's grain field. Fimpern's wife went to Küenle and demanded he get his cows out of her field, to which he responded by calling her a "used up witch."[47] As was usual in such cases, Küenle claimed Frau Fimpern had also called him insulting names. There was only one witness to this confrontation, the cowherder, who testified that he had only heard the witch insult. In a similar conflict, the widow Neffen hit one of Hans Huober's cows when it went over part of her field.[48] Huober testified "that along with terrible swearing, [the widow] hit the steer hard and in an unchristian way, with a large three-sided stick." The widow's daughter had also hit the steer with a stick. The widow did not deny hitting the animal, but she did not believe they had hurt it badly. Several witnesses testified in this case. One, Johannes Werger, could only pass on hearsay, stating that he had heard that the widow and Huober's wife had exchanged insults. Johannes Werger testified that he was in a neighboring field and had heard the two women "gruesomely insulting each other" and that he had seen the blows. The widow Neff won the case.

Other kinds of disputes also occurred in the fields. Johannes Schroff unjustly threw Anna Weberin to the ground when she was collecting "winter pears" from the ground on his property, something everyone was allowed to do.[49] Johannes Sulger, a fisherman, and Stoffel Hamman, a boatman, fought over the placement of a garden fence in 1713, hitting each other with fence posts.[50] This was the latest act in a dispute going back at least four years.

The disputes in these cases reflect the usual disputes in rural villages, over property boundaries, paths and rights of way ("*Weg und Steg*"), the grazing of animals, and the rights of access to woods and other common property. Of course, disputes of these kinds often played out in court, at meetings of the commune, or in tavern disputes. But they also could take place on the spot, in the fields themselves. In those moments, long-standing disputes might be referenced or, as one woman said in 1714, "she had of course spoken in anger."[51]

[46] Greenshields, *An Economy of Violence in Early Modern France*, p. 75. Also referenced above, Chapter 2.

[47] HStAS B486/Bd 18, 75r–76r.

[48] GLAK 61/6958, March 18, 1671.

[49] GLAK 61/7600, September 22, 1672.

[50] GLAK 61/7606, pp. 11v–12r.

[51] GLAK 61/5174, n.p. April 21, 1714.

Conflicts and violence also occurred outside villages, not just during processions, but at mills and at markets in nearby towns, as well as on the roads in the region. In fact, it is striking how many cases from these settings ended up in the various courts. One factor was that the various lordships wanted to assert their jurisdiction over their territories, including the spaces between villages and towns. Mapping projects, for example the ones undertaken by Salem in the early eighteenth century, are another indication of this interest.[52] Also, people who had been insulted, or had been victims of violence on the road or at a distant marketplace, may have felt their best recourse was to take a case to court. After all, practices of community-based mediation and reconciliation were probably not easily available in disputes that occurred in other towns or on a lonely road in the region.

Cases could come to court when a dispute between subjects took place at a market in another jurisdiction. In 1713, Jacob Bonawer brought a slander suit against Ursula Mestmerin in the court at Mainau, stating that Mestmerin had called him a scoundrel at the grain market in Constance.[53] She had added "grain thieves like him should go to the gallows." Mestmerin defended herself by saying "she had been unable to get any grain at the grain house, because of the many Swiss (buying there) and she had said out of anger that there were so many grain Jews (*Kornjuden*) that it would be better if some were punished, [because] they are driving up the prices...but she had not meant Bonawer." Mestmerin was ordered to apologize to Bonawer and also to not opine about the grain trading of the Swiss.

This case involved two Mainau subjects who brought their dispute before the Mainau court. A more complex dispute came before the *Oberamt* in Salem in 1696, once again involving insults used at a market, which was after all a very public setting.[54] On September 16 of that year, at the annual fair (*Jahrmarkt*) in Markdorf, the local butcher, Kudermann, had confronted Conrad Dreher from Wehrhausen, a subject of Salem. Kudermann was upset that Dreher had called him a scoundrel and had referred to a fine Kudermann had received the year before. The two men confronted each other again several days later at a wedding in Bermatingen, exchanging an impressive string of insults. There were jurisdictional issues in this case, but the Salem *Oberamtmann* pointed to a general agreement between Markdorf and Salem that allowed Salem to punish Dreher, which the *Oberamtmann* did.

The concerns of the authorities for maintaining the safety of roads can be seen in a 1712 case heard at the Mainau court.[55] On the road between Staad and Constance, two local farmers attacked the sacristan from Altnau. The sacristan testified that they stole the small amount of money he had with him and attacked him physically, ruining his shirt and tearing his beard. The attackers resorted to

[52] GLAK 98/2314, 98/2315, 98/2317, 98/2319.
[53] GLAK 61/7606, pp. 44r–44.
[54] GLAK 61/13337, pp. 364–7.
[55] GLAK 61/7606, pp. 32r–v, 47v.

the time-honored excuse that they had been drunk and, in any case, "the fight was not really so rough." But the Mainau authorities expressed concern about "*pro violatione pacis et viae publicae*" (the violation of the peace of the public road) and decided to send the case on to the prince, the Commander of the Mainau House of the Teutonic Knights, an indication of the high importance attached to protecting travelers. The two drunk *Bauern* found themselves in more trouble than if they had fought on the village streets or in the tavern.

Conflicts on the road were often more violent than those on the streets of towns and villages. We have already seen Simon Strigel beat his wife Johanna Silberin on an isolated road, only to have two men come to her rescue. Perhaps it was hyperbole, but one of the men told Silberin he feared that Strigel would kill her.[56] Jacob Hueber and Jerg Schrof, both from Litzelstetten, fought on the road home from Constance.[57] After initially gaining the upper hand, Hueber let down his guard and Schrof drew a knife and attempted to cut Hueber's throat. "If he had not turned his head as he was being cut [testified Hueber], he would have been killed." Schrof of course pleaded drunkenness, but he was imprisoned, fined heavily, and forbidden from carrying a knife in public in the future.

A 1706 fight on a road became more dangerous because both parties were riding horses.[58] Johannes Mäder, a servant, filed a complaint against Jacob Metzger, the *Wirt* in Heiligenberg. Mäder testified that he had a girl with him and that Metzger rode up and ripped the apron from the girl, saying he would return it "if she would let him grope (*greifen*) her." When she refused, Metzger did return the apron, but it fell to the ground and then the girl fell off the horse trying to retrieve it. Metzger attempted to have his horse jump over the girl, but it stepped on her, injuring her quite badly. Metzger then compounded his crime by insulting Mäder and threatening two men who came to help. Metzger responded by saying "they were making more of the thing than it was" and deployed the excuse that he had been drunk. He stated he was sorry the girl was hurt and was willing to come to an agreement with the victim. He was fined three *Gulden*, a hefty fine.

Similarly, Hans Georg Hueber grabbed Bartolome Schiesser by the hair and then "rode over him" with his horse on the road home to Bermatingen in November 1699.[59] Hueber had felt that Schiesser insulted him earlier in the day, when Schiesser and others accused him, Hueber, of throwing a glass of wine behind the oven at a tavern. "The tavern keeper had reminded the farmers that they should drink the wine and not throw it away; it is a gift from God." The men also impugned Huober and his father's honor. When Schiesser refused to greet Hueber on the road later that evening, Hueber got angry and violent.

[56] See above, Chapter 3.
[57] GLAK 61/7606, pp. 19v–20v. March 18, 1711.
[58] GLAK 61/13346, pp. 323–5.
[59] GLAK 61/13340, pp. 393–6.

These kinds of confrontations were not unusual on the road. On the return trip from a pilgrimage to Hegne in May 1712, Johannes Schulter's daughter told everyone that Hans Jerg Minderlin had vomited from drunkenness at the shrine.[60] Minderlin was insulted by this statement, as well as by the girl reminding Minderlin's sister of her punishment with the stocks the previous week. Minderlin admitted that he had lost his temper and struck Schulter's daughter with "several slaps," although Schulter testified that she had been knocked to the ground several times. In another case, the court minutes do not explain what five men were fighting about on the road home in August 1703, but they were all fined by the court at Mainau.[61] The man who bit another man's hand and feet received a double fine.

A case adjudicated in several sittings at Mainau in March and April 1661 provides an excellent example of the interplay between the authorities' interest in keeping the roads safe and the local people's sensitivity to insult.[62] The defendant was Johannes Reuss, a resident of Dingelsdorf. When a drunken Reuss stumbled into the tavern in Dingelsdorf, Christoff Baitz, a merchant from Riedlingen, who was spending the night at the tavern, pointed him out to a local friend of his, Johannes Romer. Baitz told Romer that earlier that evening, while riding from Constance to Dingelsdorf, he had encountered Reuss, who was holding a club and demanded that he stop. In Baitz's telling, he had pulled his sword (*Degen*, rapier), spurred his horse, and attempted to ride past Reuss, who held up his club in a threatening way. Baitz struck the club with his sword, hitting Reuss's finger. Reuss' story was different. Yes, he had been on the road, but he had fallen down just before Baitz came by.

> He [Reuss] had called out 'who goes there,' but Baitz had right away insulted him as a highway robber, and also called him a murderer. When he [Reuss], denied this, saying he is an honorable man and a subject of Mainau and born in Dingelsdorf, then Baitz rode back at him, with his sword drawn and rode up to him, so he got up, holding his club over his head, and Baitz struck at him, which he parried with his club. He, Reuss, called after him that he would find him and they would see about those insults.

When the two men confronted each other at the tavern in Dingelsdorf, Reuss calmed down and offered to share some wine with Baitz and make peace. Baitz, however, insisted on bringing the case to the authorities in Mainau.

The court in Mainau treated this as a case of highway robbery and a violation of public order, although Ruess clearly believed it was an issue of personal honor that could be solved by sharing some wine. The court explicitly stated it wanted to

[60] GLAK 61/7606, pp. 21v–22r.
[61] GLAK 61/7604, pp. 152–3.
[62] GLAK 61/7599, pp. 85–89, 101–3.

make an example of Reuss, especially for his use of a weapon, sentencing him to eight days in prison on bread and water. It did not forget the men's honor, however, requiring Reuss to apologize and "removing all the insults in the name of the authorities."

Mills, which were located outside of villages, were another location where conflicts could erupt. Partly this was because the all-important grain was processed there. Furthermore, people needed to trust millers, since they could not be watched while they ground the grain, and stories about millers stealing grain were common. Farmers brought their grain to the mill in labeled sacks and later returned to pick them up. When Schwalt Branstetter, the tavernkeeper's stepson in Steinbach, went to pick up his father's sack of grain at the mill in July 1703, it could not be found right away and he attacked the miller's servant, Georg Haubern, with insulting words.[63] The slander case ended up in court, although the sack had eventually been found intact.

Mills were also locations where men came together, and they were therefore public settings where disputes could be aired. It is not clear why Hans Schöchler, the baker at the monastery of Ochsenhausen, beat Michel Betscher bloody one night in 1664 at the mill in Bachen.[64] Betscher reopened hostilities "later" at the tavern in Berkheim. In August 1666, Hans Simbler, a weaver, insulted Hans Hasen at the mill in Rot, in a dispute over fishing in the millpond.[65] This dispute was also continued in the tavern later that day, but fortunately an older widow was able to explain an earlier agreement over fishing, thereby defusing the conflict. We find ourselves back at the tavern, for mills and taverns were linked, just like the road and the tavern. The mill and the tavern were predominantly male spaces and spaces dominated by propertied men as well.

Roads, and to a lesser extent markets and mills, were very much liminal spaces for early modern rural people. The inhabitants of the villages of Southwest Germany were certainly not isolated from the wider world, nor did they live their lives out without leaving their villages. They went on pilgrimages, both local ones and more regional ones. They traveled to markets in cities like Überlingen and Constance, and they interacted with the monastic communities who were their neighbors and lords. Village taverns hosted travelers of all kinds, local merchants, soldiers, Jewish horse traders, and journeymen artisans. Servants and farmhands came to the prosperous villages of upper Swabia from the mountains of Switzerland and the Swabian Alb region. Yet ultimately the experience of people remained profoundly local throughout this period, bounded by the practices, traditions, and legal systems in place. As people moved further from the center of the community, courts became more useful for the resolution of conflicts; over time courts also became more useful even within the community.

[63] HStAS B486/Bd 18, pp. 36r–37r.
[64] HStAS B486/Bd 13, pp. 341v–342r.
[65] HStAS B486/Bd 14, pp. 44r–44v.

Discussion and Publicity in the Public Space

The parties to disputes were always concerned about the public nature of those conflicts. This concern was most obvious in the case of honor disputes. An insult, slanderous talk, or any impugning of someone's honor was more damaging if it took place in front of other people, particularly if it was a large number of people. The same was true of acts of reconciliation, which also needed to be witnessed by others in order to be effective. The authorities were well aware of the importance of publicity in general, which is why punishments, especially shaming punishments like exposure in the stocks, were designed to humiliate offenders in front of their neighbors.

The careful attention paid by everyone to the audiences and actors in public spaces was closely related to a heightened awareness of the role of storytelling, gossip, and rumor in rural society. This was a concern shared by higher authorities, local officials, and the wider population. Everyone wanted to know what was being said, who was saying it, and how many people had heard the stories. In a face-to-face world characterized by oral communication, a person's honor and reputation were constantly framed and reframed by these rumors and stories.[66] Of course people with power had some ability to suppress stories and rumors, and indeed to promulgate their own truths, but so did the wider population. Testimonies in local courts show that women were particularly active in telling and spreading stories and, despite efforts to minimize their talk as "women's gossip" (*Weibergeschwätz*), this ability gave them power.[67]

The courts attended to this issue in several ways. First, under pressure from those who believed themselves to have been slandered, they demanded that people bring evidence to back up insults, accusations, and other stories spread about others. Secondly, they investigated rumors and gossip, especially when they considered them dangerous to the authorities themselves or their reputation, with the purpose of identifying and punishing those who spread the stories. Finally, the punishments they meted out were designed to label the guilty parties as dishonorable, disreputable, and thus unqualified to tell "true" stories. In the small territories of Southwest Germany, the authorities and the courts were close enough to the day-to-day realities of rural life to increasingly intervene in this level of local communication; how successful they were in suppressing rumors and gossip is harder to determine.

As Pia Holenstein and Norbert Schindler argue, the elite attack on "uncontrolled talk" was aimed at the common folk, most of all women and children.[68]

[66] Walz, "Agonale Kommunikation"; Schlögl, "Kommunikation und Vergesellschaftung under Anwesenden"; Schlögl, *Anwesende und Abwesende*.
[67] Holenstein and Schindler, "Geschwätzgeschichte(n)," esp. pp. 49–69.
[68] Holenstein and Schindler, "Geschwätzgeschichte(n)," pp. 41–7.

Already in the fifteenth century writers expressed concern about the ways gossip could damage a person's reputation, a concern further reinforced by religious reformers of all kinds in the sixteenth century. Not surprisingly, by the eighteenth century *Geschwätz* or *Klatsch*—gossip and scandal mongering—were labeled as characteristics of an irrational and dangerous popular class and unworthy of *Hausväter*, administrators, and educated men. This perspective can be seen in the work of the courts in Southwest Germany, but also in the concerns of local people, who also had good reasons for trying to control rumor and gossip.

On November 18, 1673, the Chancellor and *Oberamtmann* at the monastery at Salem were shocked to receive a letter from a number of important officials in the Imperial City of Constance, including the City Council and the commander of the Imperial garrison there.[69] The letter asked Salem officials to punish the Salem *Hofmeister*, Hans Hewdorf, for spreading fantastic rumors about Colonel von Buechenberg, one of the military commanders in Constance. The Empire was at this time embroiled in a European war that had begun in 1672 with Louis XIV's invasion of Holland. In the fall of 1673, French armies advanced into the Palatinate and Alsace, bringing the war to southern Germany.

According to the letter from Constance, Hewdorf had told a group of drinking companions at the tavern in the Salem village of Owingen that Colonel von Buechenberg was planning on betraying Constance to the French. The story was quite specific, and the Constance letter framed it as an affront to the colonel.

> [Hewdorf said] that the lord Colonel wants to surrender his post to the French, [and that] the King of France will stay incognito overnight with him. Also, the *Hofmeister* (Hewdorf) went further, insulting that the lord Colonel as a s.h. scoundrel and a thief and repeated his words, the devil should take him if he surrenders the city of Constance.

Hewdorf and several witnesses were brought to Salem to testify a couple of days later and a more elaborated version of this story emerged. Various men had participated in the discussion at the tavern, and they had discussed how the colonel was planning on leaving three gates open in Constance and that both Constance and Überlingen would be surrendered to the French the same day. Then the King of France, disguised as a knight, together with a lord from Switzerland, or perhaps with a high prelate, would ride into the city. In a further twist, some people claimed to have heard that the colonel had been arrested.

The story was far-fetched enough that the officials at Salem could dismiss it out of hand, although it surely says something about the hold Louis XIV had on the

[69] GLAK 61/13334, November 18, 1673, November 22, November 23, December 5. The *Hofmeister*, as we saw before (Chapter 2), was an administrative official at the monastery, a kind of chief operating officer.

European imagination in the late seventeenth century. The primary concern of the authorities was with the spread of this rumor and the fact that it was a libelous attack on Colonel von Buechenberg. The witnesses all claimed that the story was "common knowledge (*gemeine Sage*) in the region." Several of the tavern group were from the Swabian Alb region, and they had said that it was "common knowledge on the Alb."[70] Blasi Hallmer, a carter at Salem, said he had heard this story while waiting outside the gates of Überlingen, where he had gone to hear a sermon. Those discussing the rumor there included a young maid who spoke about "all kinds of conflicts and bad things," as well as people from at least two other Salem villages. In the end, Hewdorff and Hallmer were convicted of defaming the Colonel and punished with imprisonment.

The investigation determined that this rumor about this particular colonel was widespread across the region and beyond. While some specifics varied—would the King of France be accompanied by a Swiss nobleman or a high-ranking prelate?—the basic story was more or less the same. It was spread of course in taverns where, as Hewdorf said, men were talking about "the war and soldiers." The story was also told in other places where people gathered, as outside the city gates early in the morning. The Salem authorities wondered if it would be spread further during a region-wide procession to the shrine at Birnau. In all these settings the rumor was also debated and questioned. Hewdorf was skeptical that one man could open as many as three gates, but one of the Swabians suggested he could send his bodyguards to do so. And, of course, it was impossible for the investigators to nail down the details of the story, let alone determine who had started the rumor.

In this case Salem officials, including the prince-abbot himself, pushed this investigation forward out of alarm about their relations with important neighbors and military officers. But their concern for the honor of Colonel von Buechenberg was not really that different from their attention in 1684 to the honor of the two Schön girls, who were rumored to have cooked a mouse while naked. In that case (see above, Chapter 3), the court at Rot an der Rot also rejected the story out of hand, but had then sought to determine who had started and spread the story. Rumors, gossip, and storytelling were considered dangerous at all levels of society, for they had the potential to start or inflame conflicts, damage people's honor, and undermine peace.

David Sabean distinguishes levels of talk or storytelling (*Gerede*) in rural communities. Gossip (*Plauderei*, *Geschwätz*) was troublesome but not usually considered a serious threat to anyone, especially if it was labeled women's gossip

[70] The witnesses who testified at Salem did not know the names of these men, whom they called "the Swabians" and the "man from Laiz," a town near Sigmaringen in the Alb region.

(*Weibergeschwätz*).[71] *Geschrei*, most commonly translated as rumor, was more serious. These were stories that required a response, the kind of rumors we have seen leading to slander cases in court or to violence in the streets.[72] The word implied that the rumors were widely known, and "public" and important in the widest sense. At the broadest level, there was *Sage*, a word that meant "common knowledge."[73] This was the word used to describe the rumors about Colonel von Buechenberg at Constance. These levels of rumor were of course linked—extensive gossip could, over time, lead to full-blown rumors and even common knowledge across a whole region.

These same words appear regularly in local court records, although they are not always used as precisely as Sabean describes them. In the 1670s, the court in Mainau regularly heard cases that originated with gossip spread by women. In response to an accusation of stealing, the court opined "such a case is only women's gossip and complete nonsense [*lauter lari fari*] without any proof, and thus there will be no decision made."[74] When a dispute between several women and their maids broke out in the village of Egg, the court heard testimony and then ruled "...it is all just women's gossip...and the whole thing is dismissed by the lordship."[75] Similarly, in 1656 Martin Landegg filed a slander case against Oswald Wideman for having said in a tavern that Landegg had been previously expelled from his village.[76] When Wideman denied ever having said such a thing, Landegg backed off, stating that the whole issue was probably just "plain old women's gossip" (*lauter Weibergschwätz*).

Although courts, and some men, were inclined to dismiss conflicts and insults that originated in women's gossip, women's words were nonetheless usually investigated before being dismissed. Maria Clergin filed a slander suit against Anna Maria Messmerin, stating that Messmerin had been telling people that Clergin had had a child and had been "beaten with sticks" presumably as a punishment for bearing an illegitimate child.[77] Four witnesses testified in the case, as the court tried to trace the origins of this story. The court finally concluded:

> since the complainant can prove nothing and the accused only admits what she has heard said, the whole thing looks like women's and street gossip (*weiber und gassen geschwetz*). As a result, we consider the complainant an honorable person, since no one can say much or even a little against her, and therefore the

[71] Sabean, *Power in the Blood*, pp. 147–9. See also Holenstein and Schindler, "Geschwätzgeschichte(n)," esp. pp. 70–1.

[72] The noun *Geschrei*, from the verb *schreien* (scream, cry, shout), carries the meaning of loudness, of a widely heard rumor.

[73] Sabean, *Power in the Blood*, pp. 195–7.

[74] GLAK 61/7600, June 11, 1672. For more detail about this case, see the discussion above in Chapter 2.

[75] GLAK 61/7600, April 29, 1673.

[76] HStAS B486/Bd 13, pp. 122r–122v.

[77] GLAK 61/7600, May 4, 1675.

> lordship orders that everyone stop (repeating) such stories (*Nachreden*) about her.

Clearly, gossip or rumors of this kind were serious enough that people sometimes brought them to court. And the court could not dismiss them without an investigation, even if the case was ultimately dismissed as "just gossip." Furthermore, everyone was keenly aware that gossip could lead to more serious disputes. A 1672 exchange between two women in the village of Staad—labeled "women's gossip and exchange of words"—led to a larger conflict when one of the women accused a fisherman of stealing some fish.[78] After further testimony, the accusation turned out to be true and several men were fined. There was clearly a tension here between a tendency on the part of the authorities to dismiss women's words and the reality that women regularly brought cases and testified in court, and that their words could have consequences.

There is little doubt that people, men as well as women, feared women's words. In 1674, Barbara Zimmermännin, a seamstress from Wollmatingen, came to the court in Mainau, demanding to know why Jacob Geiss, the *Amtmann* in Litzelstetten, had forbidden her to enter his village.[79] The implications were that she was not an honorable person, and she wanted her honor restored. Geiss denied he had forbidden Zimmermännin from entering Litzelstetten, but did say that she was charging too much for her work and that "she should shut her angry/evil mouth (*böss Maul*) and stop setting people against each other." The court restored her honor, but also ruled she should not overcharge for her sewing and that she should stop gossiping and causing conflict in the village. In this case it is hard to determine which issue was more important, Zimmermännin's gossiping or the regulation of wages. Furthermore, as an outsider and a person who apparently moved from place to place for work, the seamstress appears to have been considered particularly disruptive.

Spreading gossip or passing it on could take stories from the category of gossip to a more dangerous realm of *Geschrei*, or rumor. It was obvious to everyone that someone who spread a story widely was doing significant damage to another's honor or reputation. A man was reprimanded in court for "thoughtlessly telling people" that he had seen a soldier with stolen money.[80] Johann Baumann, the *Amman* and tavernkeeper in Staad, brought charges against two women who were "telling people in various places that he was watering the wine and selling it to customers."[81] The two women claimed they had heard the story from a Georg Kertz, and Kertz said he had overheard it from the window of his house. One of the women was reported to have had her son write about the watering of the wine to the officials in Mainau. Local gossip spread to other villages and reached the

[78] GLAK 61/7600, May 7, 1672.
[79] GLAK 61/7600, August 27, 1674.
[80] GLAK 61/7600, May 11, 1672.
[81] GLAK 61/7600, June 11, 1672.

ears of the authorities, then became an accusation and a threat to someone's honor, and finally found its way to the court. Perhaps naïvely, officials and the courts seem to have believed that if they could just quash the gossip and rumors, they could limit an important source of conflict in these communities.

One more example shows both the way rumors spread and how seriously the courts investigated them. In fact, courts both lamented the danger of rumor mongering, and also often took it seriously as information about possible crimes. This seems to have been the situation in a 1672 case from the village of Nussdorf.[82] Georg Urnauer filed a slander suit against Jacob Ogglin, Michel Bonawer, and Catharina Morgin, all residents of Allmannsdorf, who had been saying that Urnauer had had an adulterous affair with the wife of the innkeeper. When called to testify, Ogglin said he had heard the whole story from Bonawer. Bonawer in turn claimed that Casper Hamman from Staad, and two other men, had "explicitly" stated the story was true. Hamman in turn said he had heard the story from several residents of Oberuhldingen when they were crossing Lake Constance together with a load of manure. Finally, Catharina Morgin testified that she had heard about the adultery from her mother, who was Urnauer's sister-in-law. Five people testified in this case, and they named five others who had passed on this rumor, from at least four different villages. The willingness of the court to hear all of this testimony points in several directions. Officials in Mainau probably wanted to find out if the adultery had taken place, so they could fine the guilty parties. Secondly, they took the slander charge seriously and wanted to know who was the source of the rumor. Finally, it seems to have been important for them, and for Urnauer the complainant, to know how and how far this rumor had spread. What they found out could not have been reassuring to Urnauer, who was hoping to quash the rumor altogether.

A case from the summer of 1684 further shows how rumors functioned. Johannes Fux from Dingelsdorf was brought to court by Jacob Bürckhofer for having called Bürckhofer's daughter a whore in the tavern there.[83] Fux admitted to the charge, but said that he did it because the rumor was spreading through the whole village that *he* had gotten Bürckhofer's daughter pregnant. The court was somewhat sympathetic to Fux's plight, especially since Bürckhofer had come after him with an ax. But the court pointed out that Fux should have attacked the "*delatores*," that is, those who had defamed him, rather than the daughter, and he was fined.[84] The court, and presumably the whole village, found that both Fux and Bürckhofer had a legitimate complaint. The rumor aimed at Fux was serious and needed to be quashed, but Fux's slander of Bürckhofer's daughter was also deserving of punishment.

[82] GLAK 61/7600, May 21, 1672, May 28, 1672.
[83] GLAK 61/7602, pp. 22v. . . . *in dem ganzen Dorff verschreyt* . . .
[84] Bürckhofer was also fined for the attack with the ax.

As Sabean argues, the term *Geschrei*, rumor, implied something more serious than gossip. The word itself indicates that the story is being shouted out, perhaps creating an uproar. The word also appears more often in the court records in the early eighteenth century than earlier. In 1702 the rumor in Egg was that Benedict Bronner had been sleeping with a servant girl from Switzerland.[85] This rumor (*Geschrei*, *Rede*) led to an investigation and Bronner's punishment. In 1711, Franz Meith charged Isar Jacob with passing on a rumor (*spargieren)* that the *Amman*'s daughter had made a promise of marriage with an unsuitable man.[86] Finally, in 1715 the *Amman* in Litzelstetten complained that Jerg Scherer and his wife "had spread rumors here and there" about him, accusing him of shortchanging them on some wages.[87] The *Amman* stated that the Scherers were constantly criticizing him for what he called "trivialities."

Of course, if rumors spread more widely, they became more dangerous. Andreas Rosenhardt filed a complaint against the musician Johannes Kop, who had told a smith that Rosenhardt's daughter was unhappy with the marriage her father had arranged.[88] Kop's defense was that he was just repeating a story he had heard from a soldier. Kop was fined, but Rosenhardt could not have been happy that his daughter's marriage was being discussed by disreputable types like musicians and soldiers. As we can see, rumors that ended up as the subject of slander cases often focused on sexual behavior. In a typical case, Hans Jekh defended himself in 1706 against Georg Müller and his mother, Ursula Sträubin, who had spread the rumor that Jekh was having sex with a maid, including talking about it to the parish priest and the authorities at Rot.[89] Jekh was no doubt particularly upset that the story had been told to his superiors.

If the rumors were about a local official, as happened in 1705 in Litzelstetten, they were taken very seriously.[90] Maria Baumgärtin had said that "it was a rumor (*Geschrey*) repeated by many" that the *Amman*, Simon Riehle, wanted to drive Johannes Schulter's children from their house and farm. The authorities in Mainau explained that the *Amman* was operating correctly in giving the lease to the farm to someone other than the Schulter children. Maria was reprimanded and punished for coming into the *Amman*'s house to make this accusation.

Stories could evolve from gossip (*Geschwätz*), to rumor (*Geschrei*), to common knowledge (*gemeine Sage*) quickly. And, in the hurly-burly of everyday life, these categories often overlapped. Indeed, as we have seen, people used a wide range of words to describe the transmission of stories. A 1711 case from the Mainau court shows the changing language used around a particular story. Basche Thumb from Millhalden filed a suit against Joseph Schrof from Allmannsdorf, stating that Schrof had spread the rumor (*habe ihne verschreyt*) that Thumb had fathered an

[85] GLAK 61/7604, pp. 116–17.
[86] GLAK 61/7606, 1711, pp. 4v–5r.
[87] GLAK 61/7606, 1715, p. 10v.
[88] GLAK 61/7606, 1712, pp. 7v–8r.
[89] HStAS B486/Bd 18, pp. 149r–149v.
[90] GLAK 61/7604, pp. 182v–183r.

illegitimate child with a widow.[91] Schrof's defense was that this story was "widely known" (*ein durchgehender rueff*) and that he had heard from another man that "the lower district was full of this rumor" (*daß die undere Gericht von diser fama voll seyen*). This story, then, was first described as a rumor, but in the court hearing it became a widely told story, even common knowledge in a whole region. Schrof was using a common form of defense in these kinds of cases, claiming he was just repeating a rumor that was (already) widely known.

Lorentz Waldraff used the same defense when he was accused by Johannes Schroff of telling people that Schroff had said that he did not want any priests in Dingelsdorf.[92] According to Waldraff, it was a commonly and widely held view (*eine gemaine durchgehende rede seye*) that Schroff held such anti-clerical views. The court in Mainau did not generally accept this defense, however. In October 1710 the court fined a woman who had accused two men of stealing fruit.[93] Her defense, that she had heard this story from another woman who said that it was "common knowledge in the community" (*in der Gemeind ein gemaine Sag*), did not persuade the court to let her go without a fine.

Public Spaces, Communication, and the Peasant Public Sphere

The spatial perspective situates interpersonal disputes concretely in everyday life, broadening our understanding of how people in the past interacted, fought, and made peace. Furthermore, where any dispute, including local political conflicts or even resistance and rebellion, took place played a role in how those conflicts were communicated. Look, for example, at the difference between the many tavern conflicts and the disputes that erupted on village streets or on the roads between settlements. The details of a street fight probably became common knowledge in the village, known by the *Dorfauge*, or "village eye," but generally did not go further unless the case went to court.[94] A fight on a lonely road might never become public. A tavern dispute also had a strong local character of course, but we have seen how words exchanged there could spread quickly and widely beyond the local community.

Beat Kümin has argued persuasively for the crucial role of the tavern (or public house) in communication in early modern Europe.[95] The evidence from Southwest Germany confirms much of his argument. Stories like the one about the colonel who would betray Constance to the French spread through tavern talk. Rumors became especially dangerous when someone repeated them in a

[91] GLAK 61/7606, 1711, pp. 17v–18v.
[92] GLAK 61/7606, 1710, pp. 34r–v.
[93] GLAK 61/7606, 1710, pp. 55r–55v.
[94] Eibach, "Das offene Haus," pp. 633–4.
[95] Kümin, *Drinking Matters*; also Beat Kümin, "Wirtshaus, Verkehr, und Kommunikationsrevolution im frühneuzeitlichen Alpenraum" in Dürr and Schwerhoff, eds. *Kirchen, Märkte, Tavernen*, pp. 376–93.

tavern in front of many people, including travelers from other places. Yet rumors about the treacherous colonel also spread in other ways, at gatherings at the gates of a city or during a pilgrimage.

An examination of the interplay between gossip, rumors, and public knowledge provides a useful window on communication at the local and regional level.[96] Various groups of people were concerned about the spread of rumors, from the parties in a dispute to the subjects of a slanderous rumor, to local officials trying to keep the peace. It was, however, not really possible to control the spread of stories of any kind. At times officials and the courts seemed surprised, even shocked, at how quickly rumors could spread. It does not perhaps surprise us that an adulterous affair became a topic of discussion in four or five villages, or that a woman could broadcast the accusation that an innkeeper was watering his wine across the region, but we should remember that the stories were mostly passed on by word of mouth.

Kümin takes his analysis of communication a step further, arguing that taverns were essential for the development of the public sphere in seventeenth- and eighteenth-century Europe.[97] This argument is a critique of Jürgen Habermas' influential study of the development of the "bourgeois public sphere."[98] Habermas posits that the tavern was replaced by the coffeeshop as the meeting place of the middle-class men who developed a new kind of public sphere in the eighteenth century. Recent studies, including Kümin's, indicate that traditional meeting places, like taverns, inns, and pubs, continued to host groups of politically engaged men across the eighteenth century and beyond. Furthermore, people of all social classes interacted in taverns, and in other places as well, and they debated and discussed political developments in their communities and region. This was true of the taverns of rural Southwest Germany, which were the nodal points of popular communication and formed the basis of a popular public sphere.[99]

The way stories spread through communities and then to other villages is just one part of how communication functioned. Interactions between the authorities and their subjects can be followed easily in the court records. People brought cases to the court, looking for a decision or a negotiated solution. Local officials, especially the village *Amtmänner*, reported violations of the law to their superiors, paying particular attention to those committed by groups of young people and marginalized people, like servants, vagabonds, and Jews. And the authorities

[96] On communication, esp. Schlögl, "Kommunikation und Vergesellschaftung under Anwesenden"; Schlögl, *Anwesende und Abwesende*. Also, Holenstein, "Klagen, anzeigen und supplizieren."

[97] Kümin, *Drinking Matters*, esp. ch. 5, pp. 185–9.

[98] Jürgen Habermas, *The Structural Transformation of the Public Sphere: An Inquiry into a Category of Bourgeois Society* (Princeton, 1991). Original German 1962.

[99] Following Kümin, *Drinking Matters*, esp. p. 11. See also Michaela Schmöltz-Häberlein, *Kleinstadtgesellschaft(en): weibliche und männliche Lebenswelten im Emmendingen des 18. Jahrhunderts* (Stuttgart, 2012).

communicated regularly with their subjects by court decisions, as well as by decrees and ordinances. Fines, imprisonment, and work punishments conveyed a message about who held power and what they thought was a serious crime. Shaming punishments and mandatory public apologies were even more obviously designed to communicate a message or make an example of someone, and at times the courts explicitly said so.

The kind of communication we see here was in many ways very traditional. Stories were passed on by word of mouth, carried by people going to market, visiting family, or by itinerant merchants. Journeymen artisans traveled from place to place, as did servants and farmworkers looking for work. People met at weddings or celebrations of baptisms. Even the kind of communication that took place through the administration of justice was not new. The Abbots of Salem or the Commanders of the House of the Teutonic Knights at Mainau had been dispensing justice for centuries. The nature of this communication, however, intensified after the Thirty Years' War. Trade increased and rural regions were tied more closely into a wider market economy. Postal systems developed and they depended on a network of taverns and stables to function properly.[100] Even smaller lordships intensified their governance, issuing ordinances and actively seeking to promote economic growth and discipline the population.[101]

The daily lives of the people who lived in the villages and small towns of Upper Swabia were affected by these changes, and they themselves participated in the intensification of communication. Again, much of this communication worked in time-honored ways. People gossiped and spread rumors, often out of plain old curiosity, but at times as a way of enforcing community norms. When women gossiped about an adulterous relationship in the community, they were surely enforcing certain norms. When stories spread about an abusive husband, or a woman who stole food, or a tavernkeeper who watered his wine, other community values—and fears—were brought into play.

Peasants also took cases to the courts in increasing numbers in the century after the Thirty Years' War. This development points to a more intensive interaction between local communities and the state. Now it is important to recognize that the state in this region was underdeveloped compared to the larger German states, not to mention France or Britain. The small principalities of the region had limited resources, almost no military or police forces, and a small bureaucracy. Furthermore, the people who ran these territories were neither physically nor socially that distant from the villagers they governed. The Cistercian abbots and monks at Salem, for example, were almost all the sons of farmers and small-town

[100] Behringer, *Im Zeichen des Merkur*.

[101] Marc Raeff, *The Well-Ordered Police State. Social and Institutional Change through Law in the Germanies and Russia, 1600–1800* (New Haven, 1983); Theodore Rabb, *The Struggle for Stability in Early Modern Europe* (Oxford, 1975); Wilson, *Heart of Europe*.

artisans of the region.[102] The communication between people and the state, then, was characterized by a certain familiarity, if not sympathy between the parties. The willingness of the courts to handle cases that might appear trivial or unimportant is one indication of this understanding.

The fate of Johanna Silberin, the innkeeper's wife from Mimmenhausen, who in the 1690s was expelled from Salem territory, is an example of these developments.[103] Even as daily life in the villages remained primarily face-to-face and personal, people were increasingly embedded in structures characterized by administrative and judicial systems organized by educated administrators around written records. Johanna ended up in deep trouble with the Salem *Oberamtsgericht* because someone, probably the secretary of the court, went back through the court minutes and found the dozen or more cases involving the *Wirtin*. The court was thereby convinced, or convinced itself, that Johanna Silberin had demonstrated a pattern of immoral and criminal behavior that demanded a severe punishment. But the closer and more intense interactions between the courts and the villages, between the state and the people, were not just the result of initiatives from above. They also responded to the needs of the population itself.

[102] On Salem, see above, Chapter 1, with secondary references.

[103] See above, Chapter 3.

6
A System of Conflict Resolution and the Search for Peace

Rural society was riddled with conflict, as we have seen in the previous chapters. Not surprisingly, people also regularly expressed a desire to maintain peace and order. Of course, this desire was common for people living in traditional societies, which generally valued, in theory at least, the maintenance of traditional social structures and ways of behaving. It is only natural that the Thirty Years' War should strengthen and highlight this desire.

We have already examined in detail the nature of conflicts in rural society in the period after 1650, as well as the ways those conflicts were adjudicated in lower courts. Rural people of all kinds, from propertied peasants and their wives, to servants and farm laborers, used the judicial system to resolve disputes and in the process shaped the courts to their needs. We also know that the courts were only one part of a system of conflict resolution that included mediation and negotiation, and various forms of self-help.

The Notion of Public Peace

Throughout its long history, the Holy Roman Empire was a structure that was supposed to keep the peace. The imperial reforms of the late fifteenth century aimed to create peace, culminating in the Emperor Maximilian's "Eternal Public Peace" (*Immerwährende Landfrieden*).[1] The most effective and most durable of the institutions of the Public Peace were judicial, the Imperial Chamber Court (*Reichskammergericht*) and the Imperial Aulic Council (*Reichshofrat*). Of course, imperial institutions and structures had failed to prevent or end the Thirty Years' War, but for much of the German elite the Peace of Westphalia (or rather the Osnabrück part of that treaty) was, as Siegrid Westphal argues, "regarded as a renewal of the Augsburg settlement and as a legal update of the Public Peace...."[2] Furthermore, after 1648 the Emperor and the Imperial Diet generally agreed on

[1] Wilson, *Heart of Europe*, ch. 12; Siegrid Westphal, "The Holy Roman Empire of the German Nation as an Order of Public Peace" *German History* 36 (2018): 401–14.

[2] Siegrid Westphal, "The Holy Roman Empire of the German Nation" *German History* 36 (2018): 409.

Keeping the Peace in the Village: Conflict and Peacemaking in Germany, 1650–1750. Marc R. Forster, Oxford University Press. © Marc R. Forster 2024. DOI: 10.1093/oso/9780198898474.003.0007

the necessity of imposing imperial bans on any polity that violated the Public Peace.[3] Although there were few cases of actually deploying these bans, Westphal nevertheless maintains "...that one can assume a broad acceptance and internalization of the terms of the whole system of public peace."[4]

Perhaps the rarified air of the constitutional history of the Holy Roman Empire tells us little about the experience of most Germans. Still, the "internalization" of the idea of *Landfrieden* among the German princes and the political elite carried over into the administration of the territories of the Empire. And imperial courts, especially the Imperial Chamber Court, influenced judicial practice throughout the Empire.[5] As Peter Wilson argues, "peasants generally developed a favourable view of the Empire's supreme courts, whose adherence to standardized procedures often contrasted with seemingly capricious seigniorial justice."[6] As the new judicial practices trickled down to territorial and local courts, common folk used them more frequently, reinforcing the process of juridification. Furthermore, many princes pursued a policy of *Bauernschutz* ("peasant protection"), which used law courts to protect peasants from "lordly exploitation." The German *Rechtsstaat* of the modern period, the state under the rule of law, was influenced by the evolution of justice in the Holy Roman Empire.[7]

One aspect of the response to the Thirty Years' War, then, was a renewed emphasis on the idea of peace at the Imperial level. A second response was the development of stronger state structures in the territories of the Empire. In the 1970s and 1980s, English language scholars could read the works of Theodore Rabb (*The Search for Stability in Early Modern Europe*, 1975) and Marc Raeff (*The Well-Ordered Police State*, 1983), both of whom saw the war as the catalyst for the development of stronger states. Rabb, a wide-ranging historian of England and the Renaissance, wrote from a broad comparative perspective. In describing the impact of the war, he quotes Blaise Pascal and John Locke, as well as Grimmelshausen, in arguing that "the revulsion against the excesses of war was one of the fundamental reasons that stability returned in the mid-seventeenth century."[8] One aspect of this drive for stability was that the "forces of control," that is, the states, used military force and more effective government to enforce peace. The war ended, witchcraft panics died out, and peasant revolts became less frequent. Rabb says, tantalizingly, that "the result [of this process] (and to some extent the cause) was a renewal of calm in the countryside. Villagers were forced to adjust to new norms imposed from above...."[9] We will return to the question

[3] A person, even a prince, could be put under the Imperial Ban, making them an outlaw and subject to arrest and execution. Perhaps the most famous ban was placed in 1621 on Frederick V, the Elector Palatinate, for accepting the title of King of Bohemia from the rebellious Bohemian estates.

[4] Westphal, "The Holy Roman Empire of the German Nation," p. 410.

[5] Wilson, *Heart of Europe*, p. 628.

[6] Wilson, *Heart of Europe*, pp. 632–7.

[7] This argument follows Wilson quite closely.

[8] Rabb, *The Struggle for Stability*, p. 124.

[9] Rabb, *The Struggle for Stability*, pp. 95–96, quote p. 96.

of the role of the rural population and whether peasants were the cause or a target of a drive for social stability and state-building.

Marc Raeff was a historian of Imperial Russia who compared state development in Russia and Germany.[10] Raeff studied *Polizei and Landesordnungen*—police and territorial ordinances—promulgated by German territorial states across the early modern period. The ordinances certainly aimed at strengthening the state by codifying law, but they also sought to actively intervene in everyday life to regulate and encourage agriculture, manufacturing, and trade. Raeff argues that "there was an uneasy compromise between the passivity of traditionalism and the dynamics of modernity" in this program.[11] Furthermore, "in the course of the seventeenth century, in addition to the rationalism and voluntarism that never disappeared, a strong note of pragmatism, or of reliance on the lessons of experience, emerges."[12] Raeff links this activist and pragmatic approach directly to the Thirty Years' War, as the "interests of the country as a whole had to be put uppermost and made the object of legislative action" as a means to repair the damages done by war.[13] Like Rabb, he argues that a primary consequence of the war was the strengthening of the state.

In his 1980 study *Das Zeitalter des Absolutismus. Gottesgnadentum und Kriegsnot*, Hartmut Lehmann focused on the negative side of the seventeenth century. For him, the crises of wars and economic downturn led to a psychology of fear and anxiety, not just during the war, but throughout the seventeenth century.[14] Lehmann's study focuses on the history of Christianity, which he sees caught in multiple tensions. One tension was between the support of absolute monarchies by established churches and the opposition of some religious groups to the state. At the same time, the history of Christianity was "also determined by the secular catastrophe of the seventeenth century, during which the question about the power of good and the power of bad was insistently placed in the world, making the search for a way out of the misery of central importance."[15]

On the one hand, Lehmann points to the negative consequences of this crisis and the wide sense of despair, distress (*Not*), and fear it engendered. This fear, he argues, fed the witch hunts and attacks on Jews. Meanwhile, religious literature focused on consolation, funeral sermons, and apocalyptic writings, as people

[10] Marc Raeff, "The Well-Ordered Police State and the Development of Modernity in Seventeenth and Eighteenth-Century Europe" *American Historical Review* 80 (1975): 1221–43.

[11] Raeff, "The Well-Ordered Police State," p. 1226.

[12] Raeff, "The Well-Ordered Police State," p. 170.

[13] Raeff, "The Well-Ordered Police State," p. 172. For a critique of Raeff, see James Van Horn Melton, "Absolutism and 'Modernity' in Early Modern Central Europe" German Studies Review (1985): 383–98.

[14] Hartmut Lehmann, *Das Zeitalter des Absolutismus. Gottesgnadentum und Kriegsnot* (1980). Lehmann was born in 1936, so his work reflects the perspective of the German post-1945 generation. It also connected to the literature on the "Crisis of the Seventeenth Century."

[15] Lehmann, *Das Zeitalter des Absolutismus*, p. 18.

waited for direct intervention from God. Lehmann posits another response as well, the development of ideas around *Leistung*, achievement, particularly through work. Lehmann's focus is on the European elite, particularly the German Protestant elite. From this perspective, the crisis of the seventeenth century, particularly the long war, changed the orientation of society and culture. Peace treaties aimed at "subordinating the great war machines...to the dictates of reason of state, while there was also a securing of political order through absolutism and a strengthening of economic conditions through mercantilism...."[16]

These grand overviews from the 1970s and 1980s are logical and persuasive, even if they reflect the modernizing theories and focus on absolutism characteristic of those times, as well as the personal experiences of the post-World War II generation. Surely the Thirty Years' War demanded a response and a search for stability and order that was not just logical, for it also meshed with cultural values of this society, such as notions of discipline and order (*Zucht und Ordnung*). In the past twenty years historians have dug deeper into German society and politics and not surprisingly have found that the memory of the war resonated not just among the political and religious elite, but at all levels of society.

As Wilson states in his history of the Holy Roman Empire, "...the Empire's political institutions and practices were rooted in society and shared its strengths and weaknesses."[17] This was a hierarchically organized society with a strong corporate element. Sheilagh Ogilvie illuminates this point further:

> The Thirty Years' War laid the basis for German absolutism, as is so often argued; it also created a resilient system of constraints on that absolutism, by forcing many German rulers to grant favours to corporate groups within their own societies in order to tax, conscript, and regulate their territories to the degree necessary to survive the war.[18]

Using the example of Württemberg, Ogilvie demonstrates that the state needed local elites in towns and villages to govern effectively. The central government in Stuttgart installed paid bureaucrats at the district level and gave pastors important roles, but at the local level guilds, the *Ehrbahrkeit* (elite) of the towns, and landowning peasants shared the governing functions, such as manning the lower courts, collecting taxes, and regulating economic activity. Most of the time these corporate bodies cooperated with the directives of the state, but they could make life very difficult for administrators if they did not support government initiatives.

[16] Lehmann, *Das Zeitalter des Absolutismus*, p. 18. [17] Wilson, *Heart of Europe*, p. 485.

[18] Sheilagh Ogilvie, "The State in Germany. A Non-Prussian View" in John Brewer and Eckhart Hellmuth, eds. *Rethinking Leviathan. The Eighteenth-Century State in Britain and Germany* (Oxford, 1999), pp. 177–8.

Like Oglivie, David Sabean's complex and nuanced discussion of *Herrschaft* (lordship) emphasizes the corporate nature of the state in Württemberg (and elsewhere), but he also points to the ways in which the population was complicit in its own domination.[19] Focusing on the practice of *Herrschaft*, Sabean argues that:

> ...we can see how community was subject to a massive interpenetration of Herrschaft at many different levels, and that the dynamic in *Herr/Knecht* relationships was not only on the side of surplus extraction but also on the side of rendering services and legitimizing both rents and peace-keeping.[20]

As is often the case with Sabean's work, there is a lot packed into that sentence. However, the last point, the question of peacekeeping and justice in the aftermath of the Thirty Years' War, highlights an important development at the local level.

Peacekeeping and Justice at the Local Level

At the level of villages and small towns, peacekeeping involved preventing and resolving conflicts. A wide range of local studies show that people used informal methods of conflict resolution—negotiation, mediation, arbitration, or violence—and that they also used formal methods, that is, they went to court.[21] These strategies were neither mutually exclusive, nor were they necessarily hierarchically understood.[22] Some disputes went quickly to court, but were then resolved informally. Other conflicts dragged on as kinds of feuds. Courts themselves could negotiate settlements or send people away without a decision, often suggesting and even ordering mediation.[23]

Peter Wettmann-Jungblut, for example, argues that drinking increased in eighteenth-century Baden, leading to an increase in conflict and violence. As this violence increased, villagers turned to local courts as a kind of "alternative public space" or "wider public space."[24] It would seem that these people did not consider courts as instruments of an interventionist state, but rather as useful tools in local

[19] Sabean, *Power in the Blood*, Introduction, esp. pp. 20–7.

[20] Sabean, *Power in the Blood*, p. 25. "Herr/Knecht relationships" refers to the ties between ruler and subject and landlord and employee.

[21] Benoît Garnot, ed. *L'Infrajudiciaire du Moyen Age à l'époque contemporaine* (Dijon, 1996); Benoît Garnot, "Justice, infrajustice, parajustice et extra justice dans la France d'Ancien Régime" *Crime, Histoire, et Sociétés* 4 (2000); Francisca Loetz, "L'Infrajudiciaire. Facetten und Bedeutung eines Konzepts" in Blauert and Schwerhoff, eds. *Kriminalitätsgeschichte*, pp. 545–62.

[22] Esp. Barbara Krug-Richter, "Konfliktregulierung"; Dinges, "Justiznutzungen als soziale Kontrolle."

[23] Schäfer, "Frieden durch Recht"; Frank, "Ehre und Gewalt im Dorf der Frühen Neuzeit."

[24] Wettmann-Jungblut, "Modern Times, Modern Crimes" in Habermas and Schwerhoff, eds. *Verbrechen im Blick*; Wettmann-Jungblut, "Gewalt und Gegengewalt."

conflict—perhaps better for peace and order than the tavern and at times more effective than mediation or negotiation.

Studies also show that local courts appear to have become increasingly popular, that is, that they were used more frequently after 1650, although this is of course very difficult to substantiate.[25] In most places the majority of cases adjudicated were brought by local people, not by officials.[26] Local courts provided inexpensive justice and reached decisions fairly quickly.[27] Another reason for their popularity was that juries and often judges were local men and the courts were "instruments of village society," as Michael Frank argues in reference to Lippe.[28] Even historians like Karl Härter, who argue that the state benefited from the greater tendency to "go to justice," admit that the population cooperated with and supported judges and other legal officials.[29] Furthermore, a successful justice system (in the sense that it was used by people and its decisions respected) had to reflect social norms to function effectively. Here, several developments appear to be occurring together. First, people used courts because they fulfilled a social need for peace-making, securing order, and maintaining community. Secondly, state officials tried to use courts to establish and strengthen norms coming "from above."[30] Third, effective courts, used frequently by villagers and townspeople, gave prestige and legitimacy to the authorities (the *Obrigkeit*) that provided them.[31]

To follow Harriet Rudolph's study of the Bishopric of Osnabrück, in the long run a good system of law and justice could contribute greatly to the process of turning subjects into obedient citizens of the state (*Staatsbürger*). However, this did not occur through social disciplining by state officials, but rather in the ongoing practice of a legal culture that emphasized the regulation of local conflict, the limitation of damages, efficiency, pragmatism, and the sensible individualization

[25] Krug-Richter, "Konfliktregulierung"; Krug-Richter, "Von Rügebrauch zur Konfliktkultur": Krug-Richter, "Von nackten Hummeln und Schandpflasten"; Barbara Krug-Richter, "'Mann müßte keine leute zuhause hangen.' Adlige Gerichtsherrschaft, soziale Kontrolle und dörfliche Kommunikation in der westfälische Herrschaft Cannstein um 1700" *Westfälische Forschungen* 48 (1998): 481–509.

[26] Hohkamp, *Herrschaft in der Herrschaft*, ch. 4.

[27] Wettmann-Jungblut, "Modern Times, Modern Crimes"; Wettmann-Jungblut, "Gewalt und Gegengewalt." Compare Crubaugh, *Balancing the Scales of Justice in Revolutionary France*.

[28] Frank, *Dörfliche Gesellschaft und Kriminalität*, p. 217.

[29] Karl Härter, *Policey und Strafjustiz in Kurmainz: Gesetzgebung, Normdurchsetzung und Sozialkontrolle im frühneuzeitlichen Territorialstaat* (Frankfurt, 2005); Karl Härter, "Strafverfahren im frühneuzeitlichen Territorialstaat. Inquisition, Entscheidungsfindung, Supplikation" in Blauert and Schwerhoff, eds. *Kriminalitätsgeschichte*, pp. 459–81.

[30] Härter calls this the work of the "pedagogical state" in his study of Kurmainz.

[31] Schäfer, "Frieden durch Recht"; Magnus Eriksson, "Gemäßigte Gewalt und andere Wege zur Interessendurchsetzung auf der Insel Unmanz bei Rügen im ausgehenden 16. und in 18. Jahrhunderts" in Eriksson and Krug-Richter, eds. *Streitkulturen*, pp. 125–55; André Holenstein, "Introduction: Empowering Interactions: Looking at Statebuilding from Below" in Holenstein et al., eds. *Empowering Interactions*, esp. pp. 16–28; Sanne Muurling, *Everyday Crime, Criminal Justice and Gender in Early Modern Bologna* (Leiden/Boston, 2021), esp. pp. 88–90.

of punishments.[32] Lower courts, says Michaela Hohkamp, were used by the population "as a way to resolve conflicts," not as "an instrument of control in the hands of the authorities."[33]

André Holenstein has linked the work of local courts with the idea of "state-building from below." The Baden courts he studied all deployed a discourse of order—or rather threatened order—to support their work at the village level. This discourse used a range of words to show the level of disorder.

> The village world was threatened and endangered by all kinds of disorder, injustices, and damaging behavior; by inequality, slovenliness, and bad housekeeping; by carelessness and delinquency, sleepiness and idleness, exuberance and excess, and by high-handedness and lack of care.[34]

This language came out of the world of the village and informed how the local courts functioned.

It is worth stepping even closer to this effort to bring peace, order, and stability by returning to look at the day-to-day functioning of a local court, this time the court at the monastery of Rot an der Rot.

The Abbey of Rot an der Rot and its Law Court

The Premonstratensian Abbey of Rot an der Rot is located in prosperous farming country in Upper Swabia, between Memmingen and Biberach. Founded in the twelfth century, in the early modern period the abbey was *Reichsunmittelbar* (an independent lordship, subject directly to the Emperor), and the monks governed a small but fairly enclosed territory of about a dozen villages. The population of the territory when it was secularized in 1803 was about 3,000.[35] Most of the village parishes were incorporated into the monastery and were served by monk-priests, rather than secular clergy. This territory had little in common with even middle-sized states of Southwest Germany like Württemberg or Baden-Durlach, let alone the large states of Prussia or Bavaria, other than the fact that the abbot had a seat in the *Reichstag* like all other princes.

[32] Harriet Rudolph, "Eine gelinde Regierungsart" in *Peinliche Strafjustiz im geistlichen Territorium. Das Hochstift Osnabrück (1716–1803)* (Konstanz, 2001), esp. pp. 35, 345–50.

[33] Hohkamp, *Herrschaft in der Herrschaft*, p. 186.

[34] Holenstein, "Ordnung und Unordnung im Dorf" in Häberlein, ed. *Devianz, Widerstand und Herrschaftspraxis in der Vormoderne*, p. 170.

[35] Hermann Tüchle, Adolph Schahl, and Joachim Feist, *850 Jahre Rot an der Rot: Geschichte und Gestalt: neue Beiträge zur Kirchen- und Kunstgeschichte der Prämonstratenser-Reichsabtei* (Sigmaringen,1976); "Rot an der Rot" in Wolfgang Zimmermann and Nicole Priesching, eds. *Württembergisches Klosterbuch. Klöster, Stifte und Ordensgemeinschaften von den Anfängen bis in die Gegenwart* (Sigmaringen, 2003).

The ties between the monastery and the local population were intimate, if not always friendly. Unrest in the fifteenth century brought a threatening crowd of local peasants into the monastery itself, and in 1456 peasant leaders negotiated an agreement with the abbot in person, giving peasants the right to pass on their tenancies to their children. Local peasants were part of the rebellious bands that plundered the monastery several times during the Peasants' War in 1524–5. There were confrontations between peasants and the monks in 1609 and 1612, with the peasants again defending their right of *Erblehen* (inheritance of tenancies) from attempts to roll back the 1456 agreement.

The Thirty Years' War brought repeated plundering of the monastery and the surrounding region. The monks abandoned the monastery for long periods of time and the region was regularly crisscrossed by campaigning armies. It was also a preferred area for quartering soldiers, and the rural population suffered severe population losses, probably between 30% and 50%.[36] In 1658, the monks examined their financial records and reported that "because of the recent war, hunger, and pestilence, everything has declined and the debts and income [listed] in the books are lost, in the amount of 30,000 *Gulden*. In particular, in the district *auf dem Berg*, one can hope for nothing, except from Thomas Teuffler."[37] The post-war period was a time of rebuilding, population recovery, and institutional renewal.

The abbey had exercised lower judicial authority (*Niedergerichtsbarkeit*) over its subjects since the founding of the monastery and gained all judicial rights when it purchased the right of high justice (*Hohe—or Blutsgerichsbarkeit*) in 1616. A full series of *Protokolle*, or minutes, survive from the district court of the monastery, the *Oberamtsgericht*, from 1648 to 1802.[38] The records of this lower court are an excellent source for the study of the experience of the population in this period, as well as of the governing methods of the lordship, the monastery of Rot.

The *Verhörprotokolle*, or hearing minutes, of this court show that this was more than a law court. Always presided over by the *Oberamtmann*, the highest secular official of the abbey, both the cellarer (*Cellarius*, *Grosskeller*) and the abbot himself were at times present. Abbot Martin Ertle (abbot 1672–1711) was particularly inclined to attend these hearings, as he did for example four times in 1684.[39] Hearings were held weekly throughout the year at the monastery, and sometimes more often. In 1684, several "extra-ordinary" hearings were held, including one

[36] These numbers continue to be disputed. See Wilson, *The Thirty Years' War*; John Thiebault, "The Rhetoric of Death and Destruction in the Thirty Years' War" *Social History* 27 (1993): 271–90.

[37] HStAS B486/Bd 13, 202v.

[38] HStAS B486/Bände 12–38. There are also some *Protokolle* from the 1550s to 1648, which I have not examined in any detail.

[39] Martin Ertle (1641–1712) was born into a farming family in the nearby Allgäu region, another way Rot was connected to the rural society around it.

off-site in the village of Haisterkirch, where an important inheritance was investigated and recorded.[40]

The recording of an inheritance reveals one of the important functions of this court. It functioned as an administrative body (or a kind of notary), recording inheritance agreements, debts, marriage contracts, and some larger property transactions. Some similar courts, for example the court of the Teutonic Knights at Mainau, were places where local people even recorded smaller purchases and sales, for example of livestock. The Abbey of Rot, in order to protect its rights over its serfs, carefully recorded each *Todfall* (*heriot*), manumission of serfs, transfer of a tenancy, and the acceptance of new serfs, mostly as a result of marriages. Beyond the protection of its feudal rights, however, the abbey was providing a basic administrative service to its subjects, a place to record transactions and agreements that kept the social and economic life of the community functioning.

We can see the mix of roles played by Rot's court if we look at an individual hearing day.[41] On February 25, 1681, the *Oberamtmann* dealt with eight cases. First, Endreas Reisch from Haslach was fined for hosting a party, with musicians, on the final Thursday of *Fastnacht* (Carnival). The young men who attended the party were also fined. Then Martin Hörle was fined 10 *Gulden* for admitting that he had dishonorably visited a maid the previous year. The *Oberamtmann* informed Martin that he was lucky not to have also been jailed. This case was followed by the recording of debt in Kirchdorf, a manumission in Unteropfingen, and the purchase and takeover of a tenancy.

After these routine matters, the court faced a more complex case involving a child born out of wedlock, a deadbeat father, and the provision of child support for the mother and baby.[42] The final two cases heard that day were more routine, one a case of the death of a tenant and the inheritance of his tenancy, the other the recording of an agreement to pay a retiring farmer an annual fee for the rest of his life.

On that February day in 1681, the court dealt with a variety of issues, some administrative and fiscal, one, the illegitimate child case, more of a negotiation, and two, the party at *Fastnacht* and the premarital sex case, that were matters of levying fines, since the guilt of the parties was not in dispute.[43] The Rot court, however, also played a directly judicial role about half of the time. It was the place where local people could bring complaints against neighbors, negotiate and adjudicate disputes and find a way to keep the peace, provide stability, and maintain order.

[40] HStAS B486/Bd 15, 198v. There were fifty hearings held during 1684, a fairly typical year.

[41] HStAS B486/Bd 15, 8r–10v.

[42] HStAS B486/Bd 15, 9v. This case will be discussed in more detail below.

[43] Here, again, I think that the guilty party saw the fine as the cost of doing business. How the guests/customers felt about their fines is harder to guess at.

I have not located any ordinances that directly proscribe how the court functioned, but it appears that the *Oberamtmann* assessed fines on his own and oversaw the recording of important agreements. But there was also a jury that made decisions in disputed cases. So, in a May 1659 case, the jury consisted of Martin Lütz, *Gerichtsamtmann* and an innkeeper in Rot itself, Hans Hanckler, another *Amtmann*, and Sebastian Schöllhorn. These were clearly important men in their communities, two of them serving as *Amtmänner*, but they were local men, aware of the local traditions and customs that came into play in many cases.

A System of Conflict Resolution

We will return to the question opened above concerning the development of the state.[44] First, however, it is important to outline the way disputes were resolved at the local level. We have already seen how conflicts proceeded, often beginning with verbal clashes, moving to physical violence, and then ending up in a court case. The sources, especially the protocols of court proceedings, of course foreground "going to justice" and obscure other forms of peacemaking such as negotiations or mediation and other forms of informal, non-judicial conflict resolution. Nevertheless, court records do provide evidence of a widespread culture that put great value on finding settlements (*Vergleiche*). In this world, the dividing line between an informal resolution and an agreement reached through the judicial system was not clear cut. One reason we know about agreements is that they were brought to the *Oberamt* to be documented and that they were recorded in the protocols of the courts, right next to the adjudication of cases of insults and tavern brawls. The courts of the monastic lordships of Rot, Mainau, and Salem recorded many marriage contracts, inheritance negotiations, and retirement agreements, as well as sales of land and livestock. In this way, the *Oberamt* functioned as a kind of notary, where rural people, mostly propertied men, could securely preserve the documentation of important settlements they had negotiated with their neighbors.

This story is, however, more complicated. Some of the agreements had not been finalized when they were brought to court, so the court hearing served as the setting for further negotiation. This was particularly the case for negotiations around debts, since creditors could, and did, use courts as a place to both record agreements and enforce payment. Demands for payment often led to the court mediating a reduction in debt or an arrangement for payment. The discussion of property sales would sometimes require the appointment of an *Unparteiischen*, an impartial person or assessor, or some other kind of arbitrator, to determine a

[44] See below, Chapter 7.

fair price or inspect property boundaries. The courts also intervened paternalistically and regularly in family disputes, seeking to encourage domestic peace. Behind all of this activity was the idea shared by rural people and officials that the goal of the system of conflict resolution was to preserve peace and order in the community.

People with property felt a need to record important agreements with the *Oberamt*. This desire dovetailed with the traditions of these monastic lordships, who had been recording property donations and transactions for centuries, since the founding of the monasteries.[45] Furthermore, after 1650 these lordships kept careful documentation of the status of their serfs, placing those records in the *Oberamtsprotokolle*. These records included manumissions, death fees, and listings of new serfs. One consequence of this notarial work is that the officials who worked at the *Oberamt*, including judicial officials and even the monks themselves, must have developed a good sense of what was happening at the villages. The court decisions they reached and the negotiations they conducted often reflect this intimate understanding of the communities they ruled over.

At the same time, we should not over-romanticize the relationship between these lordships and their subjects. By carefully recording every death of a serf at Rot and the resulting fees, the monastery made sure it got every *Pfennig* it was legally allowed. So, in 1684 the protocols state: "Georg Zedle from Haslach buys his deceased wife's cow and clothes heriot with 7 ½ *Gulden*, which he also laid down and paid off in cash."[46] On that same day in January 1684, Michael Spürgele bought his freedom from serfdom for nine *Gulden*, declaring his intention to move away. The *Oberamt* also documented that Spürgele, despite his new status fas a free man, would be subject to all fees and dues if he were to claim a part of his father's inheritance in the future.[47] These lordships were engaged in a tightening of their enforcement of serfdom, as were others across the region.[48]

The Rot minutes are particularly valuable, because they document a wide range of administrative actions mixed in with the judicial decisions. People came to the monastery to document complex marriage arrangements, as did Hans Lingen and Maria Zimerlin on April 24, 1684.[49] These were propertied people, with Maria bringing a farm tenancy to the marriage and Hans contributing 500 *Gulden* in cash. Their marriage was complicated by the fact that Maria was a widow with

[45] The Cistercian Monastery of Salem (Salmansweiler) was founded in 1136. The Premonstratensian Monastery of Rot an der Rot was founded 1146. The Mainau Commandery of the Teutonic Knights dates from 1272.

[46] HStAS B486/Bd 15, pp. 155r (January 21, 1684). This was a fairly small heriot fee. A few weeks later a man paid 22 *Gulden* after his father-in-law's death and another man paid 10 *Gulden* 15 *Kreuzer* for his father's *Todtfahl*. HStAS B486/Bd. 15, p. 157v. Fees for men were larger than for women.

[47] HStAS B486/Bd 15, p. 155r (January 21, 1684).

[48] Compare Luebke, *His Majesty's Rebels*; Sreenivasan, *The Peasants of Ottobeuern*; Hohkamp, *Herrschaft in der Herrschaft*.

[49] HStAS B486/Bd 15, pp. 161v–162v.

four children and two stepchildren from her late husband's first marriage. The marriage arrangements explained how all those children were to be treated and even discussed various scenarios involving the deaths of Hans and Maria.

Older people, if they had significant property, often needed to make complex financial arrangements at the time of their retirement from farming. In January 1684, Georg Ruessen from Bachen dispatched his wife and two "supporters" or witnesses (*Beistände*), as well as his son Otmar, to Rot to have a retirement agreement put to protocol.[50] Due to poor health, Georg was no longer able to manage his farm, which was a sought-after *Erblehenhof*, an inheritable tenancy. His retirement coincided with the impending marriage of his daughter Johanna to Jacob Hörnle, when the young couple was to take over the tenancy, valued at 770 *Gulden*. In order to make this possible, Otmar, a son from Georg's first marriage, had to be paid 115 *Gulden* in cash so that he would give up his claims to the farm. Georg also asked that Johanna house his two younger daughters, both minors, until they were 15, at which point they could choose to go into service, marry, or work for their older sister. The new couple agreed to support their elderly parents for the rest of their lives with a bed, a room, food, as well as one *Malter* rye, four *Viertel* wheat, lard, fifty eggs, and two *Viertel* of flax each year.[51] Finally, the groom's brother, currently living at the monastery of Ochsenhausen, was given money by the groom's father in exchange for relinquishing any claim to his brother's new farm.[52] Provisions were also made for payment of all fees due to Rot, for the transfer of the tenancy, the marriage, and the eventual death fees for the older Ruessens.

People also recorded their wills at Rot, often in the form of an "inheritance agreement." Hans Schön, the tavernkeeper in Berkheim, who had regularly appeared at the Rot court in the 1650s and 1660s in conflict with Hans Pfalzer, the *Amman* there, believed he was on his deathbed in May 1684.[53] He called his wife and his two sons-in-law to his bedside, as well as two important men, Georg Pfalzer, the *Amman* in Berkheim, and Hans Ruedmüller, from Bachen, as witnesses. He asked his wife if she would be willing to forgo any inheritance from his estate, "in consideration of their unsupported children." She said that she was satisfied with what she had already received from him, and "with a hand shake (*hand gegebner true*), she explicitly agreed and promised." Schön then asked the witnesses to report this promise to the monastery, "so it could be called up in the future." Schön, like Georg Rüssen, Hans Lingen, and Maria Zimerlin, wanted to

[50] HStASt B486/Bd 15, pp. 144v–147r.

[51] A *Malter* was 150 liters, a *Viertel* presumably 1/4 of that, so 37.5 liters.

[52] The sources say that this brother was "at the monastery of Ochsenhausen." Probably he was working there, but sons of *Bauern* did become monks at Ochsenhausen, so this brother might have been a monk.

[53] HStAS B486/Bd 15, p. 166v.

make sure his decisions were written down and would be available in the future, so as to avoid possible confusion or conflict.

Despite efforts to formalize and record inheritance agreements, there could always be disagreements among heirs. An example from the village of Litzelstetten, a village ruled by Mainau, can stand for many of these disputes. On May 13, 1684, Thomas Giss came to the court at Mainau to complain that his two siblings, Jacob Giss and Maria Gissin, were refusing to give him the half *Jauchert* vineyard their father had willed to Thomas.[54] Thomas pointed out that, since his father's last wishes had been witnessed by the parish priest in Dingelsdorf (a neighboring village) as well as by a Meister Melchior, then surely the *Herrschaft* had no desire to overturn the will. Furthermore, Thomas argued, he deserved special consideration since he alone had cared for their father in his last years. Jacob, in turn, argued that their father's estate was encumbered with many debts that he and Maria would have to pay off. But he left an opening for an agreement, stating that "they would not be against coming to a legal settlement and leaving a whole *Vierling* of vineyard to the *Proponenten* (i.e., Thomas)."

The court decision was a compromise that reflects the pragmatic way in which the courts engaged many issues they faced, particularly in property disputes. First, the court stated that it was not the practice or the tradition in the lordship to disinherit a legitimate heir. But, it went on to say, the Giss inheritance was difficult, because of "the great weight of debts and small size of the property." The court seized on the suggestion of Jacob Giss and ruled that Thomas would get one *Vierling* (quarter) of the disputed vineyard "free and clear," while the other two heirs would split the rest of the vineyard and all other property and house furnishings. Thomas was credited for the care he had given his father, but also reminded that he alone had profited from the use of the vineyard during his father's lifetime.

There are a number of elements of this case that illuminate the process of conflict resolution in these communities. Local notables, in this case a parish priest and another man (Meister Melchior) witnessed the father's will.[55] The dispute over the vineyard was a property issue, but other factors, such as the history of relations in the family, were considered important as well. And, although both sides argued their positions, Jacob's suggestion of a compromise shows that the parties were not averse to an agreement. The court, in turn, saw itself as a venue for such a compromise, took a pragmatic view of the framework of "practice and tradition," and ordered a settlement. It is a sign of the court's desire to bring about

[54] GLAK 61/7602, pp. 15v–16v. *Jauchert*: an old field or area measure; it was the southern Baden version of a *Morgen*, which was 36 *ares*, just over a third of a hectare. A *Viertel* was 9 ares. The English equivalent was the morning or the yoke.

[55] It is also possible that they helped write the will, since we do not know how literate the elder Giss was. They may have participated in the negotiations around the original will as well.

a peaceful solution that it explained its reasoning and gave credence to both sides' arguments.

People also recorded property sales at the *Oberamt*. Some were quite simple, like the sale of the cow in Haslach in 1668 or the sale of a piece of land for 26 *Gulden* in Wallhausen in 1710.[56] Not surprisingly, most sales recorded in the *Oberamt* protocols dealt with more involved transactions. When Michael Schüller went to sell a small field in Bonlanden to his son-in-law for 23 *Gulden*, he also recorded a number of other financial commitments, for example that Schüller would pay the interest on the 23 *Gulden* his son-in-law had to borrow to buy the land and that he would take care of various fees owed to Rot.[57] The son-in-law wanted to build a house with a tile roof on this property, and the *Oberamt* offered him half of the tiles for free and would sell him the other half for 5 *Gulden*. More often it was large sales that were documented, particularly in the early eighteenth century. Sales recorded in the Mainau Hearing Protocols (*Verhörprotokolle*) in 1710 were almost all for larger sums of money, 100 *Gulden* or more.[58]

Sales of livestock were not recorded as often in the protocols as sales of land, but disputes over livestock sales did come to the courts. Here again we see the courts grappling with the nitty-gritty of rural life. When Caspar Knecht brought a suit to the court in Mainau to force Sebastian Romer to pay for two cows he had bought, the court heard testimony about how the two cows had died from a cattle pest and that the executioner in Romer's village had declared the cows rotten (*faul*).[59] In this case the court cited the *Landesrecht*, the laws of the region, and ruled that cows could not be returned to the seller after the purchaser had possession of them for more than four weeks. Although Romer was somewhat vague about when the cows had died, the court found a middle ground by ruling that one cow had died four weeks after the sale, the other five weeks, meaning that Romer had to pay Knecht for only one of the two animals.

Later in 1687, the same court heard a case about the sale of a horse. In some ways this was a similar case, since the complainant, Georg Romer, had sold a horse to the defendant, Conrad Forster, and the horse turned out to be sick and "unusable."[60] In this case Romer had warned Forster that there was a problem with the horse, but Forster bought it anyway. When he rode the horse home, it collapsed, making it clear he could not use it to pull a plow. Forster returned the horse the next day, but refused to pay the "costs" of the sale, which in this case was the cost of the wine the two men had consumed at the tavern while negotiating

[56] HStAS B486/Bd 14, pp. 112r–v; GLAK 61/7606, p. 11v.

[57] HStAS B486/Bd 15, pp. 144r–114v. January 10, 1684.

[58] GLAK 61/7606, pp. 2r, 3v, 9r–9v, 15r–15v, 21v–22r, 23r–23v, 23v–23a.

[59] GLAK 61/7602, January 14, 1687. The executioner (*Scharfrichter*) was probably also the veterinarian. See Kathy Stuart, *Defiled Trades and Social Outcasts: Honor and Ritual Pollution in Early Modern Germany* (Cambridge, 2001).

[60] GLAK 61/7602, 1687, 8 October.

this sale. The court ruled that Forster was "by the custom of the region" allowed to return the horse, but that, as the buyer, he had to pay for the wine.

When serving as a place for people to record marriages, retirements, and inheritances, and when adjudicating sales of property and livestock, the courts operated in a space somewhere between a notarial office and a law court. In documenting cases there could be a need to clarify issues and make a ruling. In adjudicating cases, as with the livestock sales, the courts tended to seek a compromise, even while referencing both law codes and local custom. These activities were important to these lordships, since they facilitated economic activity, particular the smooth operation of the land and livestock markets. At the same time, the courts and the *Oberämter* also provided valuable services to the people, particularly the propertied men of these villages.

The rural economy of this part of Germany was heavily dependent on debt. The big farmers, the *Bauern*, who held indivisible tenant farms, mortgaged their farms to pay off the heirs who did not get land. Poorer residents might borrow small sums to get through poor harvests, or to fund the purchase of livestock. Artisans would need credit to buy tools and set up a shop. Ecclesiastical institutions, including the monasteries themselves, as well as a variety of convents and collegiate chapters, often in nearby cities like Constance, and even parish priests, lent money throughout the region.[61] Wealthy farmers and artisans also lent money to their neighbors.

In the 1650s and 1660s the region was still rebuilding after the destruction of the Thirty Years' War. In this period, we see creditors, debtors, and the courts trying to figure out how to deal with debts from before or during the war. For example, in August 1661 the city council of Pfullendorf came to the court in Mainau asking for repayment of a loan taken out by three communes in Mainau territory.[62] The debt of 100 *Gulden* dated from before the war, and the Pfullendorfer wanted the accumulated interest on the loan as well as the capital repaid. The court ruled that the debtors would pay 25 *Gulden* for all the back interest and resume regular payments. This was a considerable write-off, since the unpaid back interest was probably in the range of 200 *Gulden*.[63]

On March 24, 1662, Leonhard Mautz, a "barber" in Constance, came to the court in Mainau to try to collect a long list of small loans.[64] The court commented that the debtors were all heirs of original borrowers and that the loans were mostly guaranteed by properties that currently produced no income. Nevertheless, the court ordered that the loans be paid off within three years, but ruled that all

[61] Sreenivasan, *The Peasants of Ottobeuren*.

[62] GLAK 61/7599, p. 27.

[63] Assuming 5% annual interest and that the debt went back thirty to forty years, those back payments totaled 150–200 *Gulden*.

[64] GLAK 61/7599, pp. 44–7. He was probably a medical person, likely a surgeon. He may have been representing other creditors from Constance, or perhaps he had purchased debts from others. The loans ranged from 6 *Gulden* to 66 *Gulden*.

back interest was canceled. The court seemed to recognize the difficulty the small debtors would have, commenting that the *Oberamt* might need to revisit these debts. The court also sympathized with larger debtors. When creditors tried to collect a debt of 500 *Gulden* from the widow of a Colonel Wachtmeister, the court ordered the parties to come to a settlement (*Vergleich*) before coming back to court.[65] Even as late as 1687, the court cited the Peace of Westphalia as a reason to forgive debts dating from the late sixteenth century.[66]

Even as this society began to recover from the effects of the long war, the courts tended to protect their subjects from creditors, asking parties in debt conflicts to come to agreements or set up payment plans themselves. By the 1670s creditors were often represented by lawyers in court, putting more pressure on debtors. In October 1673 a poor widow came to court and agreed to try to pay off a debt, but was supported by the court which refused to require her to pay off the whole debt.[67] Other debtors linked any payments to the postwar economic recovery. Animus Ocklin said he could begin to pay off his debt to the St. Stephan's Chapter in Constance with three *Eimer* of wine after the harvest, which all parties found acceptable.[68] Another man agreed to pay off his debt of 45 *Gulden* "bit by bit with wine each fall."[69] It took time for the vines to start producing after the war, and debts could not be paid until the peasants began to harvest this cash crop.

The credit market was susceptible to economic downturns and wartime crises, and not just in the immediate aftermath of the Thirty Years' War. In August 1710, during the War of the Spanish Succession, representatives of creditors in Constance came to the court at Mainau and filed fourteen different cases seeking payment of interest on loans ranging from 6 to 200 *Gulden*, all held by villagers from the region around Mainau.[70] The villagers were not able to pay cash, but, with the support of the Mainau authorities, offered to make interest payments in wine. It is not clear if these wine payments were the equivalent of the cash owed, but the creditors accepted this solution. The wartime crisis, which included the quartering of soldiers and the payment of extraordinary taxes, seems to have sucked the cash out of the local economy.[71]

The most common strategy used by courts to deal with debt cases was to organize a payment schedule acceptable to both parties. When Maria Schwegerin from Staad sought to collect a debt of 53 *Gulden* from Jacob Sulger, the court, working with both parties (including many members of the Sulger family), set up

[65] GLAK 61/7599, pp. 44–7 pp. 90–3, 94–7, March 5, 13, 14, 1663.
[66] GLAK 61/7602, August 23, 1687. This debt dated from 1591.
[67] GLAK 61/7600, October 7, 1673. [68] GLAK 61/7600, October 12, 1673.
[69] GLAK 61/7600, March 7, 1676. See several similar cases: GLAK 61/7600, September 12, 1676.
[70] GLAK 61/7606, pp. 48r–50v.
[71] Even contributions, that is, payments for support of soldiers, were converted to payments in wine in 1710: GLAK 61/7606, p. 51r. In August 1710, the contribution owed by the Mainau lordship (six villages) was 1,000 *Gulden*.

a schedule to pay off the debt over three years.[72] In a typical case, Stephan Scheri, from the Thurgau region of Switzerland, came to court in 1686 in an attempt to collect a debt of 57 *Gulden*, 29 *Kreuzer*, from Crista Schulter from Dettingen.[73] Scheri testified that he had asked multiple times for payment "and in response he had received nothing more than angry words." Schulter stated that he had no means of paying, but would give something "if possible" after the upcoming harvest, if it "should be deemed legal and right." The court took this offer a step further and ordered Schulter to pay 10 *Gulden* after the harvest and continue to pay each fall until the debt was paid off. If Schulter did not comply, more legal action would be necessary.

This kind of discussion and negotiation was common in debt proceedings. Usually the courts recognized the legality of the debts, but they often ordered leniency. It was common for court decisions to talk about what was possible for debtors, as when the Mainau court commented that Jacob Ocklin should start to pay off his debt to Lorentz Mayer, but that this coming fall he could not do so, and in the future he should pay "what is possible."[74] One fear courts had was that debt burdens would force peasants to abandon their farms. Lorenz Mayer made exactly this threat, stating that he would have to leave his farm if forced to pay all of the interest on a 100 *Gulden* loan he had taken out in order to buy the farm in the first place.[75] As is common in these cases, he was ordered to pay the current interest with wine after the harvest, and was required to keep up with the payments in the future, but was forgiven the back interest.

Debt cases often played out as a kind of arbitration hearing. One of the parties, usually the creditor, brought the case to court in order to force the issue into the open. Both sides then presented their situation, often making offers of a solution. This is what happened when Johannes Mundhasten was brought to court over his small debt of 4 *Gulden* and 33 *Kreuzer*. Mundhasten offered to pay half of the debt in two years, an offer the complainant accepted.[76] The court really had no role to play here, and the "decision" states that "since the complainant is content with this, it should remain so (*soll es darbey verbleiben*)."

The Culture of Settlements (Vergleiche)

The handling of debt disputes highlights the great value this society put on finding a *Vergleich*, a settlement or resolution of a dispute. The courts reinforced these values, as the court at Salem did in January 1700 when it urged Johannes Moser to come to a settlement with Conradt Blather in a dispute over a small debt of

[72] GLAK 61/7600, May 14, 1672. [73] GLAK 61/7602, February 23, 1686.
[74] GLAK 61/7602, March 4, 1686. [75] GLAK 61/7602, August 26, 1686.
[76] GLAK 61/7602, September 7, 1686. There were 60 *Kreuzer* in a *Gulden*.

2 *Gulden*.[77] The court records are full of *Vergleiche*, settlements of all kinds of disputes, particularly over property and inheritances, as well as debts. People also sought out *Vergleiche* in cases of family conflicts, disputes within village communities, and in conflicts between the lordship and their subjects. Settlements could be reached outside of courts, previously agreed-to resolutions could be enforced or amended by court decisions, or new agreements could be negotiated in court. The positive value of *Vergleiche* was something shared across this society.[78]

A negotiation that took place at the Mainau *Oberamt* in 1684 shows the omnipresence of the idea of settlement.[79] Conrad Morgen's heirs were called to the court in order to determine how they would fulfill the corvée (*Frondienst*, unpaid labor service) duties associated with the farm they had inherited. Conrad had come to a settlement (*Vergleich*) with the Teutonic Knights on this issue in 1668, agreeing to provide six days of work with his whole male workforce. His heirs were now admonished to figure out how "they would distribute (*vergleichen*) this *Frondienst* responsibility among themselves." Johannes Morgen, representing the heirs, offered to pay the tithe on a vineyard that was currently free of tithe payments in exchange for remission of the labor duties. The court ruled that the vineyard could not be part of a settlement on this issue and that the heirs should appear with seven men to fulfill the labor duties. But this was not the final outcome, since in the margins of the protocol there is a further note that a year later the Commander at Mainau, Herr von Rincken, came to a settlement with the heirs and converted the labor duties to an annual cash payment of six *Reichstaler*.[80]

The word *Vergleich* referred in this case to a variety of settlements and agreements, between the heirs as well as between subjects and lords. The range of what people considered settlements was quite wide. In 1673 two *Hintersassen*, non-citizen residents, were charged with a number of petty crimes before the court at Mainau.[81] They denied the charges, but the court ordered them expelled from the territory. But there was a qualification. If they could reach a settlement with the village commune where they lived, they could stay. Similarly, in 1676, the monastery of Petershausen filed complaints about Mainau subjects stealing wine and wood.[82] The court did not come to a decision, but instead ordered the parties to reach a resolution.

The court sometimes spelled out the importance they placed on settlements and agreements. When Jacob Schweighardt and Jacob Öcklin appeared in court in a dispute over the medical costs incurred in a fight between their ten-year-old

[77] GLAK 61/13342, pp. 10–12.

[78] Compare John Bossy, *Disputes and Settlement Disputes and Settlements. Law and Human Relations in the West.* (Cambridge University Press, 1983); Stephen Cummins and Laura Kounine, eds. *Culture of Conflict Resolution in Early Modern Europe* (Farnham, 2016), esp. Introduction.

[79] GLAK 61/7602, pp. 7v–8v.

[80] The *Reichstaler* was a silver coin, worth about 1.2 *Gulden*.

[81] GLAK 61/7600, May 13, 1673.

[82] GLAK 61/7600, November 14, 1676.

sons, the Mainau court asked them to find an agreement.[83] "So that it does not happen that the parties go too far and out of a friendship an enmity might arise, both parties were asked if they could, with good will, come to a resolution, which they did." Such efforts to bring about friendship and peace were not always successful. The court appealed to the parties in a dispute over the beating of a cow by the cattle herder (*Kuhhirt*) to come to a *Vergleich*, but they refused.[84] Instead the parties dug in their heels and even brought up old conflicts. The court ended up fining the *Kuhhirt*, probably exacerbating the dispute rather than defusing it.

Most frequently, settlements were made in disputes about money. In 1684, the five Sulger heirs came to a settlement with the widow of the sacristan over 24 *Gulden* they owed her.[85] Agatha Ungarin, Mathis Sulger, Maria Sulgerin, and Catharina Sulgerin agreed to pay 2 *Gulden* each, and Bashe Sulger pledged 1 *Gulden*. The *Vergleich* also stipulated that they would pay the rest of the loan off after they had "made the wine into silver," that is, sold their wine. In an even smaller case, in 1670 the tavernkeeper in Oberuhldingen came to a settlement with the local shoemaker over the cost of some shoes.[86] In December 1670 the Salem *Oberamtsgericht* was also pleased to seal a settlement between two shoemakers.[87] Bartolome Hartman, from Ebratshofen, ran into Thomas Forster, from Buggensegel, in the tavern in the village of Herdwangen and they reminisced about and seem to have revived an old dispute from fourteen years before. At that time, Hartman had been an apprentice in Forster's shop and Forster had called him a "dog's etc." in his impatience with Hartman's mistakes. Hartman brought a slander complaint to the court, but once there Hartman and Forster "came to a resolution and became good friends."

A large portion of the settlements and resolutions in the court minutes were cases of family disputes. In these cases, the courts demonstrated a kind of paternalism, as they worked to reconcile families, heirs, and even young unmarried couples. The belief that the family was the building block of society was certainly behind these efforts at peacemaking, but perhaps there was also an idea that ties of emotion might make reconciliation easier between family members.

Local authorities, as well as the courts, were concerned with men who were failing as heads of household (*Hausväter*). The key concept here was *hausen*, an untranslatable verb that encompassed various aspects of domestic economy. A man who provided for his family, was honorable in the community, and treated his household firmly but peacefully, was said to *hausen* well.[88] When Anna Wöschen brought her husband Johannes Junckere to court in 1670, she said she wanted him to *hausen* like a true father.[89] In 1672, local authorities cited

[83] GLAK 61/7600, September 9, 1673. [84] GLAK 61/7600, November 24, 1673.
[85] GLAK 61/7602, pp. 35r–35v. [86] GLAK 61/13334, p. 69. [87] GLAK 61/13334, p. 77.
[88] Sabean, *Power in the Blood*, p. 155. Also, Mack Walker, *German Home Towns. Community, State, and General Estate. 1648–1871* (Ithaca, 1971).
[89] GLAK 61/13334, p. 49. For more detail, see Chapter 1.

Jacob Hagenbach, from Mimmenhausen, before the court in Salem due to his poor *Haushaltung* (domestic economy, housekeeping).[90] As was alleged in most of these cases, Hagenbach drank too much, wasting his money and time in the tavern.[91] And, just as in the case of Junkere, the court sought an unofficial solution, admonishing Hagenbach to do better if he wanted to avoid punishment.

In 1706, the *Obervogt* was sent by the Prince-Bishop of Constance to speak to Sebastian Rohmer of Wollmatingen.[92] Rohmer was told that he needed to improve his behavior and his housekeeping. Rohmer had come to the attention of the authorities because he did not keep his dog tied up and let it wander freely in the woods. He was punished with eight days in prison on bread and water. Finally, he was told to vacate his farm in favor of his son, something that he had previously agreed to, but then had reneged on.

Most of the family disputes that came to the court for resolution and most of the agreements the courts facilitated were between members of extended families. Often these were multigenerational conflicts, disputes between retired fathers and their sons or sons-in-law, between widows and the younger generation, or between siblings living in the same house. *Vergleiche* were supposed to settle and regulate these difficult tensions, and we can assume that they usually did. When they did not work, people sometimes went to court, and the courts, rather than make a judicial decision, usually sought out a new agreement or some other kind of resolution. Interestingly, courts often encouraged the breakup of living arrangements among members of extended families, displaying an understanding of the psychological difficulties of such domestic arrangements.

The negotiations around the retirement of a farmer were often fairly complex. When Georg Aichhaimb of Allmannsdorf retired from a heritable tenancy in 1685, he turned the farm over to his stepchildren and their spouses.[93] They agreed to give him six *Gulden* a year over five years, pay for his housing, and they gave him the use of a small vineyard as well. Since Georg was going to live with his son-in-law in the village of Staad, the parties agreed that if Georg died before the five years of payments were complete, then the son-in-law would receive the balance. In that situation, the son-in-law would also keep the vineyard as collateral until the money was paid off. This *Vergleich* was carefully recorded in the Mainau court protocols.

It appears that Georg Aichhaimb and his family reached a settlement without conflict, although of course we cannot know what sort of family discussions took place to reach an agreement. We also do not know what Aichhaimb's life was like in the ensuing years. Ulrich Haidlauff, "old and decrepit," lived with his second

[90] GLAK 61/13334, December 5, 1673.

[91] Roper, *Oedipus and the Devil*, chs 5 and 7.

[92] GLAK 61/13268, pp. 108–9. This "discussion" is recorded in the protocols of the *Frevelgericht* in Wollmatigen. The sources do not explain where this meeting took place.

[93] GLAK 61/7602, p. 34v.

wife, Madlen Schwegerin.[94] Ulrich's daughter Maria filed a complaint that Schwegerin treated Ulrich poorly and did not give him enough food and drink. Furthermore, Madlen did not let Maria visit, so that Maria "would not see and make public that she [Madlen] was not giving [Ulrich] what he needed and deserved." Madlen's defense was that Ulrich was so "unreasonable" that he was hard to take care of and she could not feed him more, since he did not want more food. Both women said they had been insulted by the other.

The court at Mainau admonished Maria and Madlen to apologize for the insults. The court also ruled that Madlen needed to care better for Ulrich and that the authorities would regularly send someone to check up on Ulrich and see if he was being well treated. "If not, the property of the father will be taken out of the hands of the stepmother and, along with the sick father, given to someone else." Here we see the court intervening in the care of an older person and threatening (or proposing) a solution, with the aim of changing Madlen's behavior. The court's ruling reflects a pragmatic understanding of the situation, hence the reference to Ulrich's property, as well as a grasp of the dynamics of the relations between stepmother and daughter. From a distance of 350 years, however, we might have some sympathy for Madlen and the difficulties of eldercare.

The transition of authority on a farm did not always proceed smoothly. Michel Debronner from Lipperatsreute and his son-in-law Jacob Heggelbacher had agreed to run Debronner's farm together, but they found themselves in constant conflict.[95] Debronner complained he was not given enough food and that Heggelbacher did not respect his decisions about the farm. Heggelbacher in turn resented feeding not just Michel, but Michel's five children as well. They asked the court to mediate (*Vermitteln*). The Mainau court made an interesting decision. They stated that the problem in this household was in fact Jacob Heggelbacher's mother, and she was ordered to move out and find her own residence. Then the court admonished "the father-in-law and his son-in-law to live and work together peacefully" if they did not want further intervention from the authorities.[96] The resolution, then, was to blame a woman and warn the men in the family to behave more peacefully.

It is unlikely that the authorities were surprised that domestic harmony was hard to maintain, especially in the context of multiple marriages. Georg Simbler and his stepbrother Jacob Gerthoffer lived in the same house and constantly

[94] GLAK 61/7600, April 15, 1673. Actually, we only know for sure that Madlen was the stepmother of his daughter Maria.

[95] GLAK 61/7606, pp. 62r–v.

[96] The court protocols usually identified people by their position in the family in these kinds of cases ("the father-in-law," "the stepmother," and so on). It is possible to surmise the sympathies of the court by looking at the perspective they take in a case. For example, in the Haidlauff case above the court referred to Madlen Schwegerin as "the stepmother" most of the time, seeming to take the point of view (and the side) of the daughter, Maria.

quarreled.[97] Gerthoffer claimed that Simbler owed him more money from their father's inheritance, but the records showed that Simbler had paid him off properly. As a result, the Rot court ruled that Gerthoffer had to leave his brother (Simbler) and his wife in peace. If he failed to do so, the court would relieve the Simblers from the duty to feed and house the younger Gerthoffer, an obligation that was probably part of their mutual father's will.

The courts regularly and explicitly expressed a desire for settlements within families. In a 1687 case involving a property dispute between an older couple and their nieces and nephews, the Mainau court opined "the complainants... need to behave better toward their sister's children and not create such a harsh enmity."[98] The court requested that the parties settle their dispute with a peaceful partition of the property. In 1700, the court in Salem confirmed an agreement from the village of Seefelden whereby a widow paid her son-in-law 100 *Gulden*.[99] He in turn agreed "to find his own residence and move out of the little house within two days." This solution would end the "never ending strife" in which they had been living. In this case the court was confirming an agreement already made by the parties with the mediation of the local *Amman*.

This culture of settlement and conflict resolution can also be seen in the potentially difficult negotiations around child support payments for illegitimate children. In early October of 1706, the *Oberamtsgericht* in Rot recorded a "*deflorations Vergleich*," a "deflowering settlement."[100] This case was partly about the payment made to compensate a woman for the loss of her virginity, and partly about the support and custody of the child. There was little disagreement between the parties about the facts. Sometime in December 1705, Georg Müller had gotten Anna Maria Waldvogel, a servant in the village of Conradtsweiler, pregnant. Müller admitted to having slept with Waldvogel "many times," but also said that he had never promised to marry her. Furthermore, he now refused to marry her, even when her father offered him a piece of property. Georg's father, for his part, was actively "dissuading" his son from marrying Anna Maria.

The initial response of the court was unsympathetic to the young man.

> He is sentenced to a punishment in the tower [the prison at Rot] which will be held over him until he is able to resolve this in another way. He is warned that if he does not do what is honorable for this person [*dieses mensch nit zue Ehren setzen werde*], he will be given custody of the child.

[97] HStAS B486/Bd 15, p. 202r. [98] GLAK 61/7602, November 29, 1687.

[99] GLAK 61/13341, pp. 7–8.

[100] HStAS B486/Bd 18, pp. 155v–156v. See Loetz, *A New Approach to the History of* Violence, pp. 97–115.

And, secondly, as the law requires, he will have to give her the just payment for the deflowering [*ratione deflorationis*].

Then the court told the parties to think it over and come back in a few days. They appeared in court again on October 5 after meeting with an arbitrator (*Mittelsperson*) who proposed that Müller pay Anna Maria 40 *Gulden* and that the child would be raised by the mother for the first year, and then live with the father. Anna Maria's father refused this offer, stating that she should keep the baby and that her honor was worth 150 *Gulden*. The parties took another break and returned on October 30 with a *Vergleich*. The mother would keep the child for its first five years, after which Müller would be responsible. The Müllers (father and son) would also pay 100 *Gulden*, 20 *Gulden* a year, for the deflowering and the upkeep of the child. If the father of the child died, then the Waldvogel family would keep the child, but forfeit the payments, and if the child were to die, the 100 *Gulden* would still be paid. Finally, Georg Müller was fined 9 *Gulden* for the pre-marital sex, Anna Maria Waldvogel 6 *Gulden*.[101]

This had been a fraught negotiation, with the young man rejecting the traditional solution of marrying the mother of his child and the family of the young woman defending her honor tenaciously. But the parties continued to seek a resolution, rather than asking the court for a decision. At one point the parties even said, "we do not want to burden the Chancellery (i.e., the court at Rot) further with this case." After two breaks for cooling off, the intervention of a mediator, and further negotiations, a settlement was reached, one that apparently held.

A 1681 case from the village of Engelharz also involved negotiations over the support of an illegitimate child.[102] Once again, the parents of the child were servants when the woman, referred to as Hans Schödlin's daughter in the sources, became pregnant. The father, Hans Behr's son, ran away and the young woman married another man, Martin Lachner. Lachner testified that he was willing to raise the illegitimate child as his own, but he wanted a financial contribution of 25 *Gulden* from Hans Behr, the grandfather of the baby. Grandfather Behr stated that he did not accept any legal obligation to either his son "who has gone bad" (*ubel gerahthenem*) or the child, but was willing to give 10 *Gulden* "in the name of the child." He hoped this would bring some peace, but he also commented that Lachner could wait and see if he got anything when he, Behr, died. Lachner accepted the offer of 10 *Gulden* and asked the court at Rot to enforce the agreement.

A series of court hearings in 1672 at the Mainau court played out as a drawn-out negotiation over the support of an illegitimate child. In January, Barbara

[101] In the margins of the court protocol there is a series of notes from 1706, 1707, 1708, 1709, and 1710, recording that the 20 *Gulden* was paid each year.

[102] HStAS B486/Bd 15, p. 9v.

Bauchlin and her mother brought suit against Jerg Braunbart, claiming he had impregnated Barbara.[103] Braunbart "doubted" he was the father. At a second hearing, in March, Braunbart argued that Bauchlin had become pregnant two weeks before he had sex with her, but Barbara countered that he had been with her four times.[104] The court claimed to be baffled and asked for more investigation, but it also ordered Jerg to pay wine and grain to Barbara "for the forthcoming childbirth." In June Barbara, now a mother, again appeared in court, this time with her father and the *Amman* from her village of Dingelsdorf.[105] She claimed that Jerg had promised to marry her in January and had now reneged on that promise. She still wanted to marry him, but since he refused, she decided to "declare him single" (*ihne aber ledig gesprochen*). The court (again) ordered him to pay her wine and grain for the childbirth. The parties also agreed that Jerg would pay 10 *Gulden* a year for three years to support the child. There is evidence that Jerg did not keep up with his payments, since Barbara was back in court in 1673 asking for the child support payments.[106]

All of these cases demonstrate the interplay between informal resolution, arbitration, negotiation, and formal hearings in the court. Ultimately, most cases ended in some kind of settlement, although in all of them the men refused to marry the mother of their child. This was not the most common outcome. There are many cases where the parties did marry after the woman became pregnant.[107] What is harder to know is when pregnancies resulted from sexual activity between courting couples who intended to marry in any case and when pregnancies were unexpected and unwanted. The above cases all seem to have involved servants, rather than daughters and sons of established families, and in such cases the women were less likely to have the clout to force a marriage.

The largest number of settlements recorded in the court protocols are marriage agreements and inheritance arrangements. As discussed above, these *Vergleiche* sometimes involved resolving disputes, particularly about inheritances. In most cases, however, these agreements were recorded with the aim of preventing future conflicts. Most of these involved people with extensive property and considerable future obligations to the lordship, as well as complex family situations. The practice of recording these arrangements clearly drew on the pre-existing tradition of written marriage contracts and wills. This was also the period when the Catholic Church began to consistently record baptisms, marriages, and deaths in parish registers, further contributing to the advance of written records at the village level. We also know that this was a period of growing literacy, which surely contributed to making the culture of settlement a culture of written settlements.

[103] GLAK 61/7600, January 23, 1672.
[104] GLAK 61/7600, March 21, 1672.
[105] GLAK 61/7600, June 11, 1672.
[106] GLAK 61/7600, May 27, 1673.
[107] Just some examples: GLAK 61/7600, June 11, 1672. There is more discussion in Chapter 7 of the issue of *frühzeitige Beischlaf* ("sleeping together too soon"). See also Hull, *Sexuality, State, and Civil Society*, p. 91.

Another window on the prevalence of informal resolution in the communities of Southwest Germany can be found in the references to the consultation of experts and the use of *Unparteiische*, unbiased witnesses. The use of assessors to judge the true value of property or of eyewitnesses to examine the placement of boundary markers was part of daily life. Anthony Crubaugh's study of the justices of the peace in post-Revolutionary France argues that *assesseurs* and other experts made local justice in the French countryside more efficient, less expensive, and more trustworthy than seigneurial justice in the Old Regime.[108] Yet in Germany, the system of conflict resolution deployed men to provide expert testimony and eyewitness evidence as part of traditional informal justice and also within the institutions of seigneurial justice.

In the fall of 1719, Hans Jerg Hueber bought a horse from Johannes Jehle in the village of Nussdorf.[109] Shortly after the purchase, Hueber demanded that Jehle knock 10 *Gulden* off the price of the horse, since it was blind in its right eye. Jehle rejected this request since he claimed he had told Hueber of this fault with the horse at the time of the sale. The parties explained that they had gone to Tobias Abten, the saddler (and thus knowledgeable about horses), for advice at the time of the sale. Abten testified in court that Hueber and Jehle had come, a bit drunk, to his house one evening in October. They both knew that the horse did not see well out of its right eye, and Jehle asked Abten to witness the bill of sale in case any problem developed later, as in fact it did. Jehlen was concerned, since Hueber's wife had expressed opposition to the purchase. Abten suggested to Hueber that he should go see a miller in Bermatingen who had some medicine that might help the horse. Abten, then, was both an expert witness who had been informally consulted, then signed the bill of sale, and finally testified in court. The court ruled that the sale price would be reduced by 5 *Gulden*, a compromise.

In a more straightforward case, an impartial assessor was chosen in 1681 to determine the fair price of a cow.[110] If the price was acceptable to the buyer, the sale would be finalized and recorded at Salem. An impartial person was also needed in Thengen in 1672 to settle an ongoing dispute over a path through the vineyards.[111] This man was charged by the court to find a path that did less damage to the vines. In Haslach in 1681, an *Unparteiischer* was asked to set the cost of the damages done to a vineyard there by oxen.[112] Similarly, in 1710 an impartial assessor was appointed by the court to determine the damages caused by some illegal haying.[113]

[108] Crubaugh, *Balancing the Scales of Justice*; Anthony Crubaugh, "Local Justice and Rural Society in the French Revolution" *Journal of Social History* (2000): 327–350, esp. pp. 339–40.

[109] GLAK 61/13350, pp. 472–8.

[110] GLAK 61/13335, p. 5v.

[111] GLAK 61/6958, February 23, 1672.

[112] HStAS B486/Bd 15, p. 22r. A similar case, from 1687, with a horse damaging field. GLAK 61/7602, September 13, 1687.

[113] GLAK 61/7606, pp. 23a–r.

Who were the men who did these inspections and assessments? A dispute over property boundaries between two brothers (and their wives) at the Mainau court gives us some idea.[114] This dispute led to the appointment of several nearby local officials (*Amtmänner*) to make an in-person inspection (*Augenschein*) of the fields in question. The inspection led to a quick decision in favor of the defendant in the case. In a 1681 dispute over the sale of a cow, two mediators, a smith and an innkeeper, negotiated a settlement between the parties.[115] Several inspections were reported to the court at Thengen in September 1659.[116] In one case the inspectors inspected some disputed house repairs, and in the other they determined that some boundary markers had been inadvertently moved and needed to be moved back. In these cases, it is not clear who did the inspections, but perhaps it was one or more of the jurymen at the village court there in Thengen.

These assessments and inspections show one set of practices among the spectrum of strategies used to keep the peace and resolve conflicts in rural society. Assessments and inspections were surely often used in unofficial resolutions that never reached the courts, but they were also used by courts as they sought to maintain peace. "Unofficial resolutions," what French scholars call "l'infrajudiciaire," seem to have been widely used, but the protocols of local courts are an imperfect way to learn about their prevalence.[117] Furthermore, as we have seen, the line between informal adjudication and "going to justice" is far from clear, given the way the courts functioned as sites for mediation and negotiation, as well as for decisions handed down by judges and juries.

There are, however, indications in the court records of settlements made before a dispute landed in court. Most often, these *Vergleiche* came to the attention of the court because they had been violated or needed to be restored in some way. A tantalizing entry in the Salem court protocols from June 1671 reads as follows. "Owingen: Anna Josephin Schmidlin from Owingen files a complaint against Elisabeth Schnellerin from there. It was nothing (*war nichts*)."[118] The entry was also crossed out. It is likely that there was a dispute between these two women and a court hearing had been scheduled, but the case was resolved before the parties got to court, or perhaps even as they waited for the hearing to start.

In another 1671 case from the Salem records, two men appeared in order to have the court confirm and strengthen a settlement they had already reached.[119] Jörg Kräss, master smith in Salem, had exchanged insults with Christian Knöbelspiess, who had criticized Kräss's work. In the hearing, however, both men wanted the court to proclaim a *Fridbott*, a demand for peace, so no further

[114] GLAK 61/7600, September 9, 1673. [115] HStAS B486/Bd 15, p. 7v.
[116] GLAK 61/6958, September 12, 1659.
[117] See especially Benoît Garnot, "L'ampleur et les limites de l'infrajudiciaire dans la France d'Ancien Régime (XVIe–XVIIe–XVIII siècles)" in Garnot, ed. *L'Infrajudiciaire du Moyen Age à l'epoque contemporaine.*
[118] GLAK 61/13334, p. 101. [119] GLAK 61/13334, p. 108.

conflict would occur. And the two men declared themselves "good friends" and "confirmed the peace with several glasses of wine." Here, as we have seen quite often, the court hearing and the written record of the hearing served as a complement to a more informal process of peacemaking.

Other court cases provide clear evidence of informal resolutions of disputes. When a group of cows damaged a vineyard in 1672, an agreement was reached whereby their owner compensated the owner of the vineyard by giving him a pig and the use of an ox for two days.[120] In June 1674 a case came to the Mainau court because of some confusion over a settlement that had been reached over a year before, in February 1673.[121] In this case, one of the parties misunderstood the agreement and believed he was due 100 *Gulden*, a large sum. The court examined the settlement and declared him in error. Finally, in another case of cattle running loose, two of Leopoldt Neff's steers broke a fence and trampled Joseph Greüss' ducks, who had to be slaughtered.[122] The two men came to a settlement and Neff had agreed to pay 15 *Gulden* in damages. This agreement came to court when Neff changed his mind and refused to pay. The court ruled the original agreement valid and ordered Neff to pay the 15 *Gulden* and some court fees.

From Settlements to Peace

Rural people were pragmatic about how to maintain peace in their communities and so were local officials and the courts run by the lordships. Negotiations and mediation led to settlements and agreements, many of them reached informally between the parties. Over time people also saw the value of writing the agreements down and recording them with the chancelleries of the lordships. The courts were part of this system of conflict resolution, as they also resolved disputes, negotiated settlements, and mediated conflicts.

These practices, as we have seen, did not prevent conflict and violence in the villages. Honor conflicts were endemic throughout the period and may have even become more prevalent after 1700. On the other hand, the end of the witch hunts after about 1670 did lower tensions around the use of the witch insult against women. Finally, while difficult to quantify, there seem to have been rising social tensions in this society between masters and servants, master artisans and apprentices, and between peasants with access to land and landless cottagers. This trend is in keeping with what other studies of rural society have found for this period.

[120] GLAK 61/7600, March 5, 1672. The case came to court because the ox was so badly treated by the owner of the vineyard that it had to be slaughtered and its owner now claimed damages.

[121] GLAK 61/7600, June 18, 1674.

[122] GLAK 61/13268, December 15, 1712.

The existence, even the prevalence, of violence and conflict does not mean that the desire for peace and order coming from within rural society was not an important part of popular culture. The appeal for peace, made by peers and by local officials in an attempt to stop a dispute or a fight, the regular references to shaking hands to end a conflict, the formal removal of insults and restoration of honor in courts, and the sealing of settlements over a glass of wine all reflect a strong commitment to social peace. Even honor disputes, a seemingly never-ending source of interpersonal conflict, also had a peacemaking quality to them. The goal of the parties was almost always to reach a place where all parties were once again at peace with each other. The determined effort to track down and quash rumors, on the part of the victims of slander, local officials, and the courts, also aimed at bringing a resolution and avoiding ongoing feuds.

The formulaic words of many court decisions can ring hollow to modern readers, and perhaps they rang hollow to some at the time as well. There was a ritualistic quality to the commitments to peace and the statements about friendship and community. But rituals had power and meaning, and they certainly reflected the values of the society.

Let us consider the words of Ulrich Wesch from Bachen and his neighbor, Jacob Messmer.[123] At the end of a court case about insults these men traded after Messmer's horse trampled one of Wesch's fields, they made the following statement:

> In the end they agreed to a love of peace (*amor pacis*) and in it they commit themselves to showing each other continuing friendship and neighborliness, to think about that [i.e., peace] more often. If the littlest [conflict] should nevertheless occur, they will be punished seriously and deservedly by the lordship.

Peace and order were values shared by rural people and their rulers. As the monastic lordships of Southwest Germany developed more effective state structures in the century after the Thirty Years' War, they also worked to impose their ideas of how their subjects should behave, work, and live. Local courts were one of the tools they used in this project, a project that could ultimately only succeed with the support of elements of rural society.

[123] HStAS B486/Bd 14, pp. 151r–v.

7
Social Discipline and the State Formation from Below

Rural society in Southwest Germany might seem to be an unlikely place to look for the rise of the state. Yes, a kind of modernization was happening here since these communities were not isolated from the wider world, but instead were increasingly embedded in a market economy after 1650, and some big farmers were getting rich selling agricultural products. But this was not England or Northern France, and there were no dynamic cities tied into world trade networks that would favor a stronger state. Nor was there a fiscal-military state ruthlessly intent on mobilizing resources to fund interstate rivalries. Instead, this region, like most of western and southern Germany, looked quite traditional, a place where serfdom *(Leibeigenschaft)*, while hardly onerous, remained a real part of people's lives and where the economy was agricultural and artisanal. It was governed by small lordships which, while becoming slowly more organized and effective, never developed large bureaucracies or military establishments. Towns and cities like Überlingen and Constance were traditional places as well, governed by local oligarchies and looking much like Mack Walker's German "hometowns," inward-looking and suspicious of change.[1]

At the same time, Southwest Germany was not archaic in its social and cultural structures. Farmers controlled their own land, the land and livestock markets were lively, and cash crops like wine were important. The widespread use of credit made it possible for people to take advantage of economic opportunities and trade brought rural people into a wider world. Upper Swabia also drew immigrants from poorer mountain regions in Switzerland and the Swabian Alb, most often as servants and farm laborers. The building projects taken on by all the monasteries of the region brought considerable investment that attracted artisans and construction workers to the region. The prosperity of the great abbeys like Salem and Rot after the Thirty Years' War reflected the agricultural prosperity of the region, since the income of these institutions came from rents and dues in the villages. Finally, the region was integrated into a wider Catholic world that was at once local, regional, and international. In this world, monks of peasant extraction

[1] Walker, *German Home Towns*. Forum on German Home Towns in *Central European History* 47 (2014): 482–522.

Keeping the Peace in the Village: Conflict and Peacemaking in Germany, 1650–1750. Marc R. Forster, Oxford University Press. © Marc R. Forster 2024. DOI: 10.1093/oso/9780198898474.003.0008

interacted with noble prelates, village priests encountered Jesuit intellectuals, and pilgrims traveled to shrines in neighboring villages or at more distant sites.

This study has focused on social practice at the village level. We have seen the tensions at the local level between the ubiquity of conflict and the desire for peace and order. Some of these tensions, perhaps most of them, were mitigated by a system of conflict resolution that responded to popular needs. Some of the ways conflicts were settled are hard to grasp solely on the basis of court records and other documentation created by the authorities. Still, it is clear that one path the population used was to call on local courts to solve disputes, negotiate settlements, and record existing agreements.

While a comprehensive statistical analysis of the use of courts is not possible, there are strong indications that people were going to justice in increasingly large numbers across the period 1650–1750. Furthermore, the authorities attempted to use the courts to enforce a number of disciplinary measures in their territories, which also increased the intensity of interactions between the authorities and the population.[2] From a governance or top-down perspective, these disciplinary policies, which emphasized the enforcement of public order, the regulation of sexual activity, and the obedience of subjects to state officials, were part of a drive toward a stronger state, even when that state was a small ecclesiastical principality. This rather low-key state-building could not, however, happen without the participation of important elements of local society. Disciplinary measures, such as the monitoring of sexual behavior, were favored by local elites, including propertied farmers, heads of households, innkeepers, millers, and master artisans, and as a result these people supported a more active state.[3] I would go a step further to argue that the broader use of courts by many elements of rural society is an indication of even wider support for state formation from below.

State Formation from Below

When historians examine state formation (or state-building) from below, this involves, as André Holenstein points out, both a subject of study—the popular classes or the people more generally—and the study of their influence on the process of state development.[4] This perspective is a critique of older narratives of "the rise of the state," which focus on the activity of monarchs, government officials, and the military in strengthening central power. This older perspective has been undermined by studies that emphasize the weaknesses of the early modern

[2] Intensity of interactions: Rudolph, *"Eine gelinde Regierungsart"*; Hohkamp, *Herrschaft in der Herrschaft*. More generally, Schlögl, *Anwesende und Abwesende*.

[3] This is a theme in Roper, *Oedipus and the Devil*; Robisheaux, *Rural Society and the Search for Order*; Sabean, *Power in the Blood*, ch. 3.

[4] Holenstein, "Introduction" in Holenstein et al., eds. *Empowering Interactions*, esp. p. 3.

state, especially its inability to implement power at the local level.[5] Furthermore, studies have shown that royal absolutism was not a prerequisite for a strong state, as the case of Great Britain shows.[6] In the German context, an older focus on the study of Prussia in particular, as well as the larger states like Bavaria and Württemberg, has been supplemented by an understanding of the diversity of state formation in the German lands.

While the important collection *Empowering Interactions* conceptualizes state development as "state-building from below," state formation is a better term for what happened in Southwest Germany.[7] State formation centers analysis on the dynamic and complex process that led to the development of more effective state institutions which included, as Steve Hindle emphasizes, widespread popular participation in governance.[8] State-building is, by definition, a top-down process. As we will see, state-building of this kind occurred in the smaller German territories, but state formation more accurately describes the broader and more effective process of state development that emerged out of daily life and the practices of governing at the local level.

Scholars of early modern England have been in the forefront of studying the function of the state at the local level. As Hindle, among others, has shown, early modern England was governed by the "rural middling sort" who practiced "self-government at the King's command."[9] The role of local officials as intermediaries between state and society in German territories is also well studied. David Sabean's examination of rural society in Württemberg frequently points to the challenges faced by village headmen, called *Schultheissen* there, who had to publicize and enforce measures coming from the central government, while also representing villagers to the higher authorities.[10] The *Amtmänner*, the village mayors, played a similar role in the villages of Southwest Germany.

Furthermore, the English common law tradition and the ways the medieval English monarchy used the legal system to strengthen the power of the king has led historians of England to highlight the importance of the judicial system everywhere. Where historians of France have focused on informal forms of conflict resolution (*l'infrajudiciaire*) and have generally asserted that royal and seigneurial courts were part of an interfering and distant state, English historians have identified a "juridical state" that was both widely available and well

[5] For the "Myth of Absolutism," the classic study is: William Beik, *Absolutism and Society in Seventeenth-Century France. State Power and the Provincial Aristocracy in Languedoc* (Cambridge, 1985). See also Nicolas Henshall, *The Myth of Absolutism: Change and Continuity in Early Modern European Monarchy* (New York and London, 1992); Wim Blockmans, "Citizens and their Rulers" in Holenstein et al., eds. *Empowering Interactions*, esp. p. 283.

[6] John Brewer, *The Sinews of Power. War, Money, and the English state, 1688–1783* (London, 1989).

[7] Holenstein et al., eds. *Empowering Interactions*.

[8] Hindle, "Law, Law Enforcement and State Formation in Early Modern England," pp. 211–12.

[9] Hindle, "Law, Law Enforcement and State Formation in Early Modern England," p. 213; Hindle, *The State and Social Change in Early Modern England*.

[10] Sabean, *Power in the Blood*, esp. pp. 12–20. See also Holenstein, "Introduction," esp. pp. 21–2.

integrated into English society.[11] To give one example, Bernard Capp argues that the ecclesiastical court in the parish of Sileby in the 1630s aimed to restore Christian charity and harmony in the community.[12] The court gave people from all social classes a hearing as well, even if the "better sort" received some preferential treatment. Ultimately, as Hindle says, "The state, it should be emphasized, gained its legitimacy on the basis of its effectiveness as a forum for the resolution of conflict."[13]

The small states of Southwest Germany were geographically fragmented and lightly governed. Much of the income of monastic lordships like Salem, Rot, and Mainau came from rents on landed property and, to a lesser extent, from fees associated with serfdom, as well as some indirect taxes. Their bureaucracies were small, they had no military establishment, and they depended on local people to govern the villages. As we have seen, however, these micro-states did have a judicial system consisting of village and district courts. Like England, these were "juridical states."

As we have seen, this judicial system was part of a wider system of conflict resolution and was well integrated into the rural society it served. Cases were usually handled in pragmatic ways that emphasized the restoration of peace, the maintenance of order, and the reduction of conflict. Judges at the *Oberamtsgerichten* (district courts) at Mainau, Rot, and Salem understood how village communities functioned, as well as the ins and outs of the economic system. The "village courts" at Wollmatingen and Thengen were even closer to the people who used them. Furthermore, because the courts were local, they adjudicated cases quickly and at a low cost. Finally, there is little evidence of opposition to the decisions these courts reached and only very scattered reference to the parties appealing the cases to higher jurisdictions. At a basic level, the people seem to have considered these courts' decisions just and fair.

Holenstein emphasizes that the state developed in the early modern period through an interactive process in which the subjects had a major role.

> Such processes occurred because specific state instances reacted to complex social problems, because they answered to the demands and claims of various groups and members of the society, because they rendered services to these groups and helped bring about what these groups expected from a higher political power—for instance the settling of disputes and the solution of conflicts,

[11] Garnot, ed., *L'Infrajudiciaire du Moyen Age à l'époque contemporaine*. Hindle, "Law, Law Enforcement and State Formation." For a less positive view of the role of courts, see Tim Stretton, "Written Obligations, Litigation, and Neighbourliness" in Steve Hindle et al., eds. *Remaking English* Society (Cambridge, 2013).

[12] Bernard Capp, "Life, Love, and Litigation: Sileby in the 1630s" *Past and Present* 182 (2004): 55–83.

[13] Hindle, "Law, Law Enforcement and State Formation," pp. 212–13.

support for carrying through specific interests, or the implementation of specific concepts of public and social order.[14]

All these elements, the settling of disputes and the implementation of "specific concepts" of order and peace, were part of the work of courts studied here. And this work surely had the effect of enhancing popular appreciation for the authorities that provided this service. At the same time, this point needs some qualification, and we should keep in mind the complex role of courts. Not surprisingly, the courts tended to favor powerful social groups in rural society, particularly large farmers and male heads of families. There were also times when courts did attempt to enforce social disciplinary measures favored by political elites and, in this Catholic region, by the Church itself. These measures came to the villages in the form of attempts to discipline sexual behavior above all, but also in efforts to rein in the disorderly behavior of young people, discourage the use of popular magic, and enforce obedience to all state authorities.

Social Discipline: Regulating Sex

On the surface, the disciplining of sexual activity appears to be a classic case of Church and state elites attempting to impose behavioral norms on the wider population, in short, of social disciplining in the sense of Gerhard Oestreich.[15] Oestreich's model presents an activist state, usually drawing on the precepts of a state Church that used coercive measures to enforce moral behavior. This was a break from a traditional concern for the social consequences of deviant behavior, which informed the way village and town communities looked at disciplining the population. As Isabel Hull astutely notes, in traditional society parents and *Gemeinde* elites focused on preventing sexual behavior that might result in unwanted pregnancies that threatened inheritance structures and local subsistence levels.[16] Furthermore, Hull argues that "the German absolutist territorial states appear in a much closer symbiosis with their 'subjects' than the social-disciplinary model suggests" and that government policy was "nuanced, sensitive to local circumstances, and flexible."[17] Hull believes that the disciplining of sexual behavior undertaken by the courts of Southwest Germany had this pragmatic character, rather than the moralizing perspective of Church and state elites.

[14] Holenstein, "Introduction," esp. p. 5. Also see Neils Grüne, "Local Demand for Order and Government Intervention. Social Group Conflicts as Statebuilding Factors in the Villages of the Rhine Palatinate, c. 1760–1810" in Holenstein et al., eds. *Empowering Interactions*.

[15] Gerhard Oestreich, *Geist und Gestalt des frühmodernen Staates* (Berlin, 1969); R. Po-chia Hsia, *Social Discipline in the Reformation. Central Europe 1550–1750* (New York: 1989); Hull, *Sexuality, State, and Civil Society*, pp. 53–5.

[16] Hull, *Sexuality, State, and Civil Society*, p. 10.

[17] Hull, *Sexuality, State, and Civil Society*, ch. 2, esp. pp. 55–6.

This perspective does not mean that the treatment of people was never harsh or coercive. When it came to the attention of the authorities, illegal sexual behavior by servants and farm laborers was often severely punished. Adultery was also punished, not only by the courts, but more often by the wider community, as we have seen in the discussion of honor disputes. However, pre-marital sex was a more complex issue, since sexual relations between courting couples were generally tolerated by families and the village community. If a pregnancy resulted, the young couple was expected to marry, so long as their families agreed and the match was socially appropriate. Pregnant servants, however, were very vulnerable and often a marriage did not happen. Sex between betrothed couples, known as "sleeping together too soon" (*frühzeitiger Beischlaf, früher Beischlaf*), was usually identified when babies were born less than nine months after a wedding. This situation was common (indeed possibly almost universal) and regularly punished with a fine and sometimes a shaming punishment.[18]

Pre-marital sex, often referred to as "fornication," was routinely shown to be punished in the records of the village court in Wollmatingen. For example, in January 1675 the court met in a special session to punish a woman who had gotten pregnant outside of marriage. She was fined 5 *Gulden* and given a "church penance" that involved kneeling in the front of the church during Sunday services and was given the option of paying a larger fine (7 1/2 *Gulden*) to avoid the shaming punishment. The court noted that she was "willing to marry."[19] A 1679 case was even more straightforward. Barbara Zimmermann got pregnant by a soldier in Constance and agreed to marry him.[20] In 1670 another couple was fined for "sins of the flesh with each other" (*fleischlich miteinander versündigt*).[21] The court expressed the hope that they would marry.

A more complicated case from 1661 shows that marriage was usually the goal of the courts and of families in cases of pre-marital sex.[22] Ursula Jüngin began this case by filing suit against Jacob Klingenberger, stating he had long courted her and had promised to marry her before he had sex with her. Now Ursula was pregnant and wanted to marry. Jacob denied having promised marriage and said "he could not know who had gotten her pregnant" since he claimed that Ursula had also slept with another man, Hans Georg Sautter. Sautter denied having sex with Ursula and the court ordered Klingenberger to be punished and referred the case to the ecclesiastical court.[23]

[18] Hull calls this practice "premarital coitus," but that phrase does not capture the difference between pre-marital sex or extra-marital sex and sexual relations between couples who were planning on marrying. Hull, *Sexuality, State, and Civil Society*, esp. pp. 69–70. I will call this practice "pre-marital intimacy" to distinguish it from the larger category of pre-marital sex.

[19] GLAK 61/13268, January 12, 1675.

[20] GLAK 61/13268, May 13, 1679.

[21] GLAK 61/13268, March 8, 1670.

[22] GLAK 61/7599, pp. 3–4, 8–11.

[23] Klingenberger went to "the tower," i.e., the prison. Sautter was also punished, with the stocks, for lying.

A month later Klingenberger filed a slander suit against Catherina Jüngin, Ursula's sister. Catherina had been telling people that Klingenberger had had sex with Ursula, and he had told her that she should let him "have his will with her" since he knew how to avoid getting her pregnant. Klingenberger had then explained in detail how he would practice *coitus interruptus*. Furthermore, if for some reason Ursula should get pregnant, Hans said that he knew a good abortionist in Constance. Klingenberger initially denied that he had said and done what Ursula reported, but eventually had to give in, since Ursula was able to testify to exact dates and places where their liaison had taken place. The court decision was succinct. Klingenberger and Ursula Jüngin were each to pay a fine, make a (long) pilgrimage to Einsiedeln in Switzerland, and get married within eight days.

These cases usually resulted from the investigation of a pregnant woman, or as a result of someone reporting sexual activity, as in the Jüngin/Klingenberger relationship. One can certainly assume that many of these situations never came to court and that families arranged marriages (or compensation) among themselves. In this area, as in other aspects of life, informal resolutions and settlements were common and preferred. Settlements were easy if the couple agreed to marry and the families were supportive; if there was a disagreement over a promise of marriage, or significant social differences between the parties, or if the parents objected, then a settlement was more difficult.

These lower courts occasionally dealt with disputes over promises of marriage, as in the case above, but jurisdiction over marriage promises ultimately lay with the ecclesiastical court of the Bishops of Constance. In some cases, promises of marriage could be disputed, even without sex between the parties. In a March 1675 case, a couple was "together" but had not had sex and the woman testified that the man had promised to marry her.[24] Now the potential groom was having second thoughts, so the Mainau court ordered him to come to a decision within eight days. The reasons for his hesitation became more apparent when the man's family appeared in court and stated that the potential bride's family and friends "did not have a good name." The court ruled that he could get out of the marriage promise with a (large) payment of 30 *Gulden*. After this, the case disappears from the records, suggesting that a settlement was reached informally.

As they did with other issues, lower courts functioned as places for people to reach agreements about marriage promises. Görg Brunner from Allmannsdorf was brought to court by Anna Suterin and Maria Walbartin who testified that Görg had promised to marry both of them and then slept with both of them (*und darauff beyde beschlaffen*).[25] A settlement was reached at the court at Mainau whereby Görg agreed to marry Maria and paid Anna 20 *Gulden* "for having promised her." All parties agreed, and a "contract" was drawn up in three copies,

[24] GLAK 61/7600, March 5, 1672, March 6, 1672.

[25] GLAK 61/7600, March 10, 1674.

one for each of the women and one for the ecclesiastical court. Here, again, we see that the authorities were interested in resolving the dispute and establishing a marriage. No one was punished for the pre-marital sex.

In the summer of 1669, Jörg Geiger and Maria Poplerin "in accordance with a promise, took each other in marriage."[26] Jörg and Maria also exchanged gifts, another crucial element of any marriage. He gave her ½ *Reichstaler* and she gave him a *Pater Noster* (a rosary) and a handkerchief. The couple then consummated the marriage in a garden in Maria's home village of Tüfingen, although there is no mention of a church service. Maria admitted that they had intimate relations at least five times that summer. But in the fall the couple determined they did not want to marry after all, and Maria decided to marry someone else. They returned the gifts, although there was a dispute over how much of the money Maria should return. Also, the couple had apparently been able to keep their "marriage" secret. Maria's father was shocked when the *Amman* in Tüfingen told him Maria would remain a "whore" until her marriage had been celebrated "in the church and on the street." The court in Salem did fine the couple for their sexual behavior, but more significantly ordered them to get back together.[27] Here, again, as Hull emphasizes, the authorities were less interested in punishing pre-marital sexual behavior than they were in encouraging and preserving marriages.

In February 1661, the *Oberamtsgericht* in Rot heard extensive testimony about a disputed marriage promise.[28] This case was somewhat different from most of these kinds of cases, since it involved a widow, Agatha Wonhäsin, who had considered a marriage to Michael Gröckh. The couple admitted to having sex on multiple occasions. Despite this, the marriage negotiations with Gröckh did not go well and Agatha broke them off and married a different man. She had inherited a farm from her late husband and did not want to concede control of it to Gröckh, and there were other disputes as well. The court ordered both parties punished quite harshly, with large fines, for having sex outside of marriage. However, the Abbot of Rot intervened personally in this case.

> After this, on the 10th of March, His Reverence [the abbot] spoke as follows to this Agatha, in the company of her new husband, Georg Kargen. His Grace would have every reason to drive them out of Eppen because of their sins of the flesh, but since many and important intercessions on their behalf have come in, His Grace has also considered that we are all sinful people and that one person today [and] another tomorrow might fall. As a result, the authorities are more inclined to forgiveness (*misercordia*) than to severity.

[26] GLAK 61/1333, pp. 53–4.

[27] Both the court at Salem and the one at Mainau took testimony about marriage promises and sometimes worked out agreements. They also forwarded cases to the ecclesiastical court. See, for example, GLAK 61/7602, pp. 1r–3v, 31r–31v.

[28] HStAS B486/Bd 14, 131r–132v.

The abbot "suspended" the punishments and allowed Agatha and her husband to keep the farm in Eppen. The abbot's statement of forgiveness and his meditation on human sinfulness shows a kind of down-to-earth engagement with sexual crimes, an understanding of realities of rural society, and a practical application of Catholic pastoral theology.[29]

Neither the authorities nor the established and propertied families had an interest in punishing pre-marital sexual activity, as long as it led to marriage. The same people did want to prevent other possible consequences of sex outside of marriage, especially the birth of illegitimate children who might become a burden on the community.[30] One problematic group were servants and farm laborers, particularly maids. As we have already seen, female servants were always vulnerable to sexual advances by the men in the household, from the master, the sons of the master, as well as the other servants.

The experience of Christin Rüedlin is perhaps typical and illuminates the difficulties faced by female servants.[31] In 1672, Christin was serving in Dingelsdorf when she was visited at night by Martin Weiler on two occasions. She testified that Weiler lay on her bed and spoke to her about marriage. She did not say yes, but he nevertheless "strongly pressured her to do the *actam Fornicatoriam*" and even tried to use force. Weiler said he had been encouraged by Christin's brother to seek her hand in marriage and stated "that he hoped no one could prove that he had wanted to force her." Under further questioning, Christin admitted to having sex "often" with another man, Christoph Scherer. The court delayed announcing its punishment of Christin, but fined Weiler. In a further twist, the court reminded Weiler, perhaps as a kind of warning, that he had previously gotten his maid Margaretha Kesslerin pregnant and she had been banished from the territory the previous February.[32]

Christin was no doubt punished for having sex with Scherer, but perhaps they married. Weiler had appeared before the court on multiple occasions, including a fine for excessive celebrating during carnival and for a brawl with Christoph Scherer, Christin Rüedlin's lover.[33] He seems to have considered female servants easy targets, which they were. Did Weiler really want to marry Christin, or was the offer of marriage a ploy to get her to sleep with him? In any case, he was considered a bit of a troublemaker by the court at Mainau, but it was the maids who suffered the most serious consequences of pre-marital sex.

[29] See Louis Châtellier, *Religion of the Poor* (Cambridge, 1997); Forster, *Catholic Revival in the Age of the Baroque*.

[30] Hull, *Sexuality, State, and Civil Society*, pp. 36–41.

[31] GLAK 61/7600, December 3, 1672.

[32] GLAK 61/7600, February 9, 1672, March 26, 1672, April 22, 1672. Kesslerin's brothers came to her defense and tried to force Weiler to marry her. They were unsuccessful, partly because there was testimony that another man had also been found in Kesslerin's bed. Weiler was ordered to pay Kesslerin 6 *Gulden* and to provide for the upkeep of the child.

[33] GLAK 61/7600, December 3, 1672.

Female servants were vulnerable for obvious reasons, particularly the power dynamic in hierarchically organized households. Servants may also have been more closely supervised than the other members of the household. Hans, a servant in Dingelsdorf, was fined in July 1685 for going "upstairs" in the town hall in Egg and sleeping with Catherine Thumbin, the servant there.[34] Catherine was put in stocks outside the church during Mass. Furthermore, under normal circumstances a female servant had little chance of marrying the master of the house or an inheriting son. The dynamic was somewhat different if both the woman and the man were servants or if the man was some other kind of outsider, perhaps a soldier.

Pregnancy brought sexual activity outside of marriage to the attention of the authorities. The village court in Wollmatingen laconically noted in 1682 that a servant there had gotten pregnant.[35] Both the woman and the man who got her pregnant were given fines, but there is no discussion of a marriage. In 1701 Jacob Diesslin found himself facing multiple charges at the Wollmatingen court.[36] Barbara Stockherin, his former maid, said he had promised to marry her and then gotten her pregnant. Meanwhile, he was also charged with getting his wife pregnant "too soon," that is, before their wedding. Jacob paid hefty fines, 20 Pounds for Barbara's pregnancy and 40 Pounds for his wife's early pregnancy. The consequences of these pregnancies for the women were predictably different. Both were to stand before the church with a burning candle, but Barbara, the maid, was banished from the territory as well. Barbara announced in court that she was taking her case to the ecclesiastical court in an attempt to get further compensation from Diesslin for breaking a marriage promise.

In the period after 1700, the authorities became stricter in dealing with premarital sex. In 1702, also in Wollmatingen, Sebastian Romer and his former maid, Catherina Romerin, had "each made the other suspect."[37] Sebastian was fined, but Catherina was banished from the territory until she could show an attestation of good behavior. In 1714 another servant was banished for a year for getting pregnant.[38]

Another case, from December 1725 in Wollmatingen, is an example of the *Frevelgericht* there responding to sexual crimes very severely. Martin Stadelhoffer, from one of the established families in the village, had spent three nights with Catherina Haimin, a *Hintersässin*, that is, a non-citizen resident.[39] Their crime was compounded by the fact that their last night together was on Holy Trinity Day and they missed Mass that day. Both were ordered to perform six days of

[34] GLAK 61/7602, p. 50v. Hans was not given a last name in the court records.

[35] GLAK 61/13268, April 7, 1682.

[36] GLAK 61/13268, January 28, 1701.

[37] GLAK 61/13268, January 14, 1702. *so in ein also anderem suspect gemacht haben*. Although they had the same last names, there is no indication that Sebastian and Catherina were related, nor any accusation of incest.

[38] GLAK 61/13268, January 22, 1714.

[39] GLAK 61/13268, p. 314 v.

forced labor, pay a church fine in cash, and attend daily Mass, both morning and evenings, for four weeks. If they "frequented" each other again, Catherina would be expelled from the village. Surprisingly, if they decided to marry, Martin would lose his citizenship in Wollmatingen and they would both be sent away, "...and they could go together wherever they wished." The punishments imply that the peasant jurors in Wollmatingen were more concerned with the failure to attend Mass than with the sexual behavior. They also discouraged the couple from marrying, apparently out of concern that this was a mésalliance.

This harsh response is quite different from the rulings of the Salem court in the 1670s. In January 1670 a couple was convicted of pre-marital sexual activity. They stated they wanted to marry and were fined 5 *Gulden* each.[40] Two years later a couple was pregnant, they agreed to marry, and were given only a "church penance," probably a shaming punishment.[41] Another couple, who were already married, were found to have gotten pregnant before their wedding.[42] For this crime (*zu fruhe Impraegnation*, "too early impregnation") they were fined 6 *Gulden* which they were allowed to pay over time.

These examples show the overlap between cases of pre-marital sexual behavior and the legally distinct category of "sleeping together too soon" (*Frühzeitiger Beischlaf*), that is, sex between (what we might call) committed couples who had made a marriage promise. As mentioned before, these cases of pre-marital intimacy came to the court when a baby was born less than nine months after a wedding, although sometimes the protocols are not clear how the sexual activity came to the attention of the authorities. Of course, this category of sexual crime hinged on the validity of a marriage promise, which could be disputed by one of the parties, usually the man.

The unclear boundaries between the categories of pre-marital sex, pre-marital intimacy, and even adultery, gave courts, families, and wider communities some leeway in how to deal with particular situations. When Maria Landissen was "going around highly pregnant" in June 1672, she and Hans Baumann agreed to marry.[43] The couple had committed "fornication" months before, but the Mainau court treated their situation as a common case of "sleeping together too soon." The fine, 5 Pounds and a church penance, was standard. The couple could then be treated like any other couple that had slept together during courting, rather than as people who had engaged in casual sex and had unexpectedly become pregnant.

The court at Wollmatingen recorded quite a few cases involving "sleeping together too soon" between 1670 and the 1720s. The jury in a village court like this one likely knew a lot about what was happening among the young people, so some of the cases may not have been cases of a pregnant bride. On the other hand, fines were often larger if there was a pregnancy. The 1715 marriage of Johannes

[40] GLAK 61/13334, p. 22. [41] GLAK 61/13334, p. 115.
[42] GLAK 61/13334, p. 47. June 27, 1670. [43] GLAK 61/7600, June 11, 1672.

Köner und Catharina Weberin brought this and several other issues into the open.[44] The parish priest complained to the court that,

> this bride and groom (*Hochzeitsleute*) have been sleeping together for four years, which everyone in the community knows about. And when he warned them a year before to stop this misbehavior (*Ungebür*), they promised him, with tears in their eyes, that they would [stop]. But during this past Lent they slept together three times, and each time the bride's ten to twelve-year-old sister was in the bed with them.

The couple admitted to all of this and was fined 3 Pounds, as well as two pounds of wax for the church. The fine would be 40 Pounds if Catharina turned out to be pregnant.

The greater fine if the bride was pregnant demonstrates the concern that the couple was setting a bad public example. When a baby was born less than nine months after the wedding, it also provided indisputable evidence of pre-marital sex, therefore justifying a larger fine. The role of the parish priest here is also interesting. He was the informant in this case, bringing to the court a situation that the rest of the village community apparently tolerated. The threatened fine of 40 Pounds (about 50 *Gulden*) also shows how seriously the authorities had come to take this crime by the early eighteenth century.

This list of cases makes even clearer the increasing punishments for pre-marital intimacy. The standard fine went up to 20 Pounds by the late 1680s and then to 40 Pounds after about 1700. Banishing the couple, which first appears in the sources in 1720, was an even more serious punishment. As with all cases of banishment, it is not clear if this punishment was actually enforced, or if it could be bought off with a fine. The July 1721 case seems to imply this was possible.

The "church penances" mentioned in the decisions were at times specified as standing in front of the church holding a candle during Mass. At other times, the nature of the penance was not mentioned and in others there was no mention of a church penance at all. Such punishments were probably standard in those cases, at least for the woman. As we saw above, cases could be, and probably often were, identified by the parish priest, since he was expected to consult the parish records at the time of a baptism to see when (or if) the parents had married.[45] In this area, church and state cooperated to discipline the population. What is hard to determine, however, is if these penalties changed the way unmarried couples behaved, or if these efforts at disciplining the population became just a way of collecting more fines.

[44] GLAK 61/13268, pp. 177r–177v.

[45] John Bossy, "The Counter-Reformation and the People of Catholic Europe" *Past and Present* 47 (1970): 53.

Table 7.1 Punishments for Pre-Marital Intimacy (frühzeitigen Beischlaf) at the Frevelgericht in Wollmatingen

November 11, 1670: **3 *Gulden*** or a church penance.[46]

February 6, 1672: **3 *Gulden*,** 9 *Batzen* and church penance.

November 19, 1672: **2 *Gulden*** and church penance.

November 19, 1672: **2 Pounds** and church penance.

December 19, 1672: **1 *Gulden*, 12 *Batzen*,** 1lb wax and church penance.

August 21, 1677: **20 *Gulden*.** Fine doubled for initially denying the charge.

October 25, 1678: **20 *Gulden*.** Forbidden to have a public church wedding, due to second degree consanguinity.

October 26, 1680: **10 *Gulden*.** Woman gets church penance.

February 8, 1681: **10 *Gulden*.**

October 23, 1683: **10 Pounds** (= 11 *Gulden*, 6 *Batzen*, 4 *Pfennige*).

April 15, 1684: **20 Pounds** (= 26 *Gulden*, 10 *Batzen*). Larger fine due to fourth degree consanguinity.

October 31, 1684: **10 Pounds.**

August 30, 1687: **20 Pounds.**

August 30, 1687: **40 Pounds.**

August 19, 1690: no punishment specified.

October 20, 1692: **20 Pounds.** Fine lowered because they were poor.

January 28, 1701: **40 Pounds.**

April 15, 1715 (p. 639): **3 Pounds** and some wax. 40 Pounds if she turns out to be pregnant.

October 29, 1720 (p. 289r): Banished for one year.

July 21, 1721 (p. 292r): **40 Pounds** or banished for a year. Ordered to marry.

September 22, 1723 (p. 304v): Banished for one year.

Notes

1 Pound = ca. 1.25 *Gulden*

Source: GLAK 61/13268

This chart shows a few patterns in the fines given for pre-marital intimacy. These fines were certainly large, especially for poorer villagers. However, courts exercised some discretion in levying them, as in the 1681 case above. The husband and father, a worker at the monastery at Rot, was fined only 3 *Gulden* and ordered to work off the rest of the fine with a mason there.[47] The moderation of fines, or their conversion to work punishments, was not unusual since these local courts had a good sense of people's social and economic position.

[46] A church penance usually meant standing in front of the church holding a candle during Sunday services.

[47] HStAS B486/Bd 15, p. 21r.

Table 7.2 Penalties for Pre-Marital Intimacy at Various Courts

Year	Fine	Other	Court	Source
1668	10 *Gulden*	-	Rot	HSTAS B486/Bd 14, p. 121r
1669	18 *Gulden*	-	Rot	HSTAS B486/Bd 14, pp. 142r–142v
1669	18 *Gulden*	-	Rot	HSTAS B486/Bd 14, p. 147v
1669	18 *Gulden*	-	Rot	HSTAS B486/Bd 14, p. 147v
1670	6 *Gulden*	-	Salem	GLAK 61/13334, p. 47
1671	3 *Reichstaler*	-	Salem	GLAK 61/13334, p. 84
1681	3 *Gulden*	Work, 3 days	Rot	HSTAS B486/Bd 15, p. 21r
1681	10 *Gulden*	-	Rot	HSTAS B486/Bd 15, p. 28r
1685	6 Pounds	-	Mainau	GLAK 61/7602, p. 51v
1685	6 Pounds	-	Mainau	GLAK 61/7602, p. 51v
1685	6 Pounds	-	Mainau	GLAK 61/7602, 1685, 31 December
1687	5 Pounds	Penance	Mainau	GLAK 61/7602, 1687, 17 November
1696	5 *Gulden*	-	Salem	GLAK 61/13337, p. 156
1710	10 Pounds	-	Mainau	GLAK 61/7606, pp. 62v–63r

Other exceptions and special arrangements were also possible. The court at Mainau was shocked to hear from the *Amman* in Staad about Ursula Messmerin and Johannes Hulger's wedding.[48] The bride "like other honorable virgins had gone with the crown to the church and the street," but then eight weeks later gave birth to a daughter. The court told the couple that wearing the crown was a "great crime" and an insult to honorable people. In the decision, the court stated:

> We certainly have reason, as an example to others, to give these people a public punishment, such as displaying them with a straw crown as well as other punishments. In consideration of the friendship and the affection [we have] for both of their parents, they be spared that, but they still have to pay a fine of 5 Pounds each.

This rather modest punishment contrasts with the strong language used in the court to reprimand the couple. The status of the two families may also explain a kind of apology by the *Amman*, who stated that he was bringing this case out of "duty" and "obedience" to the lordship. Perhaps he did not want to hand out punishments to this couple on his own, or perhaps he suspected the authorities did not want to punish these families.

Other kinds of extra-marital sexual activity were less complicated to deal with, mostly because state officials, the courts, parish priests, and village elites all agreed about the dangers of adultery, prostitution, and other sexual "crimes."[49] In fact, the centrality of the insults "whore" and "adulterer" shows that an abhorrence of these violations was shared across all of society. We have seen how the whore

[48] GLAK 61/7602, November 17, 1687.

[49] Hull, *Sexuality, State, and Civil Society*, esp. pp. 53–65.

insult defined women's honor and forced them (and their families) to routinely defend their sexual behavior. We have also seen that the punishments for premarital sex fell heavier on women, especially if they were also servants or maids. It is very rare, for example, to see men, even farm laborers or other non-citizens, banished; this was a regular punishment for women who did not have important family connections, especially after 1700. Even in cases of sexual activity between betrothed couples, the women often faced shaming punishments, while the men were only fined.[50]

The unequal treatment of men and women becomes even more apparent when we examine adultery cases. Women bore the burden of unwanted pregnancies in situations that did not lead to marriage or if the man denied paternity. When Maria Merckin slept with Martin Thumb in 1685, she became pregnant, giving birth to a child.[51] In April 1687 Maria delivered the child to Martin's house, where he would be responsible for supporting it. Martin, however, went to court, stating that he did not want the child "to keep him from finding his future good luck." He testified that Maria had slept with at least six other men before him and furthermore that the child was born twelve weeks too early for him to have been the father. Maria did not testify in her defense and the court ruled that she was "a public whore" (*offentliche Scorta*) and that the child would be returned to her and Martin freed of any obligation to support it.

The strategy used by Martin Thumb, to deny paternity by claiming the baby's mother had been with (many) other men, was common. This is what happened to Lisabeth Hensin in 1670.[52] She came to court obviously pregnant (*Gross Schwanger*) and testified that Ochsenhans, a Swiss servant living in the village of Urnau, was the father. Ochsenhans retorted "that he was not alone as the father, since he had fought with another servant in her bedroom." Lisabeth now changed her strategy, stating "she did not want the fool anyway, she wants the other servant, named Massen, he is the real father." This exchange did not help her, however. The court ruled "the s.h. whore must, before sunset, leave the territory."

In the early 1670s, the Salem court routinely pre-judged cases like this one by labeling pregnant single women as "whores" even before they took any testimony. The sad case of Anna Gräffin illustrates the trap women, especially women without family or resources, could find themselves in.[53] Anna was from Switzerland, where her husband had died six years previously. She admitted to having been banished from her "fatherland" for prostitution. She had settled in Urnau, in Salem territory, where she worked as a servant. When Anna became pregnant, by Hans Mannen, a shepherd and a married man, she realized she was in a bad

[50] Hull, *Sexuality, State, and Civil Society*, p. 28.

[51] GLAK 61/7602, April 19, 1687. The case was characterized as one of *simplex adulterium*, that is, only one party was married. It is not clear whether Martin or Maria was married. Neither is described as single.

[52] GLAK 61/13334, p. 51.

[53] GLAK 61/13334, p. 94. March 4, 1671.

situation. "Out of desperation, she seduced the servant Mathis Aman [who was single] with the idea of making the child honorable and in order to get the servant as a husband." The court punished both men with prison sentences and work punishments. Anna, "the s.v. whore," was banished.

The Salem court seemed to operate with a cynical consistency, expelling pregnant women from the lordship, thereby saving on the cost of supporting an impoverished family with children. The fact that these cases were forwarded to the courts by local officials and parish priests indicates that there was a coalition of people who sought to discipline poor and unattached women. We can also see how the casual, but targeted, use of the term whore disguised a more complex lived experience, particularly for servants and other relatively powerless women. The word was also powerful, for it was everywhere in the daily life of the village and highlighted the central dichotomy between honor and dishonor in rural culture. The pregnant Anna Gräffin knew this well when she tried to "make her child honorable" by finding a man to marry.

There were many different situations that led women to be disciplined for their sexual behavior. Anna Geygerin came in person to the court at Mainau in an attempt to enforce an agreement she believed she had with the father of her child.[54] Anna had initially stated that Hans Bruelman was the father of her child and had married him, but after going to confession she "remembered" that Georg Walbarth was in fact the father. She also produced witnesses to a meeting where Walbarth had promised to help Anna's husband find a job and where he had committed to payments of flour to support the child. In court, however, Walbarth had denied any agreement, although he admitted to an eight-year sexual relationship with Anna. The court's decision is somewhat shocking. Walbarth was fined 8 Pounds for having sex with Anna for eight years while Anna was banished forever from the lordship. Anna Geygerin, her conscience pricked by her confessor, decided to tell the truth about her baby's paternity and found a husband who was willing to raise another man's child. Nevertheless, she was banished.

The campaign to discipline sexual behavior was, however, more complex than it appears on the surface. Although women bore the brunt of the disciplinary measures, men were also punished. Also in 1670, just a few months before Anna Gräffin was banished, Jacob Sauter was expelled from Salem territory for getting Catherina Dürrin pregnant.[55] Jacob's punishment was particularly severe, since he and Catherina were cousins. Jacob's claim that he did not know their grandmothers were sisters did not impress the court.

Adultery was clearly tolerated in certain situations, as in the case above of the eight-year relationship between Anna Geygerin and Georg Walbarth. Perhaps the community had also accepted a couple that was cited by the parish priest in 1672

[54] GLAK 61/7600, June 25, 1672.

[55] GLAK 61/13334, p. 88. January 21, 1671.

for living together outside of marriage.[56] Single women with children were also at times left in peace, as was for instance Maria Stufelin, who lived in Bermatingen with her six-year-old son.[57] Maria had family in the village and the court in Salem rejected a request from a resident to have her sent away. As long as she behaved properly, it ruled, she would be tolerated.

As with the cases of sex between betrothed couples, the evidence from these court records indicates a stricter attitude toward adultery in the eighteenth century. By this time, banishment was used as a matter of course, even in unclear cases. In 1710 a pregnant Maria Gislin came to court to try to enforce a marriage promise from Joseph Schwickhardt.[58] Joseph denied he had made such a promise and, as was typical in these cases, claimed that Maria had been with other men. He also testified that Maria had tried to abort the baby, which he said took away any desire he had to marry her. Maria was banished. At that same court session in Mainau, Maria Hubennestlerin from Dettingen suffered the same fate, even though she claimed a man had broken into her house and taken her by force.[59]

Maria Hubennestlerin's experience was surely more common than the sources indicate. One reason for the limited number of sexual crimes in these records is that rape charges would have been taken to a higher criminal court. Another is of course that sexual assaults are under-reported across history.[60] The small number of such cases that do appear nevertheless reveal some of the salient aspects of the regulation of sexual behavior. On the one hand, these courts investigated allegations of sexual assault seriously, at least in the cases that appear in the records. On the other hand, the victims of assaults were usually punished for adultery or fornication, in similar ways as consenting adulterers. The sexual act itself was the crime, and the courts and local officials operated under the assumption that women were both primarily responsible for allowing sex to happen and more dishonored when it did.

There are three cases of sexual assaults and/or rapes in the records I have examined. All of them were considered a form of adultery by the courts. The first is a 1670 case from the Salem *Oberamtsgericht*.[61] The victim in this case, Margaretha Herzogin, was particularly vulnerable. A 13-year-old servant in the village of Diesendorf, Margaretha had been sent away from her home village in Switzerland by an "evil stepmother" to serve as a nanny (*Kindsmagt*) for the postmaster. Margaretha testified that in her first week there a "foreign man" whom she did not know fondled her, took off her shirt, and asked her to come away with him. She referred to him as a *Herr*, that is a man of status or a gentleman. He was identified in court as Balthasar Maximilian Bäsch, a high official in the nearby

[56] GLAK 61/13334, p. 113. Another cohabitation case: HStAS B486/Bd 14, p. 120v. December 3, 1668.

[57] GLAK 61/13334, August 11, 1673.

[58] GLAK 61/7606, p. 15v.

[59] GLAK 61/7606, pp. 15v–16r.

[60] Loetz, *A New Approach to the History of Violence.*

[61] GLAK 61/13334, pp. 81–2.

lordship of Stadion.[62] Bäsch paid the postmaster 1 *Gulden* to hire Margaretha away to serve as nanny for his family. He took her first to Salem, then overnight to the inn in the Salem village of Weildorf. Margaretha described in detail how he assaulted her in the tavern. Bäsch denied "sleeping" with the girl, although he admitted to touching her "through her blouse." A witness at the inn testified that he had seen "that in the night he [Bäsch] had wanted to complete the act, but cannot say for sure if he actually did." Bäsch eventually admitted that he had "been unable to do the act." This defense was of course an attempt to avoid a conviction for rape.

The Salem court investigated this case thoroughly and showed no compunction about recording the detailed testimony from a 13-year-old servant girl about several sexual assaults. Reading them is not easy for a modern reader and one might surmise this was a difficult day in the court as well. But the final decision reflected the differences in social status between the parties, as well as the sexual politics of the era. Bäsch was given a large fine of 70 *Gulden*, but it was reduced "out of mercy" and he only paid 20 *Gulden*. Margaretha Herzogin was put in the stocks for a day, since she was considered guilty of illegal sexual activity. Punishment with the stocks also implied that Margaretha had committed a sin that needed to be punished publicly.[63]

Barbara Freyerin, age 22, was somewhat less vulnerable than Margaretha Herzogin.[64] She was the daughter of an established farmer, and her testimony reflects her sense of indignation. Several days before coming to court, late in the night after the parish festival in Neufrach and Obristenweyler, Barbara had been "led" into an excluded part of the tavern garden by two men, both of whom, as the minutes state, "did the fleshly work with her on the ground." The first man, Peter Rawer, admitted to the act, but denied he had promised to marry her, as Margaretha had testified. The second man, Lorentz Rawer, claimed he had just "grabbed her" and nothing else. A witness said he had seen Barbara with her clothes in disarray. The court did not explicitly call this event an assault, although Barbara clearly did, since she filed a complaint. Furthermore, the language of "leading her" and "grabbing her" implies the use of force. The two men were given time in prison and Barbara Freyerin was put in the stocks. Beyond that, the court decided to wait and see if "the maid" showed signs of pregnancy before proceeding any further.

The final of these cases, from June 1685, is labeled in the Mainau court records as the "Wallhausen unseemly events."[65] In fact, though, witnesses and the court considered this to be a case of sexual assault. The farmer's daughter, Johanna

[62] His full title was *Stadionischer Oberamtmann und Ratsdirector*. "High District Official and Director of the Council."

[63] Loetz, *A New Approach to the History of Violence*, p. 150.

[64] GLAK 61/13334, October 13, 1673.

[65] GLAK 61/7602, pp. 39v–42r. *Wallhaußischer Ungebihrlichs handel.*

Xanterin, became drunk at a wedding and was led to a bed in a neighboring house to sleep off the drink. Peter Bühler, a farmhand in the village, was discovered by other guests assaulting the drunk and sleeping girl. Both Johanna and Peter (referred to in much of the testimony as "the old man") denied that anything had happened. Two young people, a man and a woman, interrupted the act, drove off Bühler, and covered the half-naked girl. One of them, Maria Bonerin, testified that Johanna had appeared to be asleep, but Maria was sure she was pretending. Another witness, Maria Demblerin, a widow, stated under oath that "the old married man" had cried out "Johanna you are mine, I love you," and Maria had insulted him as an old goat. Even after this testimony, both "delinquents" (i.e., Peter and Johanna) "shamelessly" denied their guilt.

The court released Johanna Xanterin and sent her home. Peter Bühler was tossed into jail, where he continued to deny any guilt. After six days in prison, he was banished from the lordship. Clearly Johanna benefited from her family's social status, even though she was considered guilty at some level by the court. We get a sense of the community response to this widely known event from Maria Bonerin's and Maria Demblerin's testimonies. Both women were sure Johanna was pretending to be asleep and unaware of what was happening; and they therefore considered her guilty of adultery. Whatever "really happened" that June night in 1685, a young woman caught in a sexually compromised situation was presumed guilty. Johanna, daughter of an important family, was let off, unlike the 13-year-old servant with no family in the community. If the response of the two Marias is any indication, however, one might imagine that Johanna's honor was damaged by this incident.

The disciplining of sexual activity was shared by the state, embodied by local officials and local courts, the Catholic Church, in the person of the parish priest, and by the local community. We can see in all the above cases how these different forces interacted. In most cases, there was a kind of shared purpose, a desire to protect marriage and prevent disorderly procreation.[66] In some areas, for example in the regulation of pre-marital intimacy, a kind of compromise was reached between the social needs of the community and the regulatory desires of the Church and state. Betrothed young people slept together and had sex before the wedding and their families paid fines if they became pregnant or were found out. In other situations, people with powerful families could mitigate punishments, but servants, farm laborers, outsiders of all kinds, and of course single women suspected of prostitution were subject to serious punishments, including banishment. We do see what Hull calls "a creeping criminalization of sin" and, in the early eighteenth century, a more secular concern for the material consequences of irregular sexual activity.[67]

[66] Hull, *Sexuality, State, and Civil Society*, pp. 50–2.
[67] Hull, *Sexuality, State, and Civil Society*, pp. 66–8.

Preventing Disorder

We have already seen that both the authorities and local communities put a high value on peace and order. Disorderly people, especially young men, servants, and transient people, had to be watched carefully. Disorderly spaces like taverns and the streets required constant supervision. And problematic times, nighttime especially, but also holidays of various kinds and even Sundays, had to be controlled. As with the disciplining of sexual behavior, none of this regulatory activity was new in the seventeenth century, nor could it happen without the participation of the local community.

The records of the *Frevelgericht* in Wollmatingen provide a valuable window into disciplinary efforts at the village level and the interaction between state initiatives and the activity of local officials. These court records clearly show how difficult it was to prevent violence, disorder, and drunkenness. As historians have come to recognize, state mandates, increased punishments, and exhortations by local officials could do little to change behavior and were in any case not always obeyed.[68] There was nevertheless a serious and concerted effort to try to regulate streets and public spaces, particularly at night.

Drunk and disorderly people, especially men, were a regular presence in Wollmatingen, as they were in all villages. An episode in May 1723, however, seems to epitomize a new focus of village authorities on public order. The *Amman* brought to the court a series of charges, all of which resulted from "the great insolence of the young men [*junge Burschen*] during the *Nacht Fron*."[69] The *Nacht Fron* was a celebration that took place after the completion of labor services (*Fron*) and may well have had an element of protest.[70] From the *Amman*'s perspective, this was a night of chaos. First, around 11 p.m. Wilhelm Sautter, the *Kiefferknecht*, threw pieces of wood (*Scheütter*) at Anton Thrumer, who apparently pursued Sautter through the streets, eventually catching him and turning him over to the watch. Meanwhile, Antoni Sauter was admonished by the night watchmen to go home and responded (according to the watchmen) with a barrage of insults.[71]

The *Amman* then reported on a series of what we might consider youthful pranks on the same evening. Two young men made off with a pail from the well in front of the tavern. Another knocked over a milk pail and yelled insults in front of the night watchman's house, threatening also to overturn a cart full of manure. The local authorities were clearly disturbed by this behavior. One indication of their concern was the punishments they gave to the troublemakers, including a

[68] Schlumbohm, "Gesetze, die nicht durchgesetzt werden."

[69] GLAK 61/13268, pp. 300r–302v.

[70] This celebration seems to have involved the throw on pieces of wood, perhaps the burning *Scheiben* used in the *Funkenbrand* and other celebrations involving fires.

[71] See above, Chapter 2, for more about those insults.

couple of days in the tower for several of them. At its session the court also read out a princely ordinance forbidding young men to be on the streets after 10 p.m. As was the case everywhere in early modern Europe, young, unmarried men were a problem for public order.[72]

For both state officials and village leaders, young people, especially young men, behaving badly on the streets of the village at night and disobeying the appointed authorities needed to be controlled. If the evidence of court records in Wollmatingen is any indication, this was a difficult if not impossible task. Holidays remained a time for dancing, drinking, and courting as men continued drinking in taverns past the 10 p.m. closing time. The noise and brawling in the streets did not abate.

In the early eighteenth century the village leaders in Wollmatingen became deeply concerned about what was happening at night in the village. Perhaps this concern was not new, but in the first decades of the new century they reorganized the night watch in the village and attempted to improve the watch's performance, while the village court gave greater punishments to violations that occurred at night. The night watch was reorganized in December 1717.[73] This was a duty that rotated among the citizens of the village, and a fine was set for those who failed to show up for duty. The watchmen were given specific locations to stand at as they kept the peace. They were also expected to call out the hours through the night.[74] This was important to remind people that the taverns closed at 10 p.m. during the summer and earlier in the winter.

The Wollmatingen court protocols frequently indicate if a violation occurred at night. Carnival was a nighttime event, hence its German name *Fastnacht*, and a time of public disorder.[75] Johannes Romer brandished his dagger at night on Ash Wednesday 1705 and broke windows in the *Rathaus*.[76] In 1706 four men were fined for starting a "tumult" on the night of All Saints Day in front of the parsonage.[77] Several years later a group of five young men caused a disturbance in front of the chaplain's door at night, probably the same group who had stayed past closing time at the tavern and on another occasion had spent "half the night" drinking at Andres Albrecht' house.[78]

The court was also unhappy with men calling out other men from their houses at night, as Joseph Kehrner and Georg Romer both did in 1708.[79] Johan Öglin's son stood outside the Kohlmeyer's house at night and "shockingly blasphemed."[80]

[72] Especially Natalie Davis, "The Reason of Misrule" in *Society and Culture in Early Modern France. Eight Essays* (Stanford: 1965), pp. 97–123; Peter Burke, *Popular Culture in Early Modern Europe* (New York, 1978)

[73] GLAK 61/13268, p. 187r. [74] GLAK 61/13268, p. 96.

[75] GLAK 61/13268, February 21, 1679. Anna Romerin was fined for dressing as a soldier and "during the night doing all kinds of things...." See also November 24, 1706. Two men insulting each other and fighting.

[76] GLAK 61/13268, December 14, 1703. [77] GLAK 61/13268, p. 105.

[78] GLAK 61/13268, pp. 141r–v. [79] GLAK 61/13268, p. 141v.

[80] GLAK 61/13268, p. 146r.

The emphasis in the court decisions on the nocturnal nature of these crimes points to two aspects of the efforts to bring peace and order to the village. The first was a fear of what could happen at night, whether it was violence lubricated by drinking, or crimes hidden by darkness. Secondly, most of the people punished were young men, on the loose when they did not have to work, which meant evenings and holidays. The latter were especially problematic, since a day of celebrating and drinking could lead to chaos on the streets the night of feast days.

Efforts by the governing classes to "colonize" and control nighttime activities were widespread, as Norbert Schindler and Craig Koslofsky have emphasized.[81] Ordinances, such as the one issued by the Bishop of Constance for the village of Wollmatingen, were common. The Catholic Church and its parish priests fulminated against dances and other gatherings of young people, even the closely chaperoned *Spinnstuben*, evening gatherings where women spun cloth and young people flirted. The loud demonstrations in Wollmatingen in front of the parsonage and the house of the chaplain may also indicate that young men understood the role of the Church in attempting to restrict their nighttime activities.[82] In the eighteenth century, regulations also sought to suppress what Schindler calls "the acoustic forms of demonstration," the mocking laughter, banging on pots and pans, and the "cheering" (*Jauchzen*) that was part of both street protests and celebrations, especially of weddings.[83]

Controlling the youth, patrolling village streets, and trying to keep peace and quiet at night were difficult. Neither ordinances nor stronger punishments could prevent noise, violence, and rowdy youths from disrupting the peace. But young people were not the only residents in the community, and the desire for peace and order made many take their disputes and other concerns to the courts.

Social Discipline: Suppressing "Superstition"

The courts were only peripherally concerned with evidence of popular beliefs that either contradicted Catholic teachings or might be evidence of trafficking with the devil. The witch insult, as we have seen, was common and on occasion could become an accusation of the practice of witchcraft. Courts were always skeptical of witchcraft accusations and quashed them as a matter of course. By the first decades of the eighteenth century, the witchcraft insult was just an insult.

[81] Norbert Schindler, "Nocturnal Disturbances: On the History of the Night in the Early Modern Period" in *Rebellion, Community, and Custom in Early Modern Germany* (Cambridge, 2002), ch. 5; Craig Koslofsky, *Evening's Empire. A History of the Night in Early Modern Europe* (Cambridge, 2011), esp. ch. 7.

[82] Schindler, "Nocturnal Disturbances," pp. 201–22. Medick, "Spinnstuben auf dem Dorf" in Huck, ed. *Sozialgeschichte der Freizeit.*

[83] Schindler, "Nocturnal Disturbances," pp. 210–11.

Scattered through the court records are references to beliefs in ghosts and charms and in soothsayers who could help one find a lost object. But these references are always embedded in routine court cases, involving slander, accusations of stealing, or village conflicts of other kinds. There is no evidence of an active campaign to suppress popular beliefs or "superstitions."

A 1653 case, ostensibly a standard slander case, reveals the role of prophecies and charms.[84] The case was already somewhat unusual in that Hans Kern filed a slander suit against his brother, Jacob Kern. While drinking at a tavern during a church festival, Jacob lamented that he not only had a horse die, but also a child. "This hurt him and God did not do it, but he knows who did" he went on to say. Although warned by a cousin (the *Amman*) to hold his tongue, he went on to imply that his brother Hans was guilty in the two deaths. Not surprisingly, Hans asked the court in Rot to stop Jacob from spreading these false rumors and restore his honor.

Under questioning, Jacob explained that he had consulted a passing gypsy woman, who told him he and his wife were very unlucky and would lose both a horse and a child. She had said that a harmful charm had been buried on his farm, adding that if he paid her, she could find it and dig it up. Jacob gave the woman a half *Gulden*, and she dug up a bone "from a child who had not been baptized" outside his pigsty. The bone had hairs wrapped around it, one from Jacob's wife and one from a "bad person." The gypsy woman said that the "bad person" would come to their house on the following Monday and ask for something. On the following Monday, Jacob reported that his brother's wife came to the house and asked for water. Shortly after this Jacob's wife gave birth to a child who was so small that it died immediately. Jacob then realized that his sister-in-law had helped with the birth, which made him think that the gypsy woman's prophecy had come true.

Under questioning in court, Jacob's confidence in the gypsy woman's prophecy quickly collapsed. He said that the whole story was probably a scam perpetuated by the woman and that she probably went around to gather information about people before telling fortunes. The court pointed out that Jacob had violated God's and the lordship's ordinances by consulting the fortune teller. He apologized publicly to his brother and paid a fine of 4 and a half *Gulden*, which was considerably reduced according to the wishes of both Jacob's brother and the *Amman*.

The case of the gypsy fortune teller highlights the importance of beliefs in the supernatural and also shows how they were embedded in everyday life. The belief in harmful magic (and counter magic) was part of life, but Jacob could also switch modes and critique his own beliefs in a pragmatic and commonsensical way. The court and the lordship were clear that consulting a fortune teller was illegal and against Church ordinances, but also pragmatically pointed out the damage Jacob

[84] HStAS B486/Bd 13, pp. 3v–5v. The name is hard to read, either Kern or Kem.

had done to people's honor by accusing them of harming animals and humans with magic.

On several occasions reports of diabolical pacts came to the attention of the courts. Here too the responses of both local people and the authorities were pragmatic and showed little concern about a wider attack by the forces of evil. In 1687, Jacob Messmer admitted in court to a pact with the devil, which brought him into possession of an object (*Kuenst*) that apparently gave him some power.[85] He told the court he had recently thrown the object into Lake Constance and that he was reforming his life. He was ordered to confess his sins and renounce his *pactis diabolicus* and was punished with eight days of unpaid work.

Less dangerous manifestations of the supernatural concerned the courts even less. In 1703 the court in Rot was only mildly concerned about a complaint that a smith was mixing a magical root or plant into the fodder for his cows.[86] The smith claimed there was nothing magical going on, it was just a healing plant. The court asked the apothecary in the city of Memmingen to examine the offending plant and provide a report. Nothing more is found in the documents. In 1714 a woman in the village of Allmannsdorf was put in the stocks for telling people that the ghost of her brother-in-law was haunting the house where the brother-in-law's widow was living with her new husband.[87] The crime in this case was slander.

It is certainly true that there was an effort to bring popular beliefs in line with Catholic doctrine and to deal quickly with accusations of witchcraft or pacts with the devil. The officials of the small states understood the risks that came with witch panics, which in the 1630s had devastated similar small ecclesiastical territories in southern Germany.[88] Yet, however serious these concerns might have been, the population, local officials, and the courts all treated manifestations of popular beliefs in the supernatural as a part of daily life that could be managed through the normal system of conflict resolution and negotiation.

The case of a stolen kettle in the village of Wollmatingen in 1672 is a good example of the embeddedness of popular beliefs. This case began as a standard slander charge that revealed the networks of rumor and gossip that could damage people's honor.[89] Johannes Romer brought a slander charge against Johannes Greüssen, testifying that Greüssen had started a rumor that Romer had stolen his kettle. Five witnesses testified to the spread of this accusation through an ever-widening group of women and maids who passed the story to their husbands, or at least that is what the men of Wollmatingen said.

Then the case veered off into the realm of everyday magic, as Greüssen admitted to having consulted Caspar Fessler, a *teüfels beschwörer* (a magician or soothsayer), who claimed to be able to help people find lost property. Fessler told

[85] GLAK 61/7602, April 26, 1687. There was another case of a man attempting to make a pact with the devil, from 1721. GLAK 61/7607, pp. 6r–6v.

[86] HStAS B486/Bd 18, p. 36r. [87] GLAK 61/7606, pp. 52v–52r.

[88] Midelfort, *Witch Hunting in Southwestern Germany.* [89] GLAK 61/13268, pp. 7–8, 11, 12.

Greüssen that the kettle was in the possession of a well-known man in Wollmatingen whom Greüssen trusted. After this consultation, Greüssen spread the rumor that Romer had stolen the kettle. The village court in Wollmatingen did not accept the findings of the soothsayer as evidence of a robbery and fined Greüssen for slander.

The final twist in the case came several weeks later when the court discovered that Georg Stockher of Wollmatingen had stolen Greüssen's kettle, buried it for a time in his vineyard, and then given it to his mother in another village. In the meantime, Stockher had been going around the village calling Romer the "kettle man" (*Kesselmann*), further damaging Romer's honor.[90] Stockher was punished hard, with eight days in prison, but, as a sign of his importance, his prison time was reduced after the intervention of the Prince Bishop of Constance himself, as well as from village leaders in Wollmatingen. Still, he had to apologize to Romer and Greüssen, was ordered to go without weapons, and was banned from meetings of the commune for a year. He also had to pay fines and compensation. Stealing was far worse in the view of the Wollmatingen court than consulting a soothsayer or spreading slanderous rumors.

Social Discipline: Enforcing Obedience to State Officials

Rulers and officials of the small states of Southwest Germany were aware of the development of stronger states and stronger institutions in the larger polities of the Empire and in Europe more generally. The regular French invasions of the period 1650–1750 surely focused these petty princes on the power of their powerful neighbor. Their status as imperial princes gave the abbots of Rot and Salem a loyalty to the "incubator" of the Holy Roman Empire and was central to the consciousness of the ruling elites of these territories.[91] If the prince-abbots, the monks, and their officials were often socially and physically close to their subjects, they also insisted on their status and punished disobedience and disrespect consistently.

Peter Mozner lost his job as gardener at the monastery of Rot when the cellarer, a monk, asked him to send him his assistant, a boy and perhaps his son.[92] Mozner was reported to have insulted the cellarer by saying "he would not send his boy to just any fool." In 1686 the court at Mainau put Maria Thumbin in the stocks for colorfully criticizing the lordship over the renting of a tenant farm.[93] Tavern talk could also get villagers in trouble, as in the case of Jorg Moser, who in

[90] Romer was also known as "the Swabian" in Wollmatingen, indicating that he was probably an immigrant from further north, from Württemberg or the Swabian Alb region.
[91] Wilson, *Heart of Europe*. The concept of the Holy Roman Empire as an "Incubator" comes from Walker, *German Home Towns*.
[92] HStAS B486/Bd 14, p. 136r.
[93] GLAK 61/7602, August 26, 1686.

1671 said that he did not care what the Abbot of Salem had ordered.[94] Moser's defense was to claim extreme inebriation. "When the drink is in him [Moser admitted], he is often rude and not in control of himself." The Salem court forwarded the case to the Abbot himself to determine the punishment.

In 1701 Stoffel Hani, a fisherman from Staad, committed a gross act of disrespect, earning himself a large fine.[95] Stoffel took an ordinance issued from Mainau, threw it on the ground and stomped on it, declaring "I shit on the order." When Barbara Hotzin reported him to the authorities for "disrespecting" (*despectire*) an official ordinance, he insulted her and "beat her completely blue." As with all conflicts in this society, the public nature of Stoffel's disrespect especially raised the ire of the court in Mainau, and the fine of 5 Pounds was quite large.

Most efforts to enforce obedience to the authorities revolved around the role of the *Amtmann* (*Amman* in the local parlance). We have already seen that these men were in a difficult spot. They were local men, usually propertied farmers, and, at best, the first among equals socially and economically. The *Amtmänner* were charged with enforcing the lordship's ordinances, collecting taxes, organizing labor services, and generally keeping the peace. They also interacted constantly with the communal government (the *Gemeinde*), attended its meetings, and organized its work. In one sense they were the classical representatives of what Michaela Hohkamp calls "delegated Lordship" (*deligierte Herrschaft*), men who considered themselves part of a peasant elite rather than government administrators.[96] In another way, however, they were in fact officials who were expected to enforce the lord's will.

In this latter role, the *Amtmänner* were usually protected and supported by the higher officials in Salem, Rot, and Mainau. They needed this protection, because conflicts between the *Amman* and his fellow villagers were endemic. Most often these disputes were framed as one between the commune and the *Amman*. The career of Jacob Manz, the *Amman* of Allmannsdorf in the early eighteenth century, illustrates the place of the *Amman* in the village. A 1712 case was another flagrant case of disrespect toward Manz.[97] When Joseph Mayer, the butcher, was ordered to participate in a hunt, presumably by the Teutonic Knights from Mainau, his maid Anna Reiserin said to the person who delivered the summons: "she shits (s.v) on the hunt and the Mainauer should eat it." She was denounced by two villagers, put in the stocks on the *Herrenbrugg*, the bridge that led to the island of Mainau, and banished.

In the case of Anna Reiserin, Manz appears to have had the support of important villagers. In 1721 he faced a more serious challenge, this time during a meeting of the *Gemeinde*.[98] In a discussion of taxes, Hans Sulger said "by one hundred

[94] GLAK 61/13334, pp. 111–13. [95] GLAK 61/7604, p. 146.
[96] Hohkamp, *Herrschaft in der Herrschaft*, ch. 3, esp. pp. 113–14.
[97] GLAK 61/7606, p. 54r. [98] GLAK 61/7607, pp. 57r–57v.

sacraments, he would not pay the *Contribution* until someone came and took his musket away." While this sounds like an echo of contemporary American language about the Second Amendment, most likely Sulger was claiming that as an armed citizen he was part of a local home guard and therefore not required to pay a special tax in wartime. Manz reported that this protest not only angered some of the "subjects," but that it was leading some other villagers to a similar protest. The Mainau *Oberamt* supported Manz and Sulger was sentenced to a jail term.

In these cases, Manz was acting to defend the lordship's policies and its reputation. In other situations, the *Amman* came under attack or became embroiled in village conflicts himself. In 1701 Manz sharply attacked Jacob Forster during a meeting of the commune, accusing Forster of stealing money, fruit, and wine when he was *Pfleger*, that is, manager of communal property.[99] In 1710, Johann Galley called Manz a scoundrel and a thief in the course of his duties.[100] The same year, Manz was accused of cheating the villagers of Allmannsdorf, apparently not for the first time, by Basche Bombgartner.[101] The court at Mainau knew Bombgartner as a troublemaker and fined him 5 Pounds for this attack.

Manz may have been a particularly active *Amman*, enforcing ordinances, supervising communal officials, and collecting taxes diligently. At the same time, he was not an outsider in Allmannsdorf and faced the same insults and criticisms that other *Bauern* dealt with. In fact, his power and his official role gave him, and all *Amtmänner*, the opportunity for corruption and thus made them vulnerable to denunciation before state officials. The officials in Mainau mostly supported Manz, but not without investigating accusations of malfeasance. This dynamic could make almost any *Amman* unpopular.

Other *Amtmänner* faced more substantive charges of corruption and abuse of their position. In 1701 representatives of the *Gemeinde* of Lippertsreute made the journey to Mainau to file a complaint against their *Amman*, Sebastian Vögele.[102] They accused Vögele of failing to warn them when soldiers were coming to the village, which led to unnecessary difficulties. Furthermore, "he pays attention to his own interest and neglects the common interest, in such a way that he gains an advantage when the quartering of soldiers or transport services are required...." The difficulties caused by wartime conditions were only part of the issue with Vögele. He also bought and sold wine without paying the proper taxes and collected the tithe improperly and kept it for himself. The court ordered further investigation of the issues around quartering of soldiers and fined Vögele 10 Pounds for the latter two violations, which he confessed to. The fact that the *Amman* admitted to using his position to gain economically might well indicate that this sort of behavior was common. What David Sabean says about a *Schultheiss* in the Duchy of Württemberg was also true of an *Amman* in Upper

[99] GLAK 61/7604, pp. 87v–88r.
[100] GLAK 61/7606, pp. 55r.
[101] GLAK 61/7606, pp. 46r–46v.
[102] GLAK 61/7604, pp. 162r–163r.

Swabia. "An important part of his income was made up of fees and, of course, bribes, and the everyday exercise of his authority at least skirted along the edge of corruption and self-aggrandizement."[103]

Sebastian Vögele was also in a difficult position. His "subjects," that is, the people of Lippertsreute, were not always compliant. They could also appeal to the higher authorities who, although they generally supported the *Amtmänner*, were willing to rein in the worst of their behavior.[104] The *Amman* in Litzelstetten, for example, was strongly reprimanded in 1705 for speaking harshly to and insulting the honor of Martin Fux during a meeting of the *Gemeinde* there.[105] In 1704, during a French invasion, the people of Neufrach complained that their *Amman*, Christian Hafen, had fled the village, leaving them at the mercy of the invaders.[106] The Salem *Oberamt* investigated the case carefully, reprimanded all sides for their behavior, and turned the case over to the abbot for final adjudication. We do not know what the final decision was. Here, again, Sabean's description is apt. "... [S]elf-administration at the local level was coupled with detailed control from the center... local officials were at the same time embedded in the interests of the village and functioned as crucial links in the chain of feudal exaction."[107] And, unlike Sabean's Württemberg, lordships like Salem, Rot, and Mainau were small enough to allow close supervision of local conditions. The "center" was literally right down the road.

* * *

There is no evidence of determined or extensive state-building by the rulers of these small principalities. Their administrative apparatus remained underdeveloped and the number of government officials quite small. For the collection of taxes and the enforcement of ordinances, they were dependent on village-level officials who were residents of those villages. Even in areas where these micro-states attempted to discipline local society, for example around sexual behavior, they depended on the cooperation of local people for putting their policies into action. The same constraints were at work when it came to forbidding unauthorized appeals to the supernatural and keeping peace on the streets. And while state authorities were sensitive to any signs of disobedience or disrespect to the lordship, they were also suspicious of local officials and accepted remonstrances and complaints against them by local people.

[103] Sabean, *Power in the Blood*, p. 16. See also David Warren Sabean, *Kinship in Neckarhausen, 1700–1870* (Cambridge, 2010), ch. 2.

[104] Examples of support for the Amman: GLAK 61/13344, pp. 203–4, 275–7; HStAS B486/Bd 18, pp. 85r, 132v.

[105] GLAK 61/7604, pp. 191r–191v.

[106] GLAK 61/13344, pp. 283–90. The *Amman*'s wife remained behind in Neufrach and acted in his place. She was a strong-willed woman, who demanded obedience and even physically attacked several men, including grabbing Hans Nonnenmacher by the hair and smashing his head on a table.

[107] Sabean, *Power in the Blood*, p. 20.

The lower courts were centrally important to the process of state formation that did occur. First, the population came to use the courts more often in the first decades of the eighteenth century. This was surely a sign that these institutions were considered efficient, affordable enough to use, and reasonably fair. Secondly, the courts did not function primarily as tools of the state, but rather as part of a more complex system of conflict resolution on the one hand, and as a vehicle for communication between the authorities and local communities on the other. Thirdly, these interactions between the population and the state could sometimes be contentious, but most often they were routine, pragmatic, and reasonably cooperative.

This dynamic created a particular kind of state formation from below, one that grew out of the regular use of local courts and the interactions that took place there. These courts were state institutions and recognized as such by the general population; yet people did not primarily experience them as oppressive or disciplinary. Instead, they were integrated into everyday life, useful, and even valued. The states that provided them and made them work effectively for people reaped a political benefit from their work as well.[108]

[108] Note that this is different from the traditional "*unter dem Krummstab ist gut leben*" idea, which emphasizes the low tax burden in ecclesiastical states. Peter Hersche, *Müße und Verschwendung*.

Conclusion

This study examines the period 1650–1750 from the bottom up, looking at how rural people managed conflict in their communities. Of course, peasants, village artisans, and cottagers could do little about marauding armies or the quartering of soldiers. Yet they were also not passive victims, even of soldiers, as they used all the methods available to limit their depredations, including appeals to their rulers and legal action. Within their communities, rural people developed and refined ways of limiting conflict, drawing on many traditional methods of negotiation and mediation while also incorporating state institutions, particularly nearby law courts and administrative judicial institutions. The appeal to and instrumentalization of state institutions was a vital element of a process of state formation from below.

Katherine Brun's study of the territory of the Abbots of Salem in the fifteenth and sixteenth centuries demonstrates that many of the developments traced in this study had pre-Thirty Years' War antecedents. Brun examines the function of courts in the Salem territory, focusing on the *Sidelgericht*, a predecessor to the Salem *Oberamtsgericht* studied there.[1] This court also handled disputes over sales of property, debts, inheritances, and use of fields and pastures, as well as personal conflicts, including honor disputes.[2] Although individual disputes seem to have been less prevalent at the *Sidelgericht* than they were after 1650, this court was also pragmatic, local, and drew on the traditions of customary law.

Brun concludes her discussion of the court: "Salem's territorial court supported a stronger and more unified polity by incorporating diverse needs, providing an institutional setting for communication and compromise, and encouraging peace and stability in everyday situations as well as on a more symbolic level." She further develops this point in reference to the governance of Salem's territory more broadly. "This study proposes that the success of governance owes as much or more to this sense of connectedness and membership among the people than to the more typical measures of statehood, such as exclusive jurisdiction, military power, bureaucracy, or political sovereignty."[3]

Brun shows that a kind of state formation from below was underway before the cataclysm of the Thirty Years' War. It then comes as no surprise that after the war

[1] Brun, *The Abbot and His Peasants*, ch. 5.
[2] Brun, *The Abbot and His Peasants*, pp. 267–304.
[3] Brun, *The Abbot and His Peasants*, both quotes p. 330.

Keeping the Peace in the Village: Conflict and Peacemaking in Germany, 1650–1750. Marc R. Forster, Oxford University Press. © Marc R. Forster 2024. DOI: 10.1093/oso/9780198898474.003.0009

people sought to return to those traditions. The three decades of war and destruction was followed by a period of relative peace and reconstruction. This peace was in some ways short-lived, as a further series of wars brought foraging soldiers, special war taxes, plundering, and destruction, although on a smaller scale than during the Thirty Years' War.[4] Despite the realities of war, Germans at all levels of society tried to create and strengthen institutions that would keep conflict and destruction within bounds. This effort can be seen in the revival of imperial institutions such as the Imperial Chamber Court and the Aulic Court, as well as the commitment of much of the German elite to the structure of the Empire.

The goal here has been to do more than produce another narrow local study. I try to avoid "the pervasive tendency in current work on early modern peasants to advance endless variations of the same, but sole, general analytic claim, i.e. that peasants had agency," as Govind Sreenivasan has lamented. Nor is this exclusively a study that shows the specificity of conditions in a small region on the banks of Lake Constance.[5] But to understand how rural society was governed and how it governed itself, one has to examine processes on the ground and in a local context. The court protocols used here provide the kind of detailed stories that makes such a study possible.

There were broader consequences of the way rural people integrated state judicial institutions into their communities' practices of conflict resolution. Other forms of governance probably benefited from the appreciation people had for the courts. There was no popular unrest in the territories studied here in the century after 1650. These little states did not have armies and tax burdens were low, although aspects of lordship, such as the requirement to provide transport for the wine harvest, could cause tensions. The abbeys at Rot and Salem, and to a lesser extent the Teutonic Knights at Mainau, employed a large number of local people in their monastic complexes, especially in construction. The state, such as it was, was an employer rather than much of a burden. This situation was not a peculiarity of this particular region of Germany, even if it was an under-governed area. Despite its pretensions, state power was everywhere limited.

Legal institutions, whether district courts or village courts, functioned in complex ways that take us far from the world of Michel Foucault's *Discipline and Punish*. Yes, people were punished and a prison sentence in the "tower" at Rot was humiliating and probably unpleasant. The frequent use of shaming punishments, particularly for women guilty of sexual crimes, exploited the importance of honor in these communities. But rural people were not terrorized by a fear of the capital punishment or torture, as Sreenivasan's study of criminal punishment in the

[4] Emmanuel Kreike, *Scorched Earth. Environmental Warfare as a Crime against Humanity and Nature* (Princeton, 2021), esp. chs 5 and 6.

[5] Govind P. Sreenivasan, "Beyond the Village: Recent Approaches to the Social History of the Early Modern German Peasantry" *History Compass* 11/1 (2013): 50, 55.

nearby lordship of Ottobeuren shows.[6] Instead legal institutions and practices were imbedded in the life of the village, part of daily life.[7] Unlike in some other places in Europe, and in contrast to Enlightenment literature that attacked "pettyfogging lawyers" and the slow pace of justice at the Imperial Chamber Court, the courts studied here were inexpensive, worked quickly, and produced decisions that were generally respected.[8]

This study is also about more than the interactions between the authorities and local communities. The sources provide detailed accounts of how residents of villages lived with each other, across a wide range of social groups. One obvious conclusion is that conflict was endemic and it was often violent. People were attuned to insult, quick to anger, and willing to use their fists or whatever weapon was at hand. But violence was neither uncontrolled nor random. Tavern disputes, for example, had a ritual quality to them, as men moved from insults, to slapping, to fisticuffs, to "taking it outside" for more intense disputes. Conflicts between women on the streets, another common occurrence, also followed a predictable course, from basic insults, to more imaginative name-calling, to slapping and hair-pulling.

Conflict and peacekeeping were always found together, showing the value of peace for rural people, as well as the ubiquity of conflict. Villagers, especially men with authority, local officials, tavernkeepers, and members of the village council, frequently made appeals for peace to combatants. Once tempers cooled, parties usually sought a settlement of the dispute, an apology for angry words, and a restoration of honor and peace. Community relations were not always peaceful and harmonious, but people worked to find a way to share spaces and experiences with people they had often known their whole lives. As David Sabean has astutely pointed out, a community was constituted by the fact everyone was part of "the same argument, the same *raisonnement*, the same *Rede*, the same discourse...."[9]

These communities were not closed worlds; instead they constantly interacted with higher authorities, neighboring communities, more distant towns and cities, and even with invading armies and wider political events. Also, the residents of Wollmatingen, or Allmannsdorf, or any of the other villages that appear in this study, did not always close ranks against outsiders. Instead, they took disputes to court, complained to district officials about local officials or priests, and sought advantages where they could. These interactions drew the officials of these micro-states into the daily life of the village, making them part of the "shared argument"

[6] Govind Sreenivasan, "Prosecuting Injuries" *Central European History* 47 (2014).

[7] Some scholars speak of "popular legalism." Griet Vermeesch, "Reflections on the Relative Accessibility of Law Courts in Early Modern Europe" *Crime, History, and Societies* 19 (2015): 53–76, esp. pp. 66–9.

[8] The Imperial Chamber Court had a backlog of 60,000 cases by the 1770s. David Blackbourne, *The Long Nineteenth Century. A History of Germany, 1780–1918* (Oxford, 1988), p. 16.

[9] Sabean, *Power in the Blood*, p. 29.

as well. The many stories found in the court records show the deeply interactive nature of community relations and the communication between the village and its rulers. These stories also show the real lives of the common folk, with an immediacy and particularity that gives specificity to broader historical developments.

Studies have shown that other places, across Europe, experienced this kind of practical state formation from below in the century after 1650. But perhaps there is something peculiarly German here. Are we looking at one of the sources of the strong state of nineteenth- and twentieth-century Germany? Did the descendants of these combative and honor-driven yet flexible and pragmatic peasants become the "obedient Germans" of later centuries? State formation in larger states meant developing a stronger bureaucracy that worked to centralize authority and reduce the power of intermediate authorities.[10] But that path was not really available in many places in Germany, and another method was to gain loyalty to the state by providing institutions and services that people needed and wanted.

In the early nineteenth century these smaller polities were absorbed into larger states with centralizing tendencies. Salem and Mainau became part of the Grand Duchy of Baden, Rot was absorbed by the Kingdom of Württemberg. All of them became part of a united German Empire in 1871. All these states strengthened their bureaucracies and attempted to create both regional loyalties and, especially after 1871, a sense of German nationalism.[11] Regions like Upper Swabia were, on the one hand, skeptical of their new rulers, who seemed far away in Stuttgart and Karlsruhe, and usually Protestant as well. On the other hand, these regions were socially and politically conservative, especially in the *Kaiserreich*, and firmly supported the *Zentrum*, the Catholic political party. Bismarck's *Kulturkampf* did not endear these Catholic peasants to the new Empire, but German nationalism nevertheless came to run deep.[12]

Of course, it is impossible to draw a direct line from the popular participation in and support for state institutions in the century after the Thirty Years' War to the wide German respect for administrative efficiency and bureaucratic centralization in the nineteenth and twentieth centuries. Furthermore, Germans were neither as respectful or obedient in the modern era as they have been portrayed. And, as the studies from elsewhere in Europe show, the English, French, and Italians also used, respected, and instrumentalized judicial structures and other institutions to manage local conflicts.

Ann Goldberg's study of *Privatklagen*, private slander suits adjudicated in the courts of Imperial Germany, points to several continuities with the early modern

[10] Blackbourne, *The Long Nineteenth* Century, pp. 13–26.

[11] Helmut Walser Smith, *Germany: A Nation in its Time. Before, During, and after Nationalism, 1500–2000* (New York, 2020), p. 163.

[12] Margaret Lavinia Anderson, *Practicing Democracy. Elections and Political Culture in Imperial Germany* (Princeton, 2000), esp. chs 4 and 5.

era.[13] First, Germans continued to sue each other in court over insults to honor, and Goldberg identifies an "epidemic of libel litigation" in the *Kaiserreich*. The parties in these disputes were most often middle class, but artisans and peasants were also litigants. Furthermore, about a third of convicted defendants were women. In her discussion of gender, Goldberg emphasizes that "above all, a woman's honor was composed of her sexual chastity and modesty," a clear echo of early modern attitudes.[14] Furthermore, like some of the early modern rural women we have encountered, Goldberg finds that "anecdotal evidence suggests that women pursued sexual harassment offenses through libel actions."[15]

The widespread concern with honor was coupled with a juridification of honor disputes. "What is most striking about these cases is the continuity—the tenacity over centuries and within vastly different settings—of an honor culture litigated in the courts." Goldberg points out that in the nineteenth century other countries, France, England, and the US, did not regulate issues of "civility and respect" through the court system.[16] The newly united Germany, however, had a strong "legalistic culture" that included professional "honor courts" organized by professional societies, as well as the system of private complaints, that allowed people to bypass state prosecutors and file slander charges themselves.

The frequent use of courts to adjudicate personal conflicts, conflicts configured as honor conflicts, might indicate a democratization and individualization of honor in the *Kaiserreich*, as Goldberg argues.[17] However, viewed in the context of conflict and peacemaking in early modern villages, this popular legalistic culture had a longer history. Honor conflicts in the villages were already individualistic in the late seventeenth century, and the assumption that almost everyone could access local courts had a strong whiff of democracy as well. In both the villages of Southwest Germany and in Imperial Germany, we see the common people using the institutions of the state for their purposes, and in the process giving support to the state.

We return then to the idea that the state developed with the participation of the population. Yes, rulers and their advisors, administrators and bureaucrats, judges and lawyers sought to govern their territories more effectively, sometimes purely seeking more power, and certainly often in a paternalistic mode. But the state also developed in response to the needs of local communities, out of the hurly-burly of everyday life. The close examination of the rural communities at the center of this study lays out the interaction of everyday life with the processes and institutions of governance in order to grasp the nature of state formation or the "rise of the state" in a particular place and time.

[13] Goldberg, *Honor, Politics, and the Law*. See also Ann Goldberg, "Honor and the Policing of Intra-Jewish Disputes in Eighteenth- and Nineteenth-Century Germany" in Jason Coy et al., eds. *Kinship, Community, and Self. Essays in Honor of David Warren Sabean* (New York, 2015).

[14] Goldberg, *Honor, Politics, and the Law*, p. 66.

[15] Goldberg, *Honor, Politics, and the Law*, p. 68.

[16] Goldberg, *Honor, Politics, and the Law*, pp. 2–3.

[17] Goldberg, *Honor, Politics, and the Law*, pp. 10–13.

Bibliography

Primary Sources

Generallandesarchiv Karlsruhe (GLAK)

Abteilung 98, Akten Kloster Salem

2314, 2315, 2317, 2319, 3142, 3197, 3198, 3200, 3340, 3433, 3435, 3593, 3599, 4424, 4402, 4403

Abteilung 61, Salem: Oberamtsprotokolle, Gerichtsprotokolle

61/13330—61/13351 (1585–9, 1637–1750)

Abteilung 61, Deutschordenskommende Mainau: Verhörprotokolle

61/7599–61/7607 (1661–3, 1672–1721)

Abteilung 61, Hochstift Konstanz, Amt Bohlingen: Gerichtsprotokolle ("Justizprotokolle")

61/5174 (1712–31)

Abteilung 61, Hochstift Konstanz, Reichenau: Wollmatingen, Gerichts u. Frevel Protokolle

61/13267 1598–1607

61/13268 1669–1732

Abteilung 61, Hochstift Konstanz, Reichenau: Rotteln

61/6957 (1616–41)

61/6958 (1659–89)

Abteilung 61, Fürstenberg/Heiligenberg

61/6568 (1586–9)

Hauptsstaatarchiv Stuttgart (HStAS)

B486 Rot Amts und Verhörprotokolle

Bände 1–26 (1553–1740)

Secondary Sources

Anderson, Margaret Lavinia. *Practicing Democracy. Elections and Political Culture in Imperial Germany* (Princeton: Princeton University Press, 2000).

Asch, Ronald G. and Friest, Dagmar (eds.). *Staatsbildung als Kultureller Prozess: Strukturwandel und Legitimation von Herrschaft in der Fruhen Neuzeit* (Köln: Böhlau, 2005).

Auge, Oliver and Andermann Kurt (eds.). *Dorf und Gemeinde. Grundstrukturen der ländlichen Gesellschaft in Spätmittelalter und Frühneuzeit* (Ostfildern: Verlagsgruppe Patmos, 2012).

Backman, Sibylle (ed.). *Ehrkonzepte in der Frühen Neuzeit. Identitäten und Abgrenzungen* (Berlin, Boston: Akademie Verlag, 1998).

Baier, Hermann. "Die Stellung der Abtei Salem in Staat und Kirche," *Freiburger Diöcesan Archiv* 35 (1934): 131–54.

Behringer, Wolfgang. *Im Zeichen des Merkur. Reichspost und Kommunikationsrevolution in der Frühen Neuzeit* (Göttingen: Vandenhoeck & Ruprecht, 2003).

Beik, William. *Absolutism and Society in Seventeenth-Century France. State Power and the Provincial Aristocracy in Languedoc* (Cambridge: Cambridge University Press, 1985).

Berger, Stefan. *Inventing the Nation: Germany* (Oxford: Oxford University Press, 2004).

Beuke, Arnold. "In guter Zier und Kurzweil bey der Naßen angetastet. Aspekte des Konfliktaustrags in der Frühen Neuzeit," in *Praktiken des Konfliktaustrags in der Frühen Neuzeit*, Barbara Krug-Richter and Ruth-Elizabeth Mohrmann (eds.) (Münster: Rhema, 2004), pp. 119–55.

Blackbourne, David. *The Long Nineteenth Century. A History of Germany, 1780–1918* (Oxford: Oxford University Press, 1988).

Blauert, Andreas and Schwerhoff, Gerd (eds.). *Kriminalitätsgeschichte. Beiträge zur Sozial- und Kulturgeschichte der Vormoderne* (Konstanz: Universitätsverlag, 2000).

Blickle, Peter. *Deutsche Untertanen. Ein Wiederspruch* (Munich: C. H. Beck'sche Verlagsbuchhandlung, 1981).

Blockmans, Wim. "Citizens and their Rulers," in *Empowering Interactions. Political Cultures and the Emergence of the State in Europe, 1300–1900*, André Holenstein, Daniel Schläppi, and Wim Blockmans (eds.) (Burlington: Ashgate, 2009), pp. 281–91.

Bossy, John. "The Counter-Reformation and the People of Catholic Europe," *Past and Present* 47 (1970): 51–70.

Bossy, John (ed.). *Disputes and Settlements. Law and Human Relations in the West* (Cambridge: Cambridge University Press, 1983).

Bossy, John. *Christianity in the West, 1400–1700* (Oxford: Oxford University Press, 1985).

Bossy, John. *Peace in the Post-Reformation* (Cambridge: Cambridge University Press, 2012).

Brändle, Fabian. "Public Houses, Clientelism, and Faith: Strategies of Power in Early Modern Toggenburg," in *The World of the Tavern. Public Houses in Early Modern Europe*, Beat Kümin and B. Ann Tlusty (eds.) (Aldershot: Ashgate, 2002), pp. 83–94.

Brecht, Bertold. *Mutter Courage und ihre Kinder. Eine Chronik aus dem Dreißigjährigen Krieg* (Frankfurt: Suhrkamp, 2018).

Breen, Michael. "Law, Society, and the State in Early Modern France," *The Journal of Modern History* 83 (2011): 346–86.

Brewer, John. *The Sinews of Power. War, Money, and the English State, 1688–1783* (Cambridge MA: Harvard University Press, 1989).

Brun, Katherine. *The Abbot and his Peasants. Territorial Formation in Salem from the late Middle Ages to the Thirty Years' War* (Oldenburg: DeGruyter, 2013).

Burghartz, Susanna. "Geschlecht-Körper-Ehre. Überlegungen zur weiblichen Ehre in der Frühen Neuzeit am Beispiel der Basler Ehegerichtsprotokolle," in *Verletzte Ehre. Ehrkonflikte in Gesellschaften des Mittelalters und der Frühen Neuzeit*, Klaus Schreiner and Gerd Schwerhoff (eds.) (Köln: Böhlau, 1995), pp. 214–34.

Burke, Peter. *Popular Culture in Early Modern Europe* (New York: Routledge, 1978).

Capp, Bernard. "Life, Love, and Litigation: Sileby in the 1630s," *Past and Present* 182 (2004): 55–83.

Castiglione, Caroline. *Patrons and Adversaries. Nobles and Villagers in Italian Politics, 1640–1760* (Oxford: Oxford University Press, 2005).

Châtellier, Louis. *The Religion of the Poor* (Cambridge: Cambridge University Press, 1997).

Claus, Christina. "'Alles hat er versoffen'—Der Wirtshaus Besuch und seine Folgen," in *Kellnerin, a Maß. Das Wirtshaus—die weltliche Mitte des Dorfes*, Toni Drexler (ed.) (Jexhof: Bauernhofmuseum, 1997), pp. 89–101.

Creasman, Allyson. "Fighting Words: Anger, Insult, and 'Self-Help' in Early Modern German Law," *Journal of Social History* 51 (2017): 272–92.

Crubaugh, Anthony. "Local Justice and Rural Society in the French Revolution," *Journal of Social History* 34 (2000): 327–50.

Crubaugh, Anthony. *Balancing the Scales of Justice: Local Courts and Rural Society in Southwest France, 1750–1800* (University Park: Pennsylvania State University Press, 2002).

Cummins, Stephen and Kounine, Laura (eds.). *Culture of Conflict Resolution in Early Modern Europe* (Farnham: Ashgate, 2016).

Coy, Jason. *Strangers and Misfits: Banishment, Social Control, and Authority in Early Modern Europe* (Leiden: Brill, 2008).

Davis, Natalie. "The Reason of Misrule," in *Society and Culture in Early Modern France. Eight Essays* (Stanford: Stanford University Press, 1965), pp. 97–123.

Dillman, Erika. *Anselm II. Glanz und Ende eine Epoche. Eine Studie über den letzten großen Abt der Reichsabtei Salem* (Tettnang: Senn, 1987).

Dillman, Erika. *Stephan I. Fundamente des Barock. Salem an der Wende zum 18. Jahrhundert* (Tettnang: Senn, 1988).

Dillman, Erika and Schulz, Hans-Jürgen. *Salem. Geschichte und Gegenwart* (Tettnang: Senn, 1989).

Dinges, Martin. "'Weiblichkeit' im 'Männlichkeitsritualen.' Zu weiblichen Taktiken in Ehrenhandel in Paris in 18. Jahrhundert," *Francia* 18/2 (1991): 71–98.

Dinges, Martin. "Die Ehre als Thema der historische Anthropologie," in *Verletzte Ehre. Ehrkonflikte in Gesellschaften des Mittelalters und der Frühen Neuzeit*, Klaus Schreiner and Gerd Schwerhoff (eds.) (Köln: Böhlau, 1995), pp. 47–62.

Dinges, Martin. "Ehre und Geschlecht in der frühen Neuzeit," in *Ehrkonzepte in der Frühen Neuzeit. Identitäten und Abgrenzungen*, Sibylle Backmann (ed.) (Berlin, Boston: Akademie Verlag, 1998), pp. 123–47.

Dinges, Martin. "Justiznutzungen als soziale Kontrolle in der Frühen Neuzeit," in *Kriminalitätsgeschichte. Beiträge zur Sozial- und Kulturgeschichte der Vormoderne*, Andreas Blauert and Gerd Schwerhoff (eds.) (Konstanz: Universitätsverlag, 2000): 503–44.

Drexler, Toni (ed.). *Kellnerin, a Maß. Das Wirtshaus—die weltliche Mitte des Dorfes* (Jexhof: Bauernhofmuseum, 1997).

Dürr, Renate. "Die Ehre der Mägde zwischen Selbstdefinition und Fremdbestimmung," in *Ehrkonzepte in der Frühen Neuzeit. Identitäten und Abgrenzungen*, Sibylle Backman (ed.) (Berlin/Boston: Akademie Verlag, 1998): 170–84.

Dürr, Renate and Schwerhoff, Gerd (eds.). *Kirchen, Märkte und Tavernen. Erfahrungs- und Handlungsräume in der Frühen Neuzeit* (Frankfurt: Klostermann, 2005).

Eibach, Joachim. "Das offene Haus. Kommunikative Praxis im sozialen Nahraum der europäischen Frühen Neuzeit," *Zeitschrift für Historische Forschung* 38 (2011): 621–64.

Eriksson, Magnus. "Gemäßigte Gewalt und andere Wege zur Interessendurchsetzung auf der Insel Unmanz bei Rügen im ausgehenden 16. und in 18. Jahrhunderts," in *Streitkulturen. Gewalt, Konflikt und Kommunikation in der ländlichen Gesellschaft (16.–19. Jh.)*, Magnus Eriksson and Barbara Krug-Richter (eds.) (Köln: Böhlau, 2003), pp. 125–55.

Eriksson, Magnus and Krug-Richter, Barbara (eds.). *Streitkulturen. Gewalt, Konflikt und Kommunikation in der ländlichen Gesellschaft (16.–19. Jh.)* (Köln: Böhlau, 2003).

Forster, Marc R. *Catholic Revival in the Age of the Baroque: Religious Identity in Southwest Germany, 1550–1750* (Cambridge, Cambridge University Press, 2001).

Forster, Marc R. "Space, Gender, and Honor in Village Taverns," in *Public Eating, Public Drinking. Places of Consumption from Early Modern to Postmodern Times* (Food and History 7/2, 2010), Marc R. Forster and Maren Möhring (eds) (Turnhout: Brepols, 2010), pp. 15–29.

Forster, Marc R. "Women, Conflict, and Peacemaking in German Villages," in *Embodiment, Identity, and Gender in the Early Modern Age*, Amy E. Leonard and David M. Whitford (eds.) (Abingdon: Routledge, 2021), pp. 159–69.

"Forum: German Home Towns, Forty Years Later," *Central European History* 47 (2014): 482–522.

Foyster, Elizabeth. "Male Honour, Social Control and Wife Beating in Late Stuart England," *Transactions of the Royal Historical* Society 6 (1996): 215–24.

Frank, Michael. *Dörfliche Gesellschaft und Kriminalität: das Fallbeispiel Lippe 1650–1800* (Paderborn: Ferdinand Schöningh, 1995).

Frank, Michael. "Ehre und Gewalt im Dorf der Frühen Neuzeit. Das Beispiel Heiden (Grafschaft Lippe) im 17. und 18. Jahrhundert," in *Verletzte Ehre. Ehrkonflikte in Gesellschaften des Mittelalters und der Frühen Neuzeit*, Klaus Schreiner and Gerd Schwerhoff (eds.) (Köln, Böhlau, 1995), pp. 320–38.

Frank, Michael. "Satan's Servant or Authorities' Agent? Publicans in Eighteenth Century Germany," in *The World of the Tavern. Public Houses in Early Modern Europe*, Beat Kümin and B. Ann Tlusty (eds.) (Aldershot: Ashgate, 2002), pp. 12–43.

Fuchs, Ralf-Peter. *Um die Ehre: Westfälische Beleidigungsprozesse vor dem Reichskammergericht, 1525–1805* (Paderborn: Ferdinand Schöningh, 1998).

Füssell, Marion and Rüther, Stephanie. "Einleitung," in *Raum und Konflikt. Zur symbolischen Konstituierung gesellschaftlicher Ordnung im Mittelalter und in Früher Neuzeit*, Christoph Dartmann, Marion Füssell, and Stephanie Rüther (eds.) (Münster: Rhema, 2004), pp. 9–17.

Garnot, Benoît. "L'ampleur et les limites de l'infrajudiciaire dans la France d'Ancien Régime (XVIe–XVIIe–XVIII siècles)," in *L'Infrajudiciaire du Moyen Age à l'époque contemporaine*, Benoît Garnot (ed.) (Dijon: Éditions Université de Dijon, 1996), pp. 69–76.

Garnot, Benoît (ed.). *L'Infrajudiciaire du Moyen Age à l'époque contemporaine* (Dijon: Éditions Université de Dijon, 1996).

Garnot, Benoît. "Justice, infrajustice, parajustice et extra justice dans la France d'Ancien Régime," *Crime, Histoire, et Sociétés* 4 (2000): 103–20.

Gersmann, Gudrun. "Gehe hin und vertheidige dich! Injurieklagen als Mittel der Abwehr von Hexerei Verdächtigungen—ein Fallbeispiel aus dem Fürstbistum Münster," in *Ehrkonzepte in der Frühen Neuzeit. Identitäten und Abgrenzungen*, Sibylle Backman (ed.) (Berlin, Boston: Akademie Verlag, 1998), pp. 237–66.

Gersmann, Gudrun. "Ort der Kommunikation, Ort der Auseinandersetzung," in *Streitkulturen. Gewalt, Konflikt und Kommunikation in der ländlichen Gesellschaft (16.–19. Jh.)*, Magnus Eriksson and Barbara Krug-Richter (eds.) (Köln: Böhlau, 2003), pp. 249–268.

Ginzburg, Carlo. *The Cheese and the Worms. The Cosmos of a Sixteenth Century Miller* (Baltimore: The Johns Hopkins University Press, 1980).

Goldberg, Ann. *Honor, Politics, and the Law in Imperial Germany* (Cambridge University Press, 2010).

Goldberg, Ann. "Honor and the Policing of Intra-Jewish Disputes in Eighteenth- and Nineteenth-Century Germany," in *Kinship, Community, and Self. Essays in Honor of David Warren Sabean*, Jason Coy et al. (eds.) (New York, 2015), pp. 216–29.

Gowing, Laura. *Domestic Dangers. Women, Words, and Sex in Early Modern London* (Oxford University Press, 1998).

Greenshields, Malcolm. *An Economy of Violence in Early Modern France: Crime and Justice in the Haute Auvergne, 1587–1664* (University Park, PA: Pennsylvania University Press, 1994).

Grimmelshausen, Hans Jakob Christoph von. *Der abenteuerliche Simplicissimus Teutsch*. Available at: https://www.gutenberg.org/ebooks/55171.

Grüne, Neils. "Local Demand for Order and Government Intervention. Social Group Conflicts as Statebuilding Factors in the Villages of the Rhine Palatinate, c. 1760–1810," in *Empowering Interactions. Political Cultures and the Emergence of the State in Europe, 1300–1900*, André Holenstein, Daniel Schläppi, and Wim Blockmans (eds.) (Abingdon, 2009), pp. 173–86.

Haack Julia. *Der vergällte Alltag: zur Streitkultur im 18. Jahrhunderts* (Köln: Böhlau, 2008).

Habermas, Jürgen. *The Structural Transformation of the Public Sphere: An Inquiry into a Category of Bourgeois Society* (Cambridge MA: MIT Press, 1991).

Haghoe, Jeremy. *Enlightened Feudalism. Seigneurial Justice and Village Society in Eighteenth Century Northern Burgundy* (Rochester: University of Rochester Press, 2008).

Hardwick, Julie. "Early Modern Perspectives on the Long History of Domestic Violence: The Case of Seventeenth-Century France," *Journal of Modern History* 78 (2006): 1–35.

Härter, Karl. "Strafverfahren im frühneuzeitlichen Territorialstaat. Inquisition, Entscheidungsfindung, Supplikation," in *Kriminalitätsgeschichte. Beiträge zur Sozial- und Kulturgeschichte der Vormoderne*, Andreas Blauert and Gerd Schwerhoff (eds.) (Konstanz: Universitätsverlag, 2000), pp. 459–81.

Härter, Karl. *Policey und Strafjustiz in Kurmainz: Gesetzgebung, Normdurchsetzung und Sozialkontrolle im frühneuzeitlichen Territorialstaat* (Frankfurt: Klostermann, 2005).

Henshall, Nicolas. *The Myth of Absolutism: Change and Continuity in Early Modern European Monarchy* (New York and London: Routledge, 1992).

Hindle, Steve. *The State and Social Change in Early Modern England, c. 1550–1640* (Houndsmills: Palgrave, 2000).

Hindle, Steve. "Law, Law Enforcement and State Formation in Early Modern England," in *Staatsbildung als Kultureller Prozess: Strukturwandel und Legitimation von Herrschaft in der Fruhen Neuzeit*, Ronald G. Asch and Dagmar Friest (eds.) (Köln: Böhlau, 2005), pp. 209–34.

Hohkamp, Michaela. *Herrschaft in der Herrschaft. Die vorderösterreichische Obervogtei Triberg von 1737 bis 1780* (Göttingen: Vandenhoeck und Ruprecht, 1998).

Holenstein, André. "Ordnung und Unordnung im Dorf. Ordnungsdiskurse, Ordnungspraktiken und Konfliktregelungen vor dem badischen Frevelgerichten des 18 Jahrhunderts," in *Devianz, Widerstand und Herrschaftspraxis in der Vormoderne. Studien zu Konflikten im südwestdeutschen Raum (15.–18. Jahrhundert)*, Mark Häberlein (ed.) (Konstanz: Universitätsverlag, 1999), pp. 165–96.

Holenstein, André. *"Gute Policey" und lokale Gesellschaft im Staat des Ancien Régime. Das Fallbeispiel der Markgrafschaft Baden(-Durlach)* (Epfendorf/Neckar: Wallstein Verlag, 2003).

Holenstein, André. "Klagen, anzeigen und supplizieren. Kommunikative Praktiken und Konfliktlösungsverfahren in der Markgrafschaft Baden im 18. Jahrhunderts," in *Streitkulturen. Gewalt, Konflikt und Kommunikation in der ländlichen Gesellschaft (16.–19. Jh.)*, Magnus Eriksson and Barbara Krug-Richter (eds.) (Köln: Böhlau, 2003), pp. 335–69.

Holenstein, André. "Introduction: Empowering Interactions: Looking at Statebuilding from Below," in *Empowering Interactions. Political Cultures and the Emergence of the State in Europe, 1300–1900*, André Holenstein, Daniel Schläppi, and Wim Blockmans (eds.) (Burlington: Ashgate, 2009), pp. 1–31.

Holenstein, André, Schläppi, Daniel, and Blockmans, Wim (eds.). *Empowering Interactions. Political Cultures and the Emergence of the State in Europe, 1300–1900* (Burlington: Ashgate, 2009).

Holenstein, Pia, and Schindler, Norbert. "Geschwätzgeschichte(n). Ein Kulturhistorischer Plädoyer für die Rehabilitierung der unkontrollierter Rede," in *Dynamik der Tradition*, Richard van Dülmen (ed.) (Frankfurt: Fischer Verlag, 1992), pp. 41–108.

Hsia, R. Po-chia. *Social Discipline in the Reformation. Central Europe 1550–1750* (New York: Routledge and Keegan Paul, 1989).

Hull, Isabel. *Sexuality, State, and Civil Society in Germany, 1700–1815* (Ithaca: Cornell University Press, 1991).

Ingram, Martin. "Ridings, Rough Music, and the Reform of Popular Culture in Early Modern England," *Past and Present* 105 (1984): 79–113.

Jordan, John. "Rethinking Disputes and Settlements: How Historians can use Legal Anthropology," in *Cultures of Conflict Resolution in Early Modern Europe*, Stephen Cummin and Laura Kounine (eds.) (Farnham: Ashgate, 2016), pp. 17–50.

Kolb, Johann Baptist von. *Historisch-statistisch-topographisches Lexicon von dem Großherzogthum Baden*. Band 3 (Karlsruhe: Karl Friedrich Ratlotschen Buchhandlung und Hofbuchdruckerey, 1814).

Kounine, Laura. "The Witch on Trial. Narratives of Conflict and Community in Early Modern Germany," in *Cultures of Conflict Resolution in Early Modern Europe*, Stephen Cummin and Laura Kounine (eds.) (Farnham: Ashgate, 2016), pp. 230–54.

Koslofsky, Craig. *Evening's Empire. A History of the Night in Early Modern Europe* (Cambridge: Cambridge University Press, 2011).

Kramer, Karl-Sigismund. "Das Herausfordern aus dem Haus. Lebensbild eines Rechtsbrauches," *Bayerisches Jahrbuch für Volkskunde* (1956): 121–38.

Kramer, Karl-Sigismund. *Grundriß einer rechtlichen Volkskunde* (Göttingen: Schwartz, 1974).

Kramer, Karl-Sigismund. "Hohnsprake, Wrakworte, Nachschnack und Ungebür. Ehrenhändel in holsteinischen Quellen," *Kieler Blätter für Volkskunde* XVI (1984): 49–85.

Kreike, Emmanuel. *Scorched Earth. Environmental Warfare as a Crime against Humanity and Nature* (Princeton: Princeton University Press, 2021).

Krug-Richter, Barbara. "Konfliktregulierung zwischen dörflicher Sozialkontrolle und patrimonialer Gerichtsbarkeit. Das Rügegericht in der Westfalischen Gerichtsherrschaft Cannstein, 1718/19," *Historische Anthropologie* 5 (1997): 212–28.

Krug-Richter, Barbara. "'Mann müßte keine leute zuhause hangen.' Adlige Gerichtsherrschaft, soziale Kontrolle und dörfliche Kommunikation in der westfälische Herrschaft Cannstein um 1700," *Westfälische Forschungen* 48 (1998): 481–509.

Krug-Richter, Barbara. "Von nackten Hummeln und Schandpflasten. Formen und Kontexte von Rauf und Ehrenhändeln in der Westfälischen Gerichtsherrschaft Cannstein um 1700," in *Streitkulturen. Gewalt, Konflikt und Kommunikation in der ländlichen Gesellschaft (16.–19. Jh.)*, Magnus Eriksson and Barbara Krug-Richter (eds.) (Köln: Böhlau, 2003).

Krug-Richter, Barbara. "Von Rügebrauch zur Konfliktkultur. Rechtsethnologische Perspektive in der Europäische Ethnologie," *Jahrbuch für Volkskunde* N.F. 28 (2005): 27–40.

Kümin, Beat and Tlusty, B. Ann (eds.). *The World of the Tavern. Public Houses in Early Modern Europe* (Aldershot: Ashgate, 2002).

Kümin, Beat. "Wirtshaus, Verkehr, und Kommunikationsrevolution im frühneuzeitlichen Alpenraum," in *Kirchen, Märkte und Tavernen. Erfahrungs- und Handlungsräume in der Frühen Neuzeit*, Renate Dürr and Gerd Schwerhoff (eds.) (Frankfurt: Klostermann, 2005), pp. 376–93.

Kümin, Beat. *Drinking Matters. Public Houses and Social Exchange in Early Modern Central Europe* (Houndmills: Palgrave, 2007).

Lacour, Eva. *Schlagereyen und Unglücksfälle: zur historischen Psychologie und Typologie von Gewalt in der frühneuzeitlichen Eifel* (Frankfurt: Egelsbach, 2000).

Lacour, Eva. "Faces of Violence Revisited. A Typology of Violence in Early Modern Rural Germany," *Journal of Social History* 34 (2001): 649–67.

Lehmann, Hartmut. *Das Zeitalter des Absolutismus. Gottesgnadentum und Kriegsnot* (Stuttgart: Kohlhammer, 1980).

Lidman, Satu. *Zum Spektakel und Abscheu. Schand- und Ehrenstrafen als Mittel öffentlicher Disziplinierung in München um 1600* (Bern: Peter Lang, 2008).

Loetz, Francisca. "L'Infrajudiciaire. Facetten und Bedeutung eines Konzepts," in *Kriminalitätsgeschichte. Beiträge zur Sozial- und Kulturgeschichte der Vormoderne*, Andreas Blauert and Gerd Schwerhoff (eds.) (Konstanz: Universitätsverlag, 2000), pp. 545–62.

Loetz, Francisca. "A New Approach to the History of Violence," in *"Sexual Assault" and "Sexual Abuse" in Europe, 1500–1850* (Leiden and Boston: Brill, 2015).

Luebke, David Martin. *His Majesty's Rebels. Communities, Factions, and Rural Revolt in the Black Forest, 1725–1745* (Ithaca: Cornell University Press, 1997).

MacGregor, Neil. *Germany: Memories of a Nation* (London: Penguin, 2014).

Mathieu, Jon. "Statebuilding from Below—Towards a Balanced View," in *Empowering Interactions. Political Cultures and the Emergence of the State in Europe, 1300–1900*, André Holenstein, Daniel Schläppi, and Wim Blockmans (eds.) (Burlington: Ashgate, 2009), pp. 305–11.

Medick, Hans and Marschke, Benjamin (eds.). *Experiencing the Thirty Years' War. A Brief History with Documents* (Boston and New York: Bedford/St. Martins, 2013).

Medick, Hans. "Spinnstuben auf dem Dorf. Jugendliche Sexualkultur und Feierabendbrauch in der ländlichen Gesellschaft der Frühen Neuzeit," in *Sozialgeschichte der Freizeit. Untersuchungen zum Wandel der Alltagskultur in Deutschland*, G. Huck (ed.) (Wuppertal: Hammer, 1980), pp. 19–49.

Melton, James Van Horn. "Absolutism and "Modernity" in Early Modern Central Europe," *German Studies Review* 8 (1985): 383–98.

Ménétra Jacques-Louis. *Journal of My Life*. Daniel Roche, ed. (New York: Columbia University Press, 1989).

Midelfort, H. C. Erik. *Witch Hunting in Southwestern Germany, 1562–1684: The Social and Intellectual Foundations* (Stanford: Stanford University Press, 1972).

Mortimer, Geoff. *Eyewitness Accounts of the Thirty Years' War* (Houndmills: Palgrave, 2002).

Muurling, Sanne. *Everyday Crime, Criminal Justice and Gender in Early Modern Bologna* (Leiden/Boston: Brill, 2021).

Nora, Pierre. *Realms of Memory: Rethinking the French Past*, 3 vols. (New York: Columbia University Press, 1996).

Oelze, Patrick. *Recht haben und Recht behalten. Konflikte um die Gerichtsbarkeit in Schwäbisch Hall und seiner Umgebung (15.–18 Jahrhundert)* (Konstanz: UVK Verlag, 2011).

Oestreich, Gerhard. *Geist und Gestalt des frühmodernen Staates* (Berlin: Duncker und Humblot, 1969).

Ogilvie, Sheilagh. "The State in Germany. A Non-Prussian View," in *Rethinking Leviathan. The Eighteenth-Century State in Britain and Germany*, John Brewer and Eckhart Hellmuth (eds.) (Oxford: Oxford University Press, 1999), pp. 167–202.

Ogilvie, Sheilagh, Küpker, Markus, and Maegraith, Janine. "Household Debt in Early Modern Germany," *Journal of Economic History* 72 (2012): 134–67.

Peyer, Hans Conrad. *Von der Gastfreundschaft zum Gasthaus. Studien zur Gastlichkeit im Mittelalter* (Hannover: Hahn, 1987).

Rabb, Theodore. *The Struggle for Stability in Early Modern Europe* (Oxford: Oxford University Press, 1975).

Raeff, Marc. "The Well-Ordered Police State and the Development of Modernity in Seventeenth and Eighteenth-Century Europe," *American Historical Review* 80 (1975): 1221–43.

Raeff, Marc. *The Well-Ordered Police State. Social and Institutional Change through Law in the Germanies and Russia, 1600–1800* (New Haven: Yale University Press, 1983).

Rau, Susanne. "Das Wirtshaus. Zur Konstitution eines öffentlichen Raumes in der Frühen Neuzeit," in *Offen und Verborgen. Vorstellungen und Praktiken des Öffentlichen und Privaten in Mittelalter und Früher Neuzeit*, Carolina Emmelius et al. (eds.) (Göttingen: Wallstein, 2004), pp. 211–28.

Rau, Susanne. "Orte der Gastlichkeit—Orte der Kommunikation. Aspekte der Raumkonstitution von Herbergen in einer frühneuzeitlichen Stadt," in *Kirchen, Märkte und Tavernen. Erfahrungs- und Handlungsräume in der Frühen Neuzeit*, Renate Dürr and Gerd Schwerhoff (eds.) (Frankfurt: Klostermann, 2005), pp. 394–417.

Reinhard, Wolfgang. "No State Building from Below! A Critical Commentary," in *Empowering Interactions. Political Cultures and the Emergence of the State in Europe, 1300–1900*, André Holenstein, Daniel Schläppi, and Wim Blockmans (eds.) (Burlington: Ashgate, 2009), pp. 299–304.

Rieger, Arnold. "Der Schwede kommt! Der Schwede als Kinderschreck." *Stuttgarter Nachrichten*, August 10, 2009. https://www.stuttgarter-nachrichten.de/inhalt.der-schwede-kommt-der-schwede-als-kinderschreck.d1dee74c-458e-49bb-9851-a6888577429b.html.

Robisheaux, Thomas. *Rural Society and the Search for Order in Early Modern Germany* (Cambridge: Cambridge University Press, 1989).

Robisheaux, Thomas. *The Last Witch of Langenburg. Murder in a German Village* (New York and London: Norton, 2009).

Roper, Lyndal. *Oedipus and the Devil. Witchcraft, Religion, and Sexuality in Early Modern Europe* (London: Routledge, 1994).

Roper, Lyndal, *Witch Craze. Terror and Fantasy in Baroque Germany* (New Haven: Yale University Press, 2004).

Roussuaux, Xavier. "Entre accommodement local et contrôle étatique. Pratiques judiciaires et non-judiciaires dans le reglèment des conflits en Europe médiévale et modern," in *L'Infrajudicaire du Moyen Age à l'epoque contemporaine*, Benoît Garnot (ed.) (Dijon: Éditions Université de Dijon, 1996), pp. 87–108.

Rudolph, Harriet. *"Eine gelinde Regierungsart." Peinliche Strafjustiz im geistlichen Territorium. Das Hochstift Osnabrück (1716–1803)* (Konstanz: UVK Verlag, 2001).

Sabean, David Warren. *Power in the Blood. Popular Culture and Village Discourse in Early Modern Germany* (Cambridge: Cambridge University Press, 1984).

Sabean, David Warren. *Property, Production, and Family in Neckarhausen, 1700–1870* (Cambridge: Cambridge University Press, 1990).

Sabean, David Warren. "Village Court Protocols and Memory," in *Gemeinde, Reformation und Widerstand. Festschrift für Peter Blickle zum 60. Geburtstag*, Heinrich Richard Schmidt, André Holenstein, Andreas Würgler (eds.) (Tübingen: bibliotheca academica, 1998), pp. 3–24.

Sabean, David Warren. "Peasant Voices and Bureaucratic Texts," in *Little Tools of Knowledge: Historical Essays on Academic and Bureaucratic Practices*, Peter Becker and William Clark (eds.) (Ann Arbor: University of Michigan Press, 2001), pp. 67–94.

Sabean, David Warren. "Soziale Distanzierung. Ritualisierte Gestik in deutscher bürokratischer Prosa der frühen Neuzeit," *Historische Anthropologie* 4/2 (1996): 216–33.

Sabean, David Warren. *Kinship in Neckarhausen, 1700–1870* (Cambridge University Press, 2010).

Safely, Thomas Max. *Let no Man Put Asunder: The Control of Marriage in the German Southwest, 1550–1620* (Kirksville: Sixteenth Century Essays and Studies, 1984).

Schäfer, Regina. "Frieden durch Recht. Zur Funktion des Dorfgerichts in der Gemeinde," in *Dorf und Gemeinde. Grundstrukturen der ländlichen Gesellschaft in Spätmittelalter und Frühneuzeit*, Oliver Auge and Kurt Andermann (eds.) (Ostfildern: Verlagsgruppe Patmos, 2012), pp. 65–86.

Schildt, Bernd. "Der Friedensgedanke im frühneuzeitliche Dorfrecht: Das Beispiel Thüringen," *Zeitschrift der Savigny-Stiftung für Rechtsgeschichte. Germanische Abteilung* 107 (1990).

Schindler, Norbert. *Rebellion, Community, and Custom in Early Modern Germany* (Cambridge University Press, 2002).

Schlögl, Rudolf. "Kommunikation und Vergesellschaftung under Anwesenden: Formen der Sozialen und ihre Transformation in der Frühen Neuzeit," *Geschichte und Gesellschaft* 34 (2008): 155–224.

Schlögl, Rudolf. *Anwesende und Abwesende. Grundriss für eine Gesellschaftsgeschichte der Frühen Neuzeit* (Konstanz: Konstanz University Press, 2014).

Schlumbohm, Jürgen. "Gesetze, die nicht durchgesetzt werden: ein Strukturmerkmal des frühneuzeitlichen Staates?," *Geschichte und Gesellschaft* 23 (1997): 647–63.

Schmöltz-Häberlein, Michaela. *Kleinstadtgesellschaft(en): weibliche und männliche Lebenswelten im Emmendingen des 18. Jahrhunderts* (Stuttgart: Franz Steiner Verlag, 2012).

Schreiner, Klaus and Schwerhoff, Gerd (eds.). *Verletzte Ehre. Ehrkonflikte in Gesellschaften des Mittelalters und der Frühen Neuzeit* (Köln, Böhlau, 1995).

Schwerhoff, Gerd. "Das Gelage. Institutionelle Ordnungsarrangements und Machtkämpfe im frühneuzeitlichen Wirtshaus," in *Das Sichtbare und das Unsichtbare der Macht. institutionelle Prozesse in Antike, Mittelalter und Neuzeit*, Gert Melville (ed.) (Köln: Böhlau, 2005), pp. 160–76.

Schwerhoff, Gerd. "Die Große Welt im kleinen Raum," in *Kirchen, Märkte und Tavernen. Erfahrungs- und Handlungsräume in der Frühen Neuzeit*, Renate Dürr and Gerd Schwerhoff (eds.) (Frankfurt: Klostermann, 2005), pp. 367–75.

Schwerhoff, Gerd. *Historische Kriminalitätsforschung* (Frankfurt: Campus Verlag, 2011).

Smith, Helmut Walser. *Germany: A Nation in its Time. Before, During, and after Nationalism, 1500–2000* (New York: Norton, 2020).

Soergel, Philip. *Miracles and the Protestant Imagination: The Evangelical Wonder Book in Reformation Germany* (Oxford: Oxford University Press, 2012).

Sreenivasan, Govind P. "Beyond the Village: Recent Approaches to the Social History of the Early Modern German Peasantry," *History Compass* 11/1 (2013): 47–64.

Sreenivasan, Govind. *The Peasants of Ottobeuren. A Rural Society in Early Modern Europe* (Cambridge: Cambridge University Press, 2004).

Sreenivasan, Govind. "Prosecuting Injuries in Early Modern Germany (ca. 1550–1650)," *Central European History* 47 (2014): 544–84.

Stollberg-Rillinger, Barbara. "Rang vor Gericht. Zur Verrechtlichung sozialer Rangkonflikt in der frühen Neuzeit," *Zeitschrift für historische Forschung* 28 (2000): 385–418.

Stretton, Tim. "Written Obligations, Litigation and Neighbourliness," in *Remaking English Society, Social Relations, and Social Change in Early Modern England*, Steve Hindle et al. (eds.) (Cambridge: Cambridge University Press, 2013), pp. 180–210.

Stuart, Kathy. *Defiled Trades and Social Outcasts: Honor and Ritual Pollution in Early Modern Germany* (Cambridge: Cambridge University Press, 2001).

Sundin, Jan. "Cooperation, Conflict Solution, and Social Control. Civil and Ecclesiastical Justice in Preindustrial Sweden," *Historical Social Research* 37 (1986): 50–86.

Taylor, Scott. *Honor and Violence in Golden Age Spain* (New Haven: Yale University Press, 2008).

Thiebault, John. "The Rhetoric of Death and Destruction in the Thirty Years' War," *Social History* 27 (1993): 271–90.

Tlusty, B. Ann. *Bacchus and Civic Order. The Culture of Drink in Early Modern Germany* (Charlottesville: University of Virginia Press, 2001).

Tüchle, Hermann, Schahl, Adolph, and Feist, Joachim. *850 Jahre Rot an der Rot: Geschichte und Gestalt: neue Beiträge zur Kirchen- und Kunstgeschichte der Prämonstratenser-Reichsabtei* (Sigmaringen: Thorbecke 1976).

Vermeesch, Griet. "Reflections on the Relative Accessibility of Law Courts in Early Modern Europe," *Crime, History, and Societies* 19 (2015): 53–76.

Walker, Mack. *German Home Towns. Community, State, and General Estate. 1648–1871* (Ithaca: Cornell University Press, 1971).

Walz, Rainer. "Agonale Kommunikation im Dorf der Frühen Neuzeit," *Westfälische Forschung* 42 (1992): 215–51.

Wiesner-Hanks, Merry. *Women and Gender in Early Modern Europe*, 3rd edition (New York: Cambridge University Press, 2008).

Westphal, Siegrid. "The Holy Roman Empire of the German Nation as an Order of Public Peace," *German History* 36 (2018): 401–14.

Wettmann-Jungblut, Peter. "Gewalt und Gegen-Gewalt. Gewalthandeln, Alkoholkonsum und die Dynamik von Konflikten anhand eines Fallbeispiels aus dem frühneuzeitlichen Schwarzwald," in *Streitkulturen. Gewalt, Konflikt und Kommunikation in der ländlichen Gesellschaft (16.–19. Jh.)*, Magnus Eriksson and Barbara Krug-Richter (eds.) (Köln: Böhlau, 2003), pp. 17–58.

Wettmann-Jungblut, Peter. "Modern Times, Modern Crimes. Kriminalität und Strafpraxis im badischen Raum 1700–1850," in *Verbrechen im Blick. Perspektiven der neuzeitlichen Kriminalitätsgeschichte*, Rebekka Habermas and Gerd Schwerhoff (eds.) (Frankfurt: Campus Verlag, 2009), pp. 148–81.

Wilson, Lisa. *The History of Stepfamilies in Early America* (Chapel Hill: University of North Carolina Press, 2014).

Wilson, Peter. *The Thirty Years' War. Europe's Tragedy* (Cambridge, MA: Harvard University Press, 2009).

Wilson, Peter. *Heart of Europe. A History of the Holy Roman Empire* (Cambridge MA: Harvard University Press, 2016).

Wood, Andy. *The Memory of the People. Custom and Popular Senses of the Past in Early Modern England* (Cambridge: Cambridge University Press, 2013).

Zimmermann, Wolfgang and Priesching, Nicole (eds.). *Württembergisches Klosterbuch. Klöster, Stifte und Ordensgemeinschaften von den Anfängen bis in die Gegenwart* (Sigmaringen: Jan Thorbecke Verlag, 2003).

Index

For the benefit of digital users, indexed terms that span two pages (e.g., 52–53) may, on occasion, appear on only one of those pages.